# A DEAFENING SILENCE

## Hidden violence against women and children

Patrizia Romito

Translated from original Italian by Janet Eastwood

**SEPS**
SEGRETARIATO EUROPEO PER LE PUBBLICAZIONI SCIENTIFICHE

First published in Great Britain in 2008 by

The Policy Press
University of Bristol
Fourth Floor
Beacon House
Queen's Road
Bristol BS8 1QU
UK

Tel +44 (0)117 331 4054
Fax +44 (0)117 331 4093
e-mail tpp-info@bristol.ac.uk
www.policypress.org.uk

British Library Cataloguing in Publication Data
A catalogue record for this book is available from the British Library.

Library of Congress Cataloging-in-Publication Data
A catalog record for this book has been requested.

ISBN 978 1 86134 961 3 paperback
ISBN 978 1 86134 962 0 hardcover

The translation of this work has been funded by SEPS
SEGRETARIATO EUROPEO PER LE PUBBLICAZIONI SCIENTIFICHE

Via Val d'Aposa 7 - 40123 Bologna - Italy
seps@alma.unibo.it - www.seps.it

Cover design by Robin Hawes
*Front cover:* Image kindly supplied by Amnesty International Belgique francophone
Printed and bound in Great Britain by Henry Ling Limited, Dorchester

I dedicate this book, with admiration and respect, to the many women and fewer men who fight against male violence towards women and children, so that none of us loses heart: the struggle is long, the outcome uncertain and each of us is necessary.

# Contents

# Acknowledgements and preface

Although all books are difficult to write, this has been particularly so. The book deals with violence towards women and children and the methods society uses to minimise, deny and hide this violence. During the time I have taken to write it and then revise it, not a day has passed without the newspapers publishing cases of women or girls murdered by the ex-husband or fiancé they wanted to leave, children violated by men in the family, or other women, in other countries, raped or stoned to death. What is more, no occasion has passed when, speaking of these matters in public, a girl or woman has not come up to me, at the end, to tell me a similar story, in which the violence was followed by abandonment or discredit. The work of writing was so increased by this information and the pleasure, which comes simply from writing, made me almost feel guilty. Only the conviction of doing something useful, almost a commitment made to each one of these women, allowed me to continue and complete it. For these reasons, my thanks go not only to those who have contributed directly to the book, but also to those who have been close to me during these years and, with their commitment, set me an example and spurred me to go on.

First of all thanks go to the persons who believed in this project and made it possible to carry it out in its various versions: Chiara Volpato in Italy, Christine Delphy and Jacqueline Julien in France and Cynthia Cockburn in the UK. Thanks also to Philip de Bary, Commissioning Editor at The Policy Press, for his enthusiasm, expertise and generosity, and to all the staff of The Policy Press, for their passionate attention to detail and their kindness; and to Marianne Hester and Martin Calder for their useful comments.

I would not have been able to write the book if I had not spent a year at the Institute for Research on Women and Gender at Stanford University. Many ideas were developed and tested during seminars at the Institute. All the scholars present contributed with ideas, bibliographical references and encouragement. I would like to thank Lynne Henderson in particular for generously providing me with the best in the thinking of feminist jurists, and also Esther Rothblum, Marilyn Yalom and Janet Molzan Turan. Diana Russell, at Berkeley, who was one of the first to study violence against women, has been equally generous with books, ideas and suggestions.

Many friends and colleagues have read and commented on parts of the book and provided valuable ideas: I would like to thank especially Micaela Crisma and Jacqueline Julien. Christine Delphy, Karen Messing and Margherita DeMarchi have always been a valuable source of reflection and analysis, as well as irony and humour, when necessary. I would like to thank Fanny Filosof for her friendship and for finding the cover for the book. The students who have worked with me have contributed in various ways, with their work but also with the gift of their enthusiasm and their determination. Among the many I have been fortunate to know in these years, I would like to thank Chiara Lucchetta, Laura Pomicino and Francesca Quaglia, who are now young colleagues. More generally, my students have added meaning to my professional life, and allowed me to hold out and not lose enthusiasm and determination even during some difficult times.

This book, like all books on violence towards women, would not have been possible if it had not been for the extraordinary work – political, theoretical and practical – by activists throughout the world to oppose male violence. Without the women's movement, no theoretical reflection would have been possible, not even this book. I would like to thank the women of the Anti-Violence Centres of Trieste, Bologna and Belluno in particular, to whom I am bound by ties of cooperation and friendship, and my fellow members of 'La Settima Onda' Women's Association of Trieste, for their integrity, courage and sense of humour.

Thanks also to Livio Lanceri, long-time fellow traveller, for the many ways in which he has made this project possible and because he allows me to have faith in men (understood as human beings of the male sex); to Caterina Grego, for all the years of friendship, discussions and happiness; and to my mother, because she is a wonderful person and without her I would not be what I am.

And finally, a clarification. This book deals with the murder of women and children and the mechanisms society puts into operation to hide it. To support my thesis, I have had to use the knowledge and methods of disciplines that are not my own, such as history and law; it is therefore possible that, notwithstanding rereading and revising, the text contains inaccuracies or weak arguments. For this reason I would refer my readers to the words of Margaret Baldwin (1992, p 50), feminist activist and jurist:

> What I ask of you is simple but requires commitment: where my logic fails, I ask you to remember these women, and do better than I have done.

# Introduction

## Silence and noise

At the beginning of the new millennium, violence against women and children is no longer a secret, something that the victims have to hide, without hope and without means of release. We are more and more aware of the frequency and consequences of domestic violence, rape, harassment at work and child sexual abuse, phenomena for most of which there was not even a name until the 1970s. The women's movement produced awareness, knowledge and resistance; it revealed the web of complicity, often institutional, that allowed the individual violent man to continue to act, undisturbed and unpunished; it invented, proposed and at times imposed a series of measures to prevent violence. In industrialised countries and also in many developing countries there are antiviolence centres and refuges for maltreated women, almost always the result of work by feminist groups; new projects and protocols are under way; and the police and health and social workers are agreeing, and sometimes asking, to be trained in the subject of violence so that they can intervene with greater sensitivity, expertise and efficiency.

We have come a long way in the last 30 years. In many industrialised countries, there have been important changes on a legislative level. In Italy in 1981 'honour crime', which drastically reduced the penalties of anyone killing his spouse, daughter or sister, if he considered that their sexual conduct had injured 'his honour or the honour of the family', was repealed. In many European countries the so-called conjugal exemption, according to which rape committed by a husband against his wife was not considered an offence, was repealed: in 1991 in Holland, in 1994 in the UK and in 1997 in Germany. In the last two decades of the 20th century, various international organisations and numerous governments drew up important declarations defining violence against women and children as an unacceptable violation of human rights, a source of tragic consequences not only for the victims but for the whole of society, and therefore an obstacle to development. The World Bank itself has emphasised the enormous economic cost this violence involves (Pickup, 2001).

Still there is no shortage of causes for concern. As we will see later, many of these achievements are proving to be fragile or contradictory.

New laws and new social practices, introduced to prevent violence and protect victims, are proving to be ineffective, and sometimes backfire against the victims themselves. Behaviour, which has been changed with difficulty, returns to the original situation of denial of violence or blame for the victim. While there is no way of knowing if the frequency of violence has changed (in the sense of an increase or decrease) in the last few years, new forms are starting to become more visible, such as violence in adolescent couples, sexual harassment of students, 'ethnic' rapes, child pornography on the Internet, and moral, physical and sexual violence towards children by members of the church (Jones and Finkelhor, 2003). At times of discouragement, we can have the impression of being caught in a very thick web; we struggle to free ourselves, with great effort we succeed in breaking it in several places, but when we try to actually get out of it, particularly if we all want to get out, the web reforms, closes around us and envelops us again.

## Worrying trends

Let us consider sexual violence. From comparisons between various data – results of research carried out on representative samples of the population and data relating to reports, trials and related convictions – it emerges that the probability of the perpetrator of a rape being identified and put in a situation where he can do no harm is minimal. In fact, little violence is reported,[1] very little of this leads to a trial and even less ends in a conviction. In the last few years, to correct these trends, various countries have reformed the practices of health and social services, the police and the legal system; still, even though reports in some cases seem to be increasing, investigations, trials and convictions seem to be decreasing. As far as children are concerned, in the US the National Incidence Study reports that in 1986 investigations were carried out into 75% of child sexual abuse cases considered very serious; in 1993, the percentage of cases investigated had gone down to 44% (Bolen et al, 2000). The statistics of the English Home Office show a similar trend: in 1985, out of 633 reports of child sexual abuse ('offences of gross indecency with children under 14'), a conviction was made in 42% of cases; in 1995, the number of reports had doubled, but the percentage of convictions had gone down drastically to 12% (Itzin, 2000a). As regards rape, in England, cases reported to the police rose from 1,842 in 1985 to 4,589 in 1993, but the percentage of convictions more than halved, decreasing from 24% to 10% (Lees, 1997). It seems this halving cannot be attributed to a hypothetical decrease in the seriousness of the acts cited or the credibility of the reports. Sue Lees reports cases in which men accused of very serious, repeated violence, such as serial rapists, have been acquitted, notwithstanding the proof against them being overwhelming. A recent Home Office study into attrition in reported rape cases found that only 14% of rape cases reached trial stage. Even once the cases reached court, they may have been withdrawn or discontinued and in those cases where conviction did result, around half were due to a guilty plea, with an acquittal the most likely outcome in a full trial (Kelly et al, 2005). In France, the number of reports of sexual violence rose from 2,823 in 1986 to 5,068 in 1990-91; however, the percentage of convictions decreased from 22% to 14.5% (Morbois et al, 1994). At every stage (discovery, report, investigation, preparation of the case, conviction), there are various reasons that may explain the widening of the gap between the cases discovered and a positive final outcome, that is protection, release and compensation for the victim, punishment and being put in a situation where he can do no harm for the aggressor. These reasons vary from country to country, but, notwithstanding the differences, the end result is similar: women and children who are victims of sexual violence do not seem to be any more protected today than in the past.

## Break the silence?

In 2000 the European Union promoted a campaign against domestic violence adopting the slogan: 'Break the silence'. But if we listen to the victims, or rather, the survivors, we discover that many broke the silence and sought help in various ways, sometimes indirectly, at other times quite explicitly, even at the risk of suffering subsequent violence. Many accounts of paternal rape contain common elements, whether the acts occur in England, the US or Italy. The child recounts something to the grandparents, the school, friends or their parents; she is taken to hospital, because she has a sexually transmitted disease or because she has been beaten and has a broken nose, broken teeth, broken ribs, a broken eardrum, but nothing happens. As an adolescent she suffers from behavioural problems, nightmares and panic attacks, and she attempts suicide, but no one – psychiatrist, psychologist, social worker – asks her why; she is given drugs; if she talks, she is treated as a mythomaniac, defined as histrionic and accused of lying; if she goes to the police, she is ridiculed, accused of lying again, sent home and threatened (Frenken and Van Stolk, 1990; Armstrong, 1993; Russell, 1997; Rachel Pearce interviewed by Catherine Itzin, 2000). Not all abused children come up against a wall of indifference and complicity, but the fact that this can still happen today, in various contexts and countries, tells us that the heart of the problem does not lie in the silence of the victims. Research into women maltreated by their partner shows a similar trend: only a minority keeps it secret. Almost all of them talk about it, to friends, parents and institutional figures such as the doctor or police officer, but they are rarely listened to, believed and helped; they may even be insulted and threatened by the people they have asked for help (Romito, 2000; Creazzo, 2003; Walby and Allen, 2004).

The press has also contributed to breaking the silence. Cases of violence are presented, and often commented on, even by famous columnists. But how? In the last few years Italian newspapers have reported numerous episodes of women and children killed by their husband/father who could not bear to be left; sometimes the man then committed suicide. In the articles an image is confirmed of men who 'kill because they love too much' or because they 'suffer too much', leaving between the lines the connotation of possession ('if I can't have you, no one can') and revenge that these men are expressing. For example, A.M. cuts the throat of his eight-year-old daughter as 'punishment for his ex-wife' (January 2000). E.P. strangles his eight-year-old son and declares: 'I wanted to punish my wife' (May 2002). M.G. strangles his two children (September 2002) and writes to his ex-wife and mother-in-law: 'I hope your life may be a nightmare and you will live long enough to suffer remorse for this'. R.G. stabs his two children to death (April 2004) and shouts to his ex-wife: 'I killed them because of you, so you will know what it means to suffer'.[2] These articles talk generically of 'marital disputes', whereas they lack explicit references to domestic violence by men, which was most probably the reason why the women decided to separate from their husbands. If journalists investigated or listened to what the families, neighbours and the women – at least those who are still alive – said, they would often discover stories of continuous maltreatment for years. The links between violence towards wives and towards children and between violence while living together and violence after separation are now well founded. Almost two thirds of violent husbands are also violent towards their children; in about 80% of cases, the women killed have been killed by their partner after years of 'conjugal' violence, usually after separation or divorce (Edleson, 1999; Peled, 2000; Campbell et al, 2003). In Italy, there have been real massacres (for example, in October 2002 a man whose wife had left him stabbed the whole family: wife, mother-in-law, son and brother-in-law; another killed seven people: ex-wife, mother-in-law, brothers-in-law and neighbours, and killed himself) before some newspapers spoke timidly of domestic violence.

But even in 2004, referring to children being killed by their father, who was separated from his wife, a journalist wrote: 'Couples in crisis kill 15 children a year'.[3]

It is not only an Italian trend. In Quebec, from 1989 to 1998, more than 400 women and 100 children were killed by their ex–partner or father respectively, after separation or divorce. One of the most popular television broadcasts showed a programme on some of them, still in prison, presenting them as 'survivors of a family tragedy' (Dufresne, 1998).

In short, breaking the silence is acceptable as long as each act of violence is presented as isolated, and as long as the perpetrators appear to be in an exceptional situation, for example prey to uncontrollable emotions. Above all, it is acceptable to talk about violence, but never about male violence. Here, too, we have adapted to this convention so far. Also, the documents of international organisations and governments, quoted at the beginning of this chapter, talk about violence towards women and children, but almost never of male violence, even if they describe husbands raping, maltreating and killing their wives. Rereading this text and international documents, in which the adjective 'male' is added to the word violence, has the effect of a punch in the stomach, because it confronts us with a brutal reality. It is this reality we are trying to escape from when we use euphemisms or generic and imprecise terms.

In short, we have gone from silence to noise, but with what capacity to get to the bottom of male violence and prevent it? If we consider intrafamilial child sexual abuse, so-called incest, we must note that until the 1980s there was no serious study on the subject. The first work by feminist scholars such as Louise Armstrong (1978), Florence Rush (1980) and Diana Russell (1984) showed that it was in fact a frequent practice universally allowed. The most recent epidemiological research confirms this. In the US and in Europe, between 5% and 10% of children and adolescents have suffered sexual abuse by a man in the family and scholars agree on the fact that these figures represent underestimates of the phenomenon (Halpérin et al, 1996; Bolen et al, 2000). Louise Armstrong also shows us that, right from the mid-1980s, in the US we were witnessing what she defined with bitter irony as 'the birth of the incest industry', with its

> staggering array of clinicians, counsellors, therapists, researchers, authorities and experts, all with their career sighted on one of the aspects of incest and its aftermaths. (quoted in Itzin, 2000a, p 3)

Given that violent men were too numerous and often too 'normal' to be criminalised and punished, a strategy of medicalisation was adopted and experts developed the concept of 'incestuous families' to cover what Armstrong describes as 'the dreadful actuality of paternal child rape'. She also asks:

> How in just two decades did we go from total silence – from coerced secrecy, the suppression of children's experiences, such that they were not even heard – to a level of cacophony such that children's voices, women's voices, are once more not, in any purposeful sense, being heard? (quoted in Itzin, 2000a, p 3)

The cacophony is produced, as we will see later, by professionals, lobbies and individuals who are also very diverse: health workers who talk of children being nymphomaniac, seductive, histrionic or simply lying and mothers being incestuous or complicit; psychologists and lawyers supporting false memory syndrome and parental alienation syndrome, who arrange the defence of men accused of incest, sometimes in agreement with separated fathers associations; experts who have invented the concept of *failure to protect*, with which they stigmatise and punish mothers who have not been able to protect their children from the violence of their father, only to define them as hysterical, vindictive or paranoid when they report paternal sexual violence; supporters of paedophilia[4] for various reasons, who consider incest to be something positive in the name of love between adults and children or evolutionary principles, as well as artists and literary critics who present it in a positive light (*Lolita* by Vladimir Nabokov[5]) or as a good initiation to sexuality (the film *Murmur of the heart* by Louis Malle), or as the design of voracious, scheming, manipulative girls (*The liberated wife* by Abraham Yehoshua); and the 'ordinary man' (who may be a woman) who simply cannot believe it, because it cannot possibly happen so often, or admits it exists only in certain environments, but not among respectable people. Faced with this picture, Armstrong (quoted in Itzin, 2000a, p 4) concludes:

> this noise has effectively functioned to silence victims, leaving men to continue committing incest with impunity.

## Theory and practice

In this book I intend to analyse the mechanisms by which contemporary society succeeds in hiding male violence and avoiding taking all the measures necessary to prevent it. Its ambition is to go beyond a simple description to try and identify categories that allow us to read in a more concise way a reality that is often confused and threatens to crush us with the weight of its accumulated atrocities, and in this way provide a useful contribution to putting an end to the violence.

Stopping the violence is a struggle, in which very many women and more than a few men are engaged: from the victims, who have survived and are often able to draw life lessons from it, for themselves and for others, to whoever has been close to them, to all those, like doctors, nurses, psychologists, social workers, police officers, judges and teachers, who in their daily work choose to be on the side of those who have suffered and not those who have inflicted violence, to women in feminist groups (even if not always defined as such) who fight for the rights and dignity of women and children to be respected. Although I have chosen to concentrate on the violence and social strategies to hide it rather than the actions to fight it, not only do these exist and are often courageous, innovative and effective, but they form an integral part of the analysis proposed in this book. It is precisely because women are resisting, opposing and proposing alternatives, that it is necessary to find other ways, more 'modern' and articulate, to deny their rights and dignity. The complexity of the hiding strategies put into operation by society is directly proportional to the activities of the women's movement and their resistance, in a thousand different ways, on an individual and collective level (Smyth, 2002; Morgan, 2003).

If we accept the idea that stopping male violence is a fight, it then becomes inevitable that you will ask yourself whether writing a book with some theoretical ambition is the best way of engaging in it: perhaps other forms of intellectual action – popular writings, training activities, debates – may be more useful. Robin Morgan (1992), pacifist and feminist activist, journalist, writer and poet, expresses well the conflict between the desire to write (in her case a novel) and the need to do something else on the other hand ('to be at the barricades'); she also recalls how paradoxical it is to write in a world where two thirds of those who are illiterate are women. Morgan, with the secular blessing of Simone de Beauvoir, decided to write her novel, even though this meant pushing the aim of writing outreaching texts temporarily into the background, and quotes the historian Gerda Lerner (1986), who claims that women need to acquire the least 'feminine' of qualities, the intellectual arrogance to establish their own right to reorder the world.

Doing theory or trying to do it also has another significance. Violence causes suffering, anyone who has suffered it always remains wounded by it and sometimes may succumb to it. The witness also remains involved. Listening to women who have suffered violence, transcribing interviews, analysing them, writing about them, forces you to look a terrible reality in the face, brings back memories of past violence, shakes the certainty in or at least the hope for a 'just world', and inevitably makes you look at all men with suspicion and fear, even those who are not violent and hopefully never will be. In short, contact with the violence and suffering of the victims may also be devastating for the witness and may be one of the reasons behind the desire to do theory. What better way, in fact, of distancing yourself from the world? Christa Wolf (1993) says it well when she notes that aesthetics, philosophy and science, although apparently invented to enable us to get closer to reality, in fact serve to ward off this reality, to protect against it.

Writing about or doing theory may help the victims of violence to objectify the experience and may therefore become a means of healing or at least controlling the suffering (Pennebaker, 1993). This is what is maintained by bell hooks, African-American activist and writer:

> I came to theory because I was hurting – the pain was so intense that I could not go on living. I came to theory desperate, wanting to comprehend – to grasp what was happening around and within me. Most importantly, I wanted the hurt to go away. I saw in theory then a location for healing. (hooks, 1994, p 59)

Still, although this path is legitimate for those who have suffered violence, it involves some disturbing aspects for the witness. Distancing ourselves from the suffering of others and objectivising it means turning on the world that kind of gaze that not only characterises traditional science, but also forms the basis for the capacity to inflict pain, and therefore torture and violate. Reflecting on prostitution, and particularly the dozens of girls killed in the region of Green River, near Seattle, Margaret Baldwin (1992) asks herself how legitimate it is to proceed with the intellectual and rhetorical methods of writing – discussing hypotheses and counter-hypotheses brilliantly, making subtle distinctions, caring for style – when the 'material' she is writing about is the slaughter of women and children:

> The carnage: the scale of it, the dailiness of it, the seeming
> inevitability of it, the torture, the rapes, the murders, the
> beatings, the despair, the hollowing out of personality, the
> near extinguishment of hope commonly suffered by women
> in prostitution ... to render this slaughter of women a matter
> to be assessed by analytic argument ... has at times seemed
> to me an act of barbarism. (Baldwin, 1992, pp 49-50)

In the US, many activists have accused experts and academics of building their careers on the suffering of others, literally stealing the work and the knowledge produced from the victims of violence and the women who support them (Armstrong, 1996; Garrity, 2003). In Italy, the situation is, at least for the moment, very different: the funds for this type of research are limited, and anyone doing it runs the risk of ostracism by the academic world rather than renown.

In conclusion, theory is not automatically saving, liberating or revolutionary. It takes on these functions when we ask it to do so and we direct our thinking to this end. According to a phrase that has been attributed to numerous great men (from Lenin to Che Guevara, via Einstein) and, characteristically, not to any woman, nothing is more practical than a good theory. As many feminists have recognised 'if you want to change the world, you need to get your theory right' (Ramazanoglu, 1989, p 12).

### Notes

[1] In the United States, it is calculated that between 2% and 15% of sexual violence is reported. In research in Los Angeles in the 1980s, only 13% of rapes were reported to the police and only 2% of rapists were arrested (Sorenson et al, 1987). More recently, data from national research in England shows that the police were informed of no more than 13%-15% of cases of serious sexual abuse (Walby and Allen, 2004).

[2] All these articles were published by an Italian national daily newspaper (*La Repubblica*) or a Trieste daily newspaper (*Il Piccolo*).

[3] Vinci, E. (2004) 'Separated fathers, suicides increase', *La Repubblica*, 27 October.

[4] The term 'paedophilia' is inappropriate and misleading, as I will demonstrate later. I use it here because it is in current use and is not always easy to replace.

[5] In the case of *Lolita*, it was the critics rather than the author who presented the subject of the book – sexual violence by an adult man towards a child aged 12, the daughter of his wife – as something entertaining or a 'real love story' (for a criticism, see Jeffreys, 1990).

# ONE

# Violence and discrimination against women

## 1.1 The figures and their absence

This is not a book about violence against women; it is a book about responses by society to violence against women. However, having figures about violence in your hand is crucial. In fact, only by examining the extent and frequency of male violence can we appreciate the scale, determination and lack of scruples involved in covering up the violence. Only in this way does the importance of figures and statistics also become clear and, conversely, the significance and consequences of their absence. In fact, the lack of figures about violence represents a political choice and one of the means of hiding it. In her book *Sisterhood is global* (1984), an analysis of the state of the world from the point of view of women, Robin Morgan talks about the 'policy of not having figures':

> When a preface reads 'no data obtainable' [NDO] or 'no statistics obtainable' [NSO] on a given subject, it means that despite intrepid effort we could not find or gain access to the information. Those NDOs and NSOs ... form a politically revealing pattern in themselves. Again and again they arise in the categories of rape, battery, sexual harassment, incest and homosexuality; these are still the unspeakable issues in most parts of the globe. As long as they remain unspoken and under researched an enormous amount of human suffering will continue to go unacknowledged and unhealed. (Morgan, 1984, p xxiii)

Her whole book is therefore an appeal to increase research work and collect and analyse data, free from patriarchal bias, in order to uncover the truth.

Over 20 years later, we have a great deal of research, enabling us to draw a map of violence against women and children. This knowledge is the result of pressure by the women's movement and work by women in research institutions and international organisations. In many European countries, for example, research into violence carried out at a national level represents acceptance of the recommendations of the Fourth World Women's Conference in Beijing in 1995, in which the need to have statistical information was confirmed. This map is still incomplete. Although in some countries, such as the US and the UK, there is an impressive mass of data that has been collected since the 1970s by government organisations, academics and women's groups, in others, such as France and Italy, information is scarce and the first studies are much more recent (Sabbadini, 1998; Jaspard et al, 2003). On some subjects there is also a complete lack of data or it is very inaccurate. This may be because there is no desire to collect it, as in the case of murders within the context of a couple relationship, or because it is difficult to study, because it occurs in a war zone, such as the trade in children by the so-called peacekeepers of the United Nations.

Different studies also often produce differing results, in the frequency of a certain type of violence for example. It is easy to read that child sexual abuse ranges from 5% to 40% according to the studies. This big difference is explained partly by real differences (it is possible that children are abused more in a certain sociocultural context than in another), partly by differences in the definition of concepts (violence may be defined in different ways, children may be less than 12, 16 or 18 years old) and partly by differences in the methods used (face-to-face interview or anonymous questionnaire, one or many questions) (Bolen et al, 2000). These differences are inevitable and indeed are evidence that researchers are trying to refine their tools to reach more accurate and reliable results. Still, the figures on such delicate questions inevitably have a political use. In fact the discrepancy between results and even more so their absence, because of a deliberate choice, are used to discredit research revealing the high frequency of violence against women.

## 1.2 The frequency of violence

In this section I give a summary of the frequency of some types of violence; its purpose is not to give an exhaustive review so much as to give the subsequent discussion of the mechanisms for hiding it a context. A good way of starting is to consider a table provided by the World Health Organization (WHO, 1997), which has the merit of showing the continuity of violence in the life cycle of women in various cultures. Identifying various forms of violence is necessary if we want to assess its frequency and study its characteristics and consequences, but it must be remembered that this violence does not represent different categories in real life. If we consider the 16 year old raped by a much older 'fiancé', for example, is this *child sexual abuse, date rape* or *couple violence*?

**Table 1: Violence against women in their life cycle**

| BEFORE BIRTH | selective abortions, consequences of violence in pregnancy |
|---|---|
| EARLY CHILDHOOD | female infanticide, selective negligence in care, physical, sexual and psychological violence |
| LATE CHILDHOOD | forced marriage of girls, mutilation of female genitalia, physical, sexual (incest) and psychological violence, child prostitution, pornography |
| ADOLESCENCE AND ADULTHOOD | incest, 'courtship' violence (date rape, acid attacks), sex due to economic necessity, violence by partner (until death), 'dowry death', rape, femicide, rape and forced pregnancy in war, sexual harassment at work, forced prostitution[a], pornography |
| OLD AGE | murder or forced suicide of widows, physical, sexual and psychological violence |

*Note:* [a] Later I will criticise the concept of 'forced prostitution', as it implies there may be 'free' prostitution.

*Source:* WHO (1997)

## 1.2.1 Sexual violence

Women are afraid of rape and rightly so. In the US, between 15% and 24% of women have been raped as adults (Russell and Bolen, 2000; Seager, 2003). The frequency is much higher in the course of their whole lives. In one study that is considered classic because of its accuracy and care in the methods used, 44% of women reported one or more rapes or attempted rapes in the course of their lives (Russell, 1990, 1999). In fact, victims of rape are, above all, young or very young girls, under 16 in 40%-60% of cases or even under 11 in 20%-30% of cases. The frequency is particularly high among students: in the US, about half the students interviewed stated that they had suffered an experience that could be legally defined as rape and between 15% and 20% revealed a rape or attempted rape in the previous 12 months (Koss et al, 1993; Cortina et al, 1998). In England, according to data from the British Crime Survey, 24% of women interviewed had suffered sexual abuse in the course of their lives, often when they were children or adolescents, and 7% had suffered serious violence, in the majority of cases vaginal rape (Walby and Allen, 2004). We cannot tell from the current state of research if rapes are more frequent in the US or if the difference between the two countries is due to the methods used in the studies or the women interviewed being more or less reticent. Contrary to the myth of the unknown man attacking in a dark street, all the research agrees on the fact that 70%–80% of rapists are men who are well known to the woman or child: their partner, a relative, a companion or a friend of the family.

Sexual violence is even more frequent in countries where women have fewer rights. About a quarter of women in Nicaragua, Zimbabwe and India say they have been raped by a partner, as opposed to about 15% in Canada, the US and Switzerland. In South Africa, a country where violence is endemic, more than 4,000 women are raped every day (Seager, 2003). According to many researchers the real frequency could be much higher than that revealed by the statistics available in various countries, at a time when many women still relive the rape they suffered in shame and fear (Russell and Bolen, 2000).

The rape figures are frightening and it is not surprising that they have triggered fierce arguments: those who do not believe in the extent of male violence maintain that the women are lying or exaggerating and that the researchers have got it wrong and consider to be violence what is instead seduction, passionate or bad sex, and so on (Schwartz, 1997). However, we find a countercheck that sexual violence is very frequent in the fact that men interviewed with anonymous questionnaires readily admit to having committed it. In the US, a proportion of university students varying from a quarter to a half replied that they had committed at least one rape or attempted rape; in a sample of Navy recruits, 10% of those interviewed admitted that they had raped a girl (Koss and Oros, 1982; Merrill et al, 2001). In Japan, 29% of men interviewed acknowledged that they had committed sexual violence against their wife or companion (Yoshihama, 2002).

Showing the extent of sexual violence faces us with a risk. Precisely when we have to acknowledge that the frequency of rape is very high, we run the risk of trivialising and ultimately denying the violence. In other words, if so many women have been raped, then perhaps it is something that is part of life and will not have such serious consequences. But that is not how things are. Rape is an attack on the integrity of a human being, which may destroy person or undermine their identity. Those who have suffered sexual violence remain deeply wounded by it, their trust in the world is undermined to such an extent that they are often forced to change their attitudes, work and life, and this is irrespective of whether the rape was committed by a man they knew or did not know, whether or not it was accompanied by other physical violence and whether or not the victim defined it as rape (Russell, 1990; Brison, 1998; Campbell and Soeken, 1999). According to data from research carried out in France on a representative sample of women, the risk of suicide increases by 26 times in the 12 months following a rape (Jaspard et al, 2003).

Sexual violence is even more frequent in situations of war (Brownmiller, 1975). From the 1980s to date, the systematic rape of women and children by soldiers/paramilitaries has been revealed in Mexico, Guatemala, El Salvador, Haiti, Colombia, Peru, Chile, Argentina, former Yugoslavia (20,000 Muslim women raped in 1992), Cyprus, Algeria, Sierra Leone, Liberia, Sudan (50,000 girls captured by government forces to become sex slaves), Somalia, Congo, Angola, Mozambique, South Africa, Rwanda (more than 15,000 women raped in 1994), Russia, Afghanistan, India, Burma, Vietnam, Philippines, Indonesia, East Timor and New Guinea (Seager, 2003).

## 1.2.2 Violence against children

Violence against children occurs above all in the family and takes various forms. In countries such as China, India and South Korea, where there is still a strong preference for a male child, having a female, or another female, is often considered a misfortune: newborn babies and girls may be killed at birth or malnourished and neglected until they die. Better-off women tend to have an abortion when they know they are carrying a foetus of the female sex. For this reason, every year, a million fewer children are born in China than expected. Summing up these various forms of elimination, Amartya Sen (1990), winner of the Nobel prize for economics in 1998, talks of genocide of the female sex and concludes that more than 100 million children are missing from the roll call.

In the West, even though we do not witness these forms of systematic elimination of female children, violence in the family is a frequent occurrence. According to research at a national level, in Canada and Finland, about 10% of children suffer physical violence in the family; and about 20% suffer psychological violence, which means they are humiliated, insulted, ignored, forced to eat alone, clean up their father's vomit or are forgotten in bars (Sariola and Uutela, 1992; MacMillan et al, 1997). There do not seem to be great distinctions between girls and boys when it comes to the risk of suffering this violence. The studies quoted are among the few in which the perpetrator of the violence is clearly identified: they all show that fathers are more often violent than mothers, whether it is physical or psychological violence, and this is in spite of the fact that it is predominantly mothers who take care of the children and spend more time with them.[1]

Sexual violence against girls and boys is endemic. In one of the first pieces of research carried out in the US, Diana Russell (1999) discovered that 28% of women interviewed had suffered sexual abuse before the age of 12, usually by men belonging to the family circle or known to them in some way. In a national sample of young people in Britain, 21% of girls – and 11% of boys – had suffered sexual abuse before the age of 16; in the majority of cases it was abuse with physical contact and the abusers were men they knew (May-Chahal and Cawson, 2005). In Geneva, in a sample of adolescents, 20% of females had suffered sexual abuse or violence involving physical contact; in a quarter of cases it was rape. The perpetrators were their peers or adults in a position of authority; 5% of girls had suffered sexual abuse by a relative. Among adolescents in Geneva, the proportions were much higher if the definition also included abuse not involving physical contact (being exposed to exhibitionism, posing for pornographic photos and so on) (Halpérin et al, 1996). Research carried out on a vast sample of adolescents in Milan confirmed these data (Pellai, 2004).

The perpetrators of sexual violence against children are almost always men: the proportions range from 83% to 98%, according to whether the violence is committed against boys or girls (Finkelhor et al, 1990; Halpérin et al, 1996).

Physical, psychological and sexual violence often mounts up and leaves deep marks on its victims, who are more likely to suffer from depression, anxiety, post-traumatic stress syndrome and food disorders, try to commit suicide, take drugs and show signs of various somatic or psychosomatic disorders. They are also more vulnerable to the risk of suffering further violence.[2] Although some succeed in overcoming the pain of what they have lived through and making sense of what has happened, through political commitment or art[3] for example, and living a life relatively free from the weight of this experience, others remain marked by it forever. The testimony of these women tells us of devastating suffering, arrested development and clipped wings: it is a miracle that these children have overcome the pain and are able to talk about it.[4] It is important to remember this pain when, later, we analyse the discourses of paedophiles and some psychiatrists, according to which sex between adults and children and incest in particular are quite harmless.

## 1.2.3 Domestic violence

Women who are insulted, humiliated, belittled in front of their children, threatened, terrorised, controlled all the time, shut up in the house, forced to leave work and not see their friends and relatives, forced into sexual acts they do not want, with threats, blackmail and physical force, pushed, slapped, beaten repeatedly, wounded, burned, strangled: all this is called domestic violence and the aggressors are husbands, companions and fiancés or ex-husbands, companions and fiancés.

Domestic violence is understood to be a continuous series of actions, which are diverse but characterised by a common purpose: control, through psychological, economic, physical and sexual violence, of one partner over the other. It involves the other being considered not as a person, but a thing which may be at your service, kept under control, made use of when needed and on which to unleash rage and frustration. In spite of many arguments on the subject, domestic violence is to an overwhelming extent violence by a man against a woman.[5] Studies in industrialised countries, of which there are now many, show that 20–30% of women have suffered physical or sexual violence by a partner or ex-partner in the course of their lives, for periods that may last for a few months or decades; between 5% and 15% of women were suffering violence at the very time of the inquiry (Koss et al, 1994). Psychological violence is much more frequent and just as destructive. In Italy, contrary to most European countries (Hagemann-White, 2001), there are no national data on the subject: still, the results of local studies agree with international trends. In Trieste, a city in the north, among the users of various health and social services, 18% had suffered physical and sexual violence by a partner or ex-partner during their lives and 6% were suffering violence at the time of the inquiry. If we also include psychological violence, the proportions were much higher, 29% and 16% respectively (Romito and Gerin, 2002).

The figures sometimes speak with greater force than the percentages. In one year: 900,000 women in the US reported their partner for maltreatment; 28,000 did so in Peru, in a single city, Lima; there were 22,000 reports of domestic maltreatment in Spain; 32,017 women and 22,500 children sought escape in a refuge in Britain (Seager, 2003). In a single region of Italy, Emilia Romagna, in one year, about 1,500 women resorted to various anti-violence centres and refuges (Creazzo, 2003).

Although these figures are frightening, many researchers estimate that, as for rape, they represent only an underestimate of the phenomenon. A countercheck comes from research in which men were also interviewed. In New Zealand, men and women were asked the same questions about couple violence in the previous 12 months: while 15% of the former reported that they had suffered at least one act of physical or sexual violence by their partner, 21% of the latter acknowledged that they had committed them (Morris, 1997).

As confirmation of the fact that domestic violence does not consist of occasional or uncontrolled explosions of anger, caused by the frictions of living together, there is the fact that the violence also continues after the relationship has been broken off. In research carried out in Switzerland, 5% of married women reported physical or sexual violence in the previous 12 months, compared to 20% of recently separated women (Gillioz et al, 2000). Also in Trieste, the violence was about four times more frequent among separated or divorced women than among married women (Romito and Gerin, 2002). This also applies to the ultimate violence – murder. In the US, 74% of murders of women by their partners occur after separation or divorce (Seager, 2003). Women may also kill their partners, but this happens more rarely. In England and Wales, for every man killed by his partner, there are more than four women (four and a half women to be precise) killed by their partners. In the US and Canada, the ratio is 1:3.[6] A fundamental difference is that men kill their wives after committing violence against them for years, whereas women kill men after suffering violence from them for years (Jones, 2000).

Domestic violence always involves the children (Graham-Bermann and Edleson, 2001; Radford and Hester, 2006). Data from a Canadian national inquiry show that children have witnessed at least 40% of the violence by their father against their mother and, in particular, more than half the violence in which the woman feared for her life (Juristat, 1994). According to a survey carried out in the US, children witness the rape of their mother in one case in 10 (Russell, 1990). Many women are killed by their partners in front of their children (Campbell, 1992). According to representative US data at a national level, half of violent husbands are also violent towards their children (Peled, 1997, 2000).

Some types of violence against wives or girls are typical of a particular culture. According to Carol Bellamy, Executive Director of Unicef, in 1997 at least 300 women were killed by men in the family for so-called reasons of 'honour' in a single province in Pakistan, 400 in the Yemen and 97 in Egypt. More than two thirds of murders of women in the Gaza Strip and the West Bank can be ascribed to so-called reasons of honour. In India, it is estimated that more than 5,000 women are killed every year by their husband or his family for reasons connected with an inadequate dowry. In this case also, the figures are controversial, because of the attempt to pass these murders off as domestic accidents, in which the clothes of the woman caught fire while she was cooking and she was burned (Bellamy, 2000).[7] Still in India, women and girls who refuse the proposals of a man run the risk of being punished with sulphuric acid, often the low-cost kind used to fill car batteries. In Bangladesh, there has been an increase in cases of acidification: there are about 300 a year and 80% of the victims are women, almost all very young. When they do not die, these girls always suffer very severe injuries and remain horribly disfigured (Swanson, 2002).

In spite of the differences between the various phenomena described, for example between violence against women in the context of marriage or stable relationships and violence by rejected suitors, between violence of a psychological type and physical or sexual violence, between maltreatment and murder, between domestic violence and wife killing in industrialised, Western countries and developing countries, common elements are underlined with force. In various countries and cultures, many men expect to dominate and control women, accepting no opposition or refusal, and are prepared to use violence, in various forms, including until death, if women resist.

## 1.3 The figures on discrimination

In the 1970s, Simone de Beauvoir (1984) noted ironically that in France the media love to declare that feminism is dead and buried, useless because now women have got it all. Thirty years later, in the US, Robin Morgan makes the same observation: from 1969 to date, the *Time* magazine alone has declared the death of feminism at least 119 times (Morgan, 2003). According to this line of thought, violence occurs only in extreme or residual situations, and its existence did not bring into question the conviction that discrimination had been overcome. Leaving aside the right to live without violence, have women really got it all?

Let us start with political rights. Today women have the right to vote everywhere, even in Kuwait (in 2006). Still, even where they have had this right for some time, political representation of women is poor. In 2004, throughout the world, men solidly occupied 84% of the seats in national Parliaments, with limited differences between more or less developed countries (80% and 86% respectively). Sweden stands out with only 55% of Members of Parliament who are men; in the

UK 82% are men, in Italy 88%. In the first few years of 2000, 89% of ministers or deputy ministers in the world are men: 86% in more developed countries and 91% in less developed countries (Ashford and Clifton, 2005).

Unlike the vote, women have not gained reproductive rights at all. In 2004, abortion was illegal or difficult to obtain in most countries in the world. In Latin America and Africa it is illegal almost everywhere and subject to severe restrictions. In Europe it is illegal in Ireland and Malta, and subject to severe restrictions in Poland. Even where abortion is legal, the possibility of having an abortion without risk may be severely limited by the cost of the operation (as in the US) or the conscientious objection made by health staff for religious reasons or pretexts (as in Italy). In the US, in the last five years, various states have issued more than 300 measures restricting abortion. From the Reagan administration onwards, including the Clinton administration, the funds of agencies making contraception and abortion possible in developing countries have been progressively cut (Wattleton, 2003).

Every year in the world about 20 million women are forced to have an abortion illegally, often under precarious health conditions with dreadful suffering. At least half a million women, almost all in less developed countries, die every year for reasons connected with reproduction, partly in an attempt to have an abortion via illegal or unsafe means. For every woman who dies, at least 30 suffer permanent damage to their health (Seager, 2003). In general, almost everywhere the situation regarding abortion has got worse in the last few years.

On the other hand, millions of non-voluntary sterilisations have been carried out on poor women and women from black and minority ethnic communities. This happened in various countries, including Canada, Australia, Sweden and the US, until the 1960s, and in Peru, was still happening between 1996 and 2000 (Brady et al, 2001; Warin, 2005).

Let us consider access to education and paid work. In developed countries, young women now tend to have a higher level of education than men, but in less developed countries, among adults, 24% of men and 38% of women are illiterate. In Central Africa less than half the girls go to primary school.

In most of the world, the percentage of people unemployed is higher among women than among men; the great majority of those who work part time, on low salaries without the possibility of a career, are also women. In the 1990s, women continued to earn less than men, even with the same education and type of work: in industry, the salary of women represents 79% of that of men in France, 71% in Mexico and

54% in Brazil. In a sample of 32 developed countries, the percentage of women managers reaches its maximum at around 40% (Canada, Latvia, Russia and the Ukraine) (Seager, 2003).

Even in the US, perhaps the country where the feminist movement has struggled most and with greatest success for equality, official statistics for the 1990s show how the situation of women and men remains profoundly unequal. Men are more than 95% of managers in industry, 90% of newspaper editors, 90% of television executives and 80% of members of Congress. Men are 80% of the richest people in the country, and women are more than two thirds of the poor. Women earn 75% of what a man earns, even with the same level of education, professional experience and hours worked. 'Typical women's' work is still lower paid than men's: those looking after children in a nursery earn less than those looking after cars in a car park (Rhode, 1997). In Italy also, women are more often unemployed: three years after their degree, in any discipline, there are many more unemployed women than men. They are also heavily underrepresented in management jobs. At university, women are 40% of researchers (the lowest level), 26% of associate professors, 11% of full professors, 7% of deans and 3% of rectors. In the national health system women are 70% of employees, but only 7% of full-time health executives (Ingrao and Scoppa, 2001).

In the meantime, women continue to take on the overwhelming majority of unpaid work, domestic work and care. In Sweden, the US and Japan, women do approximately 30 hours of domestic work per week, men do 24, 16 and 4 hours respectively. In Italy, women workers dedicate twice as much time as men to unpaid family work (20 hours a week as opposed to 12). Adding together the time for paid work, the time for transport and for unpaid work, the total time for women exceeds that for men by about 11 hours (65 hours per week as opposed to 56). In conclusion, Italian women work two months a year more than men, earning less and accruing fewer pension rights (Saraceno, 2004).[8]

Faced with this data, there is the temptation to interpret it in a psychological and individualistic sense: it is women who, for various reasons, prefer to avoid professions that are too demanding and competitive or roles of responsibility. This is a partial interpretation that enables us to avoid confronting the brutal reality of discrimination. Many studies show how sexual harassment at work serves to exclude women from prestigious jobs or even simply jobs that are better paid than typical women's work (Faludi, 1991). In Italy, a study (La Mendola, 1995) of the criteria for employment and career paths of new graduates in large companies shows that men are almost six times more likely than women to become managers. In spite of being aware that there is a law on equality, about 40% of selectors acknowledge that they take the sex of the candidate into account during selection, and 25% explicitly state that they favour men (1% favour women). Selection in the scientific world seems to work according to similar criteria, even in more advanced countries when it comes to equality between men and women. In Sweden, a candidate of the female sex must have 2.5 times more scientific merits and publications to receive the same score as a man (Wenneras and Wold, 1997). In the US, Carolyn Heilbrun, the first woman to become a professor at Columbia University, reports similar behaviour when she recalls that to remove

> an exceedingly talented woman ... and promote in her place a quite undistinguished male candidate in a field in which we already had five tenured people ..., the old boys were cloning themselves, slipping into tenured positions young men who closely resemble them. (1997, pp 123, 125)

## 1.4 The connections between violence and discrimination

In the light of these data, it is difficult to refute the clear conclusion of the French sociologist, Colette Guillaumin (1992, p 70), according to which women are usually 'oppressed, exploited and appropriated'. For Francine Pickup (2001, p 303), researcher and activist of the Oxfam non-governmental organisation:

> the violence to which women are subject is not random, or abnormal, or defined by specific circumstances alone. It is used as a weapon to punish women for stepping beyond the gendered boundaries set for them, and to instil in them the fear of even considering doing so. It is a systematic strategy to maintain women's subordination to men.

Far from consisting of behaviour that is deviant or can be explained by the psychological problems of the individual man, male violence represents a rational means, which in order to work effectively, as in fact it does work, needs an organised system of mutual support and widespread complicity by society.

It is also clear why opposing male violence is such a formidable task: it is not just a question of changing the law and behaviour, but of bringing into question a structured and deep-seated system of control and privilege. It is not conceivable, and in fact does not happen, that those benefiting from this system will let it be dismantled or limited without opposition.

What we consider today as taken-for granted rights we have bought and paid for, in fact represent the result of long, hard and painful struggles by women, and in some societies have not been gained at all. For example, in the West, the right to education and the possibility of women gaining access to higher learning and becoming those producing knowledge is the result of a long process, in which women have had to fight tirelessly against the opinions of philosophers, moralists and writers and the 'scientific' theories of various experts, against laws and practices excluding them from the right to education, and even against the physical violence of academics opposed to their presence (Le Doeuff, 1998; Romito and Volpato, 2005). Today access has been gained to higher education, but the proportion of women university professors remains low: 18% in the US, from 11 to 13% in Italy, France and Finland, 7% in the UK and 4-5% in Austria and Ireland (Osborn, 1998). Girls tend to be better students than boys, a fact that could have simple explanations: they are more intelligent or more studious, or both these things. And yet even this fact has unleashed violent reactions: there are those who maintain that the relatively poor results of boys can be attributed to the feminisation of the teaching body, a trend for which feminism is held to be responsible, which will end by alienating boys from higher education. In Canada, the argument has turned into brutal verbal abuse towards feminist professors and women (Bouchard, 2002). At the Polytechnic of Montreal more dreadful violence occurred in 1987 with the murder of 13 students, whom their murderer, Marc Lépine, considered as feminists who had robbed him of a place that was owed to him by right.

In other contexts, it is the state that takes on the task of punishing women who dare too much. In Iran, Farrokhrou Parsa, ex-Minister for Education, was executed in 1979 after a farcical trial in which she was acknowledged as guilty of 'promotion of prostitution, corruption on earth and opposition to god'. The measures the mullahs reprimanded her with included a directive allowing pupils to go to school without the veil and setting up a commission to make text books less sexist (Afkhami, 1984, p 330). In South Africa, rapes and sexual abuse of female children and adolescents at school, by their peers or teachers, are so frequent today that they have resulted in an inquiry by the Human Rights Watch (2001). Many of these pupils abandon their studies, also because schools tend to trivialise what has happened and not take measures against the rapists; when they become pregnant, it is the same school heads who force them to leave school.

It should be said again that every time a form of control over women is brought into question, violent opposition must be expected. Sexual mutilation is a form of control over the sexuality and behaviour of women that today affects at least 100 million women, predominantly in Africa, with dramatic consequences for their psychological and physical well-being (Toubia, 1994). In Kenya, the reason that sparked off the mobilisation of various tribal and political forces for the independence of the country was an attempt by missionaries to suppress the practice of clitoridectomy in 1929 (Morgan, 1992). Even today, in many countries, girls who are not mutilated and their families come up against such devastating ostracism by society that the prospect of not practising mutilation may be insupportable or even inconceivable.

If the sexual mutilation of women and Kenya seem too far away for us, we need only recall that in the West opposition to the right to abortion has taken extreme forms of violence (Erdenet, 1992). From 1992 to 2002, in the US and Canada extreme Right-wing Christian groups killed seven people, including doctors and nurses working in clinics where abortions were carried out, tried to kill another 15 and attacked 97 clinics, bombing them or setting fire to them. Death threats, harassment and abuse towards health workers or women who were in hospital to have an abortion can be counted in thousands (Seager, 2003). Every year in the US, clinics where abortions are carried out suffer at least 3,000 acts of violence. If this happened to churches or government offices, it would be called terrorism (Juergensmeyer, 2000).

## 1.5 A model for understanding male violence

It does not follow from this analysis that all men are violent (they are not), even though observing the facts leads us to conclude that they all could be, with relative impunity, if they so wished (Hanmer, 1990). Instead it follows that all men, even those who are not violent, receive at least some of the dividends from a patriarchal system, gaining from the violence committed by some: easy access to sexual relations, free domestic services, privileged access to higher and better-paid positions at work, and the psychological benefits resulting from them.

It is still not thinkable that such a widespread phenomenon, which has branched out and diversified in time and space, could be brought back to a single cause and a single theoretical model (Delphy, 1998). So it is that, although in many cases men use violence to get what they want at once (as in rape) or to maintain a privileged position (as in the case of sexual harassment at work[9]), in others, violence or the threat of violence seem less connected to an immediate objective. Tzvetan Todorov (2000) reminds us, quoting Kant, that the exercise and abuse of power may also be ends in themselves and need no other objectives to be expressed.

In some situations, an interpretation in psychological terms may be relevant. The link between the violence a child (male) suffered in infancy and adolescence and the probability that he will use violence against women and children as an adult[10] seems to have been established, for example. In the US, in a sample of Navy recruits, young men who had suffered physical or sexual abuse when they were small were four to six times more likely to commit a rape than those who had not been victims of violence (Merrill et al, 2001). But an explanation of violence in psychological terms does not exclude an explanation in social terms. Still in the US, a study has shown that serial killers, often deeply disturbed men, act more often in those states where violence has been legitimised by society (for example where corporal punishment is tolerated at school, paramilitary groups exist, some sports fans cultivate violence and so on) (DeFronzo and Prochnow, 2004). Another element consists of the low social value of some of the victims. The police, for example, often show little interest in finding and stopping serial killers of prostitutes. In England, the police started to be interested in the Yorkshire Ripper, a serial killer who killed 13 women and seriously injured another nine in the 1980s, only when he also started to kill 'respectable' women as well as prostitutes. The head of the police force spoke to him publicly with these words:

> He has made it clear that he hates prostitutes. Many people do. We, as a police force, will continue to arrest prostitutes..... But the Ripper is now killing innocent girls. That indicates your [here speaking directly to the murderer] mental state and that you are in urgent need of medical attention. Give yourself up before another innocent woman dies. (Baldwin, 1992, p 87)

In the US, in the Green River region of Seattle, 50 young women have been killed and at least as many have disappeared from 1982 to date. Arrested in 2003, G. Ridgway had placed on the record that he 'wanted to kill as many women as possible he considered prostitutes'.[11] The police showed little care – it took them 20 years to identify the murderer – perhaps because it was almost always young black women or prostitutes who were involved (Scholder, 1993). In the 1990s another man, J. Dahmer, raped, tortured, killed and then cut into pieces many boys, who had been enticed from among adolescents who had run away from home. In spite of the neighbours having witnessed the desperate attempt of one of them to escape, wounded and mad with terror, none of them intervened because 'they were matters between homosexuals', and they let Dahmer take the boy back home. He then tortured and killed him (Scholder, 1993).

Other cases, where committing violence requires a web of complicity to be activated involving social institutions and people in authority, have to do with children killed by their fathers in retaliation for the separation that their wives wanted. In Canada, in 1993, D.R. strangled his son when on leave from prison, where he was being held because of violence against his ex-companion, leave that was granted by a judge with the consent of the public prosecutor's office and supported by a psychiatrist (Dufresne, 1998).[12]

To conclude, even when male violence is associated with the serious psychological disorders of the aggressor, for it to be committed, it is often necessary for society to legitimise or tolerate the violence, with little care for the fate of the potential victims.

## Notes

[1] According to research in Britain on a national sample of young people, 7% had suffered serious physical maltreatment and 6% serious psychological abuse, the latter occurring more frequently among girls than among boys. However, it is not specified whether the perpetrators of the violence were their mothers, fathers or both parents (May-Chahal and Cawson, 2005).

[2] There is now a great deal of research on the subject. See, for example, Mullen et al, 1996; Silverman et al, 1996; Fergusson et al, 1997; Fleming et al, 1999; Romito et al, 2001.

[3] As in the case of Louise Armstrong (1978) or Christiane Rochefort (1988), both writers and feminist activists.

[4] See, for example, the evidence collected by Herman, 1992; Russell, 1997, 1999; and Itzin, 2000a.

[5] See Thoennes and Tjaden, 1990; Whyte et al, 2000; Anderson, 2002; Walby and Allen, 2004.

[6] See the research by Soothill et al, 1999; Locke, 2000; Rennison and Welchans, 2000.

[7] For example, in 1987, the Indian government maintained that 1,572 women had been killed because of their dowry throughout the country, whereas a women's group showed that there had been 1,000 dowry deaths in the same year in the State of Gujurat alone (Spatz, 1991).

[8] According to data from the Italian Family Budgets Survey by the Bank of Italy for 2000.

[9] This also provides other secondary advantages, such as enjoyment, sexual stimulation and reinforcement of male camaraderie (Thomas and Kitzinger, 1997).

[10] See the research by Watkins and Bentovim, 1992; Malinosky-Rummell and Hansen, 1993; Maxfield and Widom, 1996.

[11] 'US killer confesses to 48 murders', *La Repubblica*, 6 November 2003.

[12] This case will be described in detail in Chapter Four. For similar cases in the UK, see Saunders, 2004.

# TWO

# The theoretical context

## 2.1 Contemporary feminism

> I always wanted to fly, feminism gave me wings. (A woman
> in a discussion group)

In this chapter I will explain briefly the theoretical references forming
the context of and guiding my work. The principal one is feminism,
as it has developed since the 1960s.[1] Without feminism, its analysis of
the oppression of women and its determination to put an end to it,
and without the concrete practices characterising it, we would not be
here discussing male violence.

In this chapter I recall some of these practices, which are particularly
relevant for studying violence. Separatism allowed women to have a
physical and mental space, in which to interact and concentrate on their
priorities without having to adapt to male expectations and priorities.
Self-knowledge, practised in small groups, caused many women to
discover that the violence they had suffered and each had lived through
in secret and shame, convinced they were alone, was instead tragically
common. Self-help groups, starting from the need to find answers to the
health problems and suffering of many women, were able to develop
radical criticism of medicine, psychology and traditional methods of
care, producing original knowledge on the subject. It is in this context
that the first centres offering support to women in rape cases and refuges
for victims of domestic violence sprang up (The Boston Women's
Health Book Collective, 1971; Schechter, 1982).

In feminism, theory and practice are intertwined and feed off each
other. It is the practices recalled above that provided inspiration for
important theoretical developments, such as epistemological breaks
with some categories of common sense. One of these breaks has to
do with the public/private dichotomy. Situations considered private,
even confidential and intimate – such as what happened in the home,
kitchen and bed – became subject to analysis, report and political action:
this happened for domestic work, sexuality and rape, for example.
Feminism also produced radical criticism of theoretical models of the
naturalistic and individualistic type, criticism that is particularly relevant

to investigating the mechanisms for hiding violence. Theories such as psychobiology and psychoanalysis identify the origin and explanation of social relationships and facts, in this case the subordination of women,[2] in nature (evolution, hormones, genes, brain structure) or individual psychology. These are deterministic models: if it is by nature that women are less given to scientific study, artistic creation or company leadership and instead more is given to care or service work, which is low paid or unpaid, if it is by nature that men are polygamous and ready for rape (as many sociobiologists maintain), then any social reform represents a useless waste of energy. Instead feminist scholars have shown that so-called instincts are the result of a social construction process as far as masculinity, femininity, sexuality, maternal and paternal behaviour are concerned: according to the succinct expression Simone de Beauvoir gave to this in the 1950s: 'You are not born a woman, you become one' (de Beauvoir, 1999).

This epistemological criticism represents a wealth of thought by many modern feminists, including materialist feminism, to which the analysis made in this book owes a great deal. It is an approach that has been developed in France since the 1970s with contributions by scholars such as Christine Delphy, Colette Guillaumin and Nicole-Claude Mathieu, using materialism above all as a method to analyse relationships between men and women in social rather than natural or psychological terms (Jackson, 1996).[3]

Feminist thought has in some cases produced and in other cases elaborated again in an original way ideas and concepts that have become essential tools for analysing and understanding reality. Here I will give a quick resumé of three of these concepts – patriarchy, gender and ideology – whereas others will be presented in the course of the text.

The term patriarchy is an ancient one and has changed in the course of history. It comes from two Greek words: *pater* (father) and *arché* (origin and command): patriarchy is therefore, literally, the authority of the father. In the contemporary feminist sense, the term patriarchy indicates a social formation in which men have power or even more simply: the power of men (Delphy, 2000).

The concept of gender may have different meanings, even in the feminist sphere. In what I am referring to this term denotes categorisation, resulting from social forces to construct men and women from the biological sex in a social context, characterised by the subordination of the latter (Mathieu, 2000). Christine Delphy (1991) proposes an even more radical position, in which the importance of biological difference is reduced. For Delphy, the crucial point is the subordinate relationship; sex is only an indicator and not a generator of the difference in power. In short, it is the gender that constructs the sex and not the other way round, or rather it is because there is a subordinate relationship between the genders that the biological sex takes on such importance.

Ideology is understood to be a set of ideas supported by concrete practices, aimed at hiding social conflict and legitimising what exists. Ideology provides a view of reality in some 'simple' way: what exists – the fact that women take on 90% of care and domestic work within the family or that men define their model of sexuality as the norm, for example – is natural, normal and therefore desirable. In short, ideology is not only partial or incorrect knowledge of the world, it is a way of representing the world so as to legitimise what exists and maintain the interests of the ruling class or group.

The ideology of rape (after all she enjoyed it, she was looking for it or she lied) serves not only to hide its frequency and ferocity, the pain of the victims and the impunity of the aggressors, but also its more general function of control, through fear, over all women (Gordon and Riger, 1989). The ideology of romantic, saving love prepares women to accept unsatisfactory heterosexual relationships, confuse violence with passion and take on care and domestic work for nothing, according to the telling English maxim 'she sank into his arms and she found herself with her arms in the sink'. In brief, the patriarchal ideology presents the subordination of women as natural, legitimate and desirable and contributes to making the reality of domination acceptable or invisible to the dominated (Delphy and Leonard, 1984; Mathieu, 1991). In this sense, sociobiology and psychoanalysis are powerful ideological tools; their extraordinary social success, in spite of internal contradictions and serious scientific limits, is indirect proof of this.

It must be underlined that, to be effective, ideology must be supported by real power. In fact, the myths about rape influence the reaction of the victims (who feel blame and suffer shame because of the violence inflicted on them) and the witnesses (40% of doctors interviewed in a study in Italy think that 'a woman cannot be raped if she does not want to be', Gonzo, 2000), but are also imposed by means of the law. In Britain, for example, based on the *corroboration rule*, during a trial involving sexual violence, judges were obliged to remind jurors of the danger of convicting someone based only on the word of the person reporting him. This law was repealed in 1994, but applying it remains at the discretion of judges, who often continue to remind jurors that 'the woman may be lying' (Lees, 1997).

## 2.2 The contribution of epistemological reflection

The antinaturalistic and antipsychologistic view of materialist feminism and its formulation of the concept of ideology are similar to the epistemological proposals of Gaston Bachelard (Bourdieu et al, 1968). Bachelard, a French philosopher of science who died in 1962, proposes a model for scientific knowledge of the world that may represent a powerful tool for criticising prevailing theories and therefore for epistemological innovation. He maintains that scientific fact is 'conquered, constructed and verified' with a hierarchy of cognitive acts applied to each phase of research, from conceptualisation to aspects that appear to be only technical. Here, what interests us most is the first stage: scientific fact is conquered by breaking with prejudices, the immediate perception of things accredited by common sense, which, precisely because it is shared, immediate and apparently intuitive, gives a powerful illusion of truth. Now, an analysis of many theories regarding women shows immediately that they are based on the most antiquated prejudices and prevailing ideology rather than scientific knowledge (Ehrenreich and English, 1979; Tavris, 1992). Bachelard offers additional tools for this analysis, which are those subversive intellectual strategies he defines as 'breaking techniques'. The principal ones include an historical–genetic analysis of scientific concepts, a tool for criticising psychologistic and naturalistic interpretative models, basing their claim of being objective on the evident ease with which they become imposed on the common consciousness, whereas instead they distance us from genuine scientific knowledge of the world. These explanations are always used to discredit behaviour the ruling class does not understand or considers deviant. You need only consider soldiers deserting and refusing to fight in the First World War being attributed to reasons of 'congenital psychological abnormality' (Bianchi, 2001a) or any behaviour by women considered to be annoying or strange being attributed to hormonal causes, such as menstruation or the menopause (Fausto-Sterling, 1992).

Another technique recommended by Bachelard is the break with everyday language, which, precisely because it is everyday, brings 'petrified social ideology' with it unobserved. In this way a housewife is talked of or was talked of as a woman who 'does not work', since the prevailing ideology considers as work only what is paid and carried out on the market; sexual violence against children is defined as 'abuse', therefore recognising the sexual use of a child by an adult as legitimate; the man who uses a prostitute is defined as a 'client', as though he were conducting a commercial transaction like any other.

The last of these breaking techniques consists of 'statistical verification'. According to Bachelard, the numerical description of reality may have an explosive effect, really unhinging the view of things from common sense. It is a proposal that powerfully shows the effect of trust, sometimes uncritical, in statistics, which is typical of the positivist approach. Inevitably, social statistics depend on the conceptualisation work carried out in the early stages, and this work may in turn be permeated with the prevailing ideology. In this way the calculation of the Gross National Product has been made traditionally without taking care and domestic work into account, the limits of which have been discussed by feminist sociologists and economists (Boserup, 1970). However, when statistical analysis produces a deviation from common sense and exercises that 'epistemological vigilance' that Bachelard considers cannot be renounced, it may represent a powerful tool for uncovering hidden aspects of reality. It is enough to quote the statistics on the division of domestic work between men and women and on the frequency of male violence against women and children.

## 2.3 Subjectivity and meaning: the contribution of psychology and social science

As already indicated, this work takes on the view of materialist feminism in opposition to psychological or biological reductionism. Still, conceiving mental activity and human behaviour exclusively in terms of social and material structures would be just as mechanistic and reductionistic. As recognised by Stevi Jackson (2001, p 288), who starts from a materialist position:

> The material and social cannot only be understood in terms of social structure. We need also to account for subjectivity and agency.

The concept of *agency*, together with the concepts of *self* and *meaning*, have become central in feminist and sociological theories in the last few years. By *human agency* we understand the capacity of the individual to intervene in a causal sense in reality. This concept is founded on some crucial questions: how social structures are created and determine the actions of individuals and what the limits are to the capacity of individuals to act independently from structural constraints, in other words, what the limits to *human agency* are. Social structures are perpetuated through human behaviour and they are not a mechanical result of the material context or ideological pressure. People think and make sense of the world around them, including their own feelings and actions, decide and act. Even faced with an objective reality, subject to ideological and material constraints, they always have a margin of freedom in the view of the world they adopt, their interpretations and actions. As Stevi Jackson (2001, p 288) writes:

> We can see ourselves as located within social structures (of gender, class and race), but nonetheless possessing agency, interpreting events, applying meaning to them.

In my investigation into the social mechanisms for hiding male violence both the role of social structures (laws, scientific theories, media system and so on) and behaviour and individual cognitive strategies will be analysed. For example, many police officers from the 'flying squad' with good direct knowledge of domestic violence against women maintain that this is 'mutual' violence (and in fact they talk of 'family arguments') and describe women as more violent than men. They maintain this representation of reality contrary to their own experience, in which with few exceptions they have never seen women being violent with men (Bascelli and Romito, 2000). What are the cognitive and social mechanisms that form the basis of these convictions?

Social psychology has developed conceptual tools to understand the methods by which we perceive and interpret the world, tools that allow us to grasp the constant human activity of construction and reconstruction of meanings and their negotiation, which happens when interacting with others and institutions. In the course of the book I will use the theory of attribution, which explains the methods by which people attribute responsibility for an event to themselves or others, stable or variable, controllable or uncontrollable causes, and models such as *coping* strategies, which are those mechanisms people put into operation when they have to deal with painful or stressful situations (Bulman and Wortman, 1977). These tools will be useful for understanding how victims can restructure reality, often according to social expectations relating to what violence is, reconstructing it in more ambiguous and less threatening terms for themselves, until sometimes they end up denying the violence completely (Phillips, 2000).

As for the role of witnesses, psychologists have tried to understand how we act faced with a situation requiring moral action or judgement, when it involves taking or not taking an action that can be censured, taking up a position on the subject or intervening in defence of the person being attacked. Often these actions have a cost: we give up something we want or which is advantageous, we lose time, we risk getting into trouble, we may suffer retaliation and so on. To resolve the moral dilemma between perceiving an injustice and not wishing to act as a consequence, human beings put into operation various cognitive strategies for 'moral release', which allow them to change the meaning of the event and therefore their behaviour. Albert Bandura (1999) lists the following:

- moral justification ('war is a necessary evil to ensure democracy', putting up a friend who is being pursued by her violent husband 'would be the right thing to do, but my family would risk getting into trouble, and my family is more important');
- euphemistic labelling (civilians killed in war are defined as 'collateral damage'; newspapers talk of 'marital disputes' instead of 'violence by husbands against their wives');
- advantageous comparisons (terrorism is justified by recalling that states now considered democratic sprang from acts of terrorism; some incestuous fathers maintain that it is better for their children to be initiated into sexuality by them than by other men);
- displacement and distribution of responsibility, encouraged by bureaucratic structures (Eichmann maintained he had only 'obeyed orders'; and who has greatest responsibility – the magistrature, social services, relatives – for a child being killed by his father, a violent ex-husband, with whom he was spending Sunday?);
- indifference or distortion of the consequences (many weapons kill without those using them dealing with the agony and death of the victim; pornography presents women who are raped as enjoying torture; many psychiatrists think that sexual abuse has no consequences for the victims);
- dehumanisation (enemies and prisoners to be gassed are defined as pigs, dogs and worms; women are defined by their anatomical parts or also as animals);
- attribution of blame ('the victim wanted it').

To explain the attempts of criminals to make their actions acceptable to others and themselves, sociologists have developed categories, some of which are similar to those listed above (Sykes and Matza, 1957). More particularly, Scully and Marolla (1984, 1985) used the categories of 'excuses and justifications' to examine how men convicted of rape and in some cases murder of the victim recounted and reconstructed the violence they had committed: 'after all they had only gone a bit too far, they had been drinking and their friends had egged them on' (excuses), or the woman 'had provoked them and she had enjoyed it after all' (justifications). In Italy, the defending lawyers in a famous rape trial (the case happened in Marcellina in 1983, in which at least 10 men were involved in kidnapping, raping and torturing two foreign girls) maintained that their clients were 'only high spirited boys involved in rustic revelry. It was only a Bacchanalian orgy....' (excuses) and that the girls had provoked them by hitch hiking (justifications) (Lagostena Bassi, 1991, p 24).

However, it is important not to fall into the temptation of reading these psychosocial mechanisms in an individualistic way. It cannot be 'by nature' or by chance that all these cognitive strategies centre on hiding, trivialising or justifying male violence. We must not forget that some of the people involved in society adhere sincerely to the patriarchal model: many men, and many women also, are convinced that it is legitimate to punish insubordination by women, whether a wild or unfaithful wife or a girl considered sexually 'loose', with violence. On the other hand, those who leave the preset tracks may incur heavy social penalties. Women who have suffered sexual violence, who define it as such and seek justice and reparation, reporting the rapist, may subsequently be cruelly victimised by lawyers and magistrates during the trial (Lees, 1997). Workers who have suffered sexual harassment are often penalised if they protest and report what has happened (Bingham and Gansler, 2002). Mothers who report incest when they are separating from their partners are defined as 'vindictive' and, for this reason, risk losing the trust of their children (on the other hand, if they do not report it, they are labelled as mothers who are complicit or give little protection, and in this case also they risk losing the trust of their children) (Myers, 1997). Relatives, friends or professionals who side with the woman or child who has been abused risk vengeance by the violent man: threats, blackmail, harassment, retaliation on a social or professional level and physical attack until death (Nelson, 2000).

## 2.4 Women are human beings

According to a traditional proverb from Milan, 'I donn hin minga gent', meaning women are not human beings. In this context, the feminist assertion by Robin Morgan (1992, p 271), 'Women are human beings, after all', acquires revolutionary significance.

Another of the ideas guiding this book is that women are human beings. Even though their condition in the patriarchy has a specific aspect, which does not rule out other specific aspects being recognised (belonging to a 'racialised' minority or being poor in a class-conscious, racist and post-colonialist society represents a condition other than being 'white' and well-to-do, for example), women are part of the human race and share experiences and reactions with other historically subordinate or oppressed groups of human beings. It is therefore possible to also examine their condition using and adapting the categories used to study other groups; in the same way it is possible to transfer categories drawn up in the context of feminism, to study women and their oppression, to other social groups. French materialist feminists, for example, used the categories of slavery and colonisation to take into account two historically crucial aspects in the oppression of women: the appropriation of women – not only their workforce in domestic production, but also their body, sexuality and 'products', which are children – and their psychological and cultural domination, including unconsciously adopting the values of those dominating, respectively (Mathieu, 1991; Guillaumin, 1992; Delphy, 1998).

The study of violence, the reactions of those suffering it and those witnessing it is a field in which comparison and analogies between different situations may be fruitful. In the course of interviewing young men about their experience of military service, for example, it was found that the episodes of bullying in which they were involved or which they had witnessed were never defined as violence but as 'pranks', even though the consequences were often serious (fractures, attempted suicide and so on).[4] In a similar way, many girls deny they have suffered rape (Phillips, 2000). In this way the refusal to accept that they are victims of violence is not a characteristic of women, but a characteristic of victims, at least in a certain historical phase of social awareness of a certain form of violence.

It is interesting to compare the reactions of women suffering violence by a man and the reactions of those who have suffered violence for reasons recognised as political. For example, Jean Améry, a Jewish member of the Resistance who was interned and survived Auschwitz, describes the experience of being hit by a police officer in the first few days of detention in Belgium in this way:

> With the first blow the detainee realises that he has been *abandoned* to his own resources: this contains in a nutshell everything that will happen later.... They are authorised to hit me in the face, the victim perceives with confused surprise, and deduces from this with certainty which is just as vague: they will do what they want with me. Outside no-one is informed and no-one will do anything for me.... right from the first blow he [the detainee] loses something which perhaps we can define provisionally as *faith in the*

*world....*The most important element of faith in the world still – and the only one relevant in our context – is the certainty that, guided by social contracts which may be written or otherwise, the other will take care of me, more specifically he will respect my physical and therefore also my metaphysical substance. The bounds of my body are the bounds of my self. The surface of my skin protects me from the outside world: if I am to have faith, my skin must only feel what I *want* it to feel.

With the first blow, however, this faith in the world collapses. With his blow the other ... imposes his physicality on me. He is upon me and in this way destroys me. It is like rape, a sexual relationship without the consent of one of the two partners ... being physically overwhelmed by the other finally becomes a form of destruction of existence. (Améry, 1996, pp 64-7 of the Italian translation)

Jean Améry was a writer and philosopher who knew how to convey incisively the fracture caused by that first blow as regards immediate experience and perception of the world. Only recently, women who have been battered or raped have been able to describe not only what happened but also produce theories from the experience they have lived through (hooks, 1997; Brison, 1998). Many great writers have suffered violence in the past also: however, it is not the direct experience or the capacity to write and analyse that women have not had until now. What they have not had is social legitimacy. Detention in a concentration camp and torture are political facts; there is a general agreement, at least in words, on the fact that they are terrible experiences, imposed on victims, which must not be repeated. Violence committed by men against women, on the other hand, especially in the context of an affectionate relationship, not only has not had the status of political violence until very recently, but battered wives and girls who have been raped have been led to be deeply ashamed of the violence suffered. Only in 2004, after 30 years of pressure from the women's movement, Amnesty International (2004), the largest of the major international organisations, defined 'private' violence against women as torture.[5]

Analogies between the response by society to the exterminations committed by the Nazis and the response by society to violence and the killing of women committed by men are many.[6] For example, although referring to the sexual behaviour of the victim in denigrating terms is a typical reaction to violence against women, making those who have suffered abuse and violence guilty is a more general social reaction. Jean Améry (1996, p 156) recalls comments such as 'if they are being arrested [the Jews] they must have done something'. Another example concerns the phenomenon of denial and trivialisation: there are historians who deny the existence of extermination camps and gas chambers and there are professionals who, as we will see, deny the extent of violence against women and children and its consequences. Still, a crucial difference lies in the fact that whereas pro-Nazi denial and anti-Semitism have been opposed and punished by society in their turn (in many European countries, denying the Holocaust is against the law, for example), no punishment by society exists for those who trivialise male violence against women and children (French, 1992). On the contrary, the media system gives credit to a pathetic image of separated ex-husbands who have killed their wives and children, presenting them as victims (Radford and Hester, 2006, p 84; Morgan, 2006), while a press campaign to support the rights of torturers and make them appear in a good light has yet to be seen.

## 2.5 An international approach

A final statement must be made regarding method rather than theory. The material discussed in this book concerns different countries, where history, culture, religion, traditions, economic development, laws, organisation of services and rates of violence also differ widely. In the majority of cases these are English-speaking countries, because it is in this geo-cultural area that the women's movement has done the greatest and earliest work on the subject of violence. Two questions arise: whether data relating to different countries can be compared with each other, and whether the results relating to a certain country can also be applied or used in some way elsewhere. It is difficult to answer these questions satisfactorily. Still, in the course of the analysis it will become clear that paths that appear to be different often lead to similar results. This convergence of results may reinforce the analysis carried out in a particular context and help to understand that the problem of male violence and the responses by society on the subject are not due to a single factor, a single law or practice. This observation may prevent concentration on one circumstantial aspect specific to one country – a certain law, a certain practice – in order to keep a more general view of the problem instead.

On the other hand, notwithstanding the difficulty in comparing different systems, comparative studies in this area have flourished in the last few years, often having as their subject the consequences of some particularly controversial measures, such as fathers' visiting rights after separation, when they are violent men, and joint custody.[7] It is thanks to the conclusions of these analyses that it is becoming possible to learn what works and what does not work: family mediation, joint custody, protection orders and programmes for violent men have existed for years in many countries and in some cases have been subject to careful assessment. Studying the results obtained in other countries may also prevent blunders and errors being made and allow possible attacks to be anticipated.

## Notes

[1] I am aware of the risk of simplification when talking of feminism as though it were a monolithic movement or thought. As it is not possible to define and discuss the various types of feminism here, I will limit myself to outlining the approach I am referring to. It must also be specified that feminism has a history starting well before the 1960s, even though it is in those years that so-called new feminism renewed its drive.

[2] This antinaturalistic analysis is not exclusive to feminism. See, for example, Rose et al (1983) and Gould (1998) for criticism of the biological explanations of the oppression of black people or the working class.

[3] This tendency is in opposition to postmodern approaches, like the so-called *cultural turn* characterised by a shift in feminism's emphasis from 'things' (like women's work and male violence) to 'words', to issues of language, representation and subjectivity (Barrett, 1992; Brodribb, 1992).

[4] 'The mechanisms of male violence: qualitative research on bullying', Lucia Beltramini, MA dissertation, Faculty of Psychology, University of Trieste, 2007.

[5] Even internment in a concentration camp was not always enough to prevent the little consideration given to some victims connected with their low social status and prejudice towards them: women and homosexuals kept quiet about their experience for a long time, for example (Todorov, 2000).

[6] Even though not always welcome. The historian Peter Novick (2001) shows how in the course of the last 50 years representatives of the Jewish community, particularly in the US, have at times underlined and at other times opposed analogies between the fate of Jews under Nazism and that of other groups interned in the extermination camps.

[7] See, for example, the work of Smart and Sevenhuijsen, 1989; Hester and Radford, 1996; Kurki-Suonio, 2000; Eriksson and Hester, 2001; Eriksson et al, 2005; Radford and Hester, 2006.

# THREE

# Tactics for hiding male violence

What do I mean by 'tactics' and 'strategies'?[1] These are mental operations – ways of seeing, conceptualising and naming reality – which materialise in behaviour, are deposited as common sense and become ideology when they centre on the interests of those in power and may be 'institutionalised' in various ways, such as laws, scientific or pseudoscientific theories and the work practices of legal and social services. These institutionalised forms influence and sometimes determine the way we perceive reality and therefore our reactions, feelings and behaviour. I define 'strategies' as complex, articulated manoeuvres, general methods for hiding male violence and allowing the status quo, privileges and male domination to be maintained; by the term 'tactics' I mean tools that may be used across the board in various strategies, without being specific to violence against women.

Talking of strategies and tactics gives the idea of an organised movement working together, in which various people combine with various means to obtain a single result: an image that is not really suited to the complexity and contradictions present in modern societies. But just because a strategy exists, it does not necessarily follow that those involved act consciously to achieve its purpose. The police officer advising a battered woman to withdraw her report against her violent husband may do so for various reasons: because he sincerely believes that it is the best way of helping her, to avoid extra work, because he is ignorant of the law, because he is convinced that a man has a right to make his wife 'toe the line', because he is also a violent husband and sympathises with the aggressor. Whatever the motive and awareness of the police officer in question, the consequences for the woman will be similar. In short, we may talk of a 'system' and strategies to maintain it, when various actions centre on the same purpose, even if those involved are not fully aware of it.

I will begin by describing the tactics, since these form the basis for the strategies (legitimising and denying violence) to work. The tactics I have identified are euphemising, dehumanising, blaming, psychologising, naturalising and separating.

## 3.1 Euphemising: the politics of language

Language is not only the tool allowing us to communicate, pass on experience, recall it and therefore construct social interactions, but it is above all the means by which we codify and conceptualise the world. The name we give to things, also usually the name others have given them, cannot but influence our perception of the things themselves and therefore our reactions and actions on the subject. In short, language is a powerful tool, which may obscure or, on the contrary, illuminate and redefine our perception of reality. The epistemologist Gaston Bachelard considers the break with everyday language as one of the principal techniques for moving from the rough and naive perception of common sense to the formulation of a problem in scientific terms. But these breaks are also necessary to take account of changing social reality. It is precisely because, as Bachelard states, the language of common sense brings 'petrified social ideology' (see Bourdieu et al, 1968) with it that feminist activists and scholars have refused to use some traditional terms and have created new ones. In the introduction to the anthology of the international feminist movement *Sisterhood is global*, Robin Morgan (1984, p xxiii) uses almost the same words as Bachelard, when she states:

> We have attempted to challenge the politics of language in terms of sex and gender ... tried to break down standard patriarchal categorisation and stereotyping of women, which is so pervasive that it becomes almost invisible in language itself.

Dale Spender (1980), an Australian researcher, recalls that to live in the world we must give it a name: names are essential for constructing reality, because without a name it is difficult to accept the existence of an object, event or feeling. To recount experiences that have remained historically invisible, such as violence against women, it has therefore been necessary to create terms and concepts that traditional language did not have. The term 'sexism', for example, was coined at the end of the 1960s in a similar way to racism to denote something that, although central to the life of women, had been without a name until then (Talbot, 1988). In the same years expressions such as *sexual harassment in the workplace* (Thomas and Kitzinger, 1997) and *femicide* were introduced. The latter term indicates cases of women killed by men exclusively because they are women; this category includes many murders by serial killers and murderers of prostitutes, but also the removal of embryos and foetuses of the female sex in countries where only the birth of a male has social value (Radford and Russell, 1992).

Although denoting reality correctly is a necessary step for reading it, understanding it and acting on it, just as crucial is revealing linguistic mechanisms for hiding it. Linguistic avoidance is a technique, deliberate or unconscious, thanks to which the perpetrators of violence against women and children – men – disappear from discourses and texts on male violence, whether these are international documents, scientific work or the popular press. Euphemising is a parallel technique, which allows a phenomenon to be labelled in an imprecise and misleading way such as to obscure the seriousness or responsibility of whoever has committed it. Let us consider, for example, the phrase 'female circumcision', which is used internationally instead of 'female sexual mutilation' out of a questionable form of respect for the more misogynistic practices of other cultures (Morgan, 1992). In reality, even in its less serious forms, genital mutilation is anatomically equivalent to partial amputation of the penis (Toubia, 1994), a practice that nobody would allow to be trivialised.

Mechanisms for euphemising and linguistic avoidance are sometimes subtle and shrewd, at other times crude, but always systematic. The results of such a process are resounding: men disappear from the discourse on violence by men against women and children. Thus we talk of 'marital disputes or conflicts' or 'domestic violence' instead of violence by husbands against wives, of 'incestuous or abusive families', 'incestuous mothers' and 'parents' instead of fathers abusing and raping their children. This distortion of language and the distortion of reality that results from it, is not a characteristic exclusive to ordinary, everyday language. Phillips and Henderson (1999) analysed a sample of articles on the subject of male violence appearing in popular and scientific journals between 1994 and 1996. Out of a total of 165 summaries and 11 articles, the expression male violence appeared only eight times, whereas code words, such as rape, abuse, violence and domestic violence were much more numerous, being used 1,044 times. The gender of the victim (female, woman) and the relevant code words (wife, victim) were also used much more often (1,179 times) than the terms 'man', 'male' and corresponding codes (abuser, perpetrator; 327 times). The authors concluded that

> when the sex of the perpetrator is not specified and the violence described only includes the identity of the female victim, male violence against women is constituted as a problem of women. Moreover, in the articles considered

in this study, code words such as domestic violence, marital violence, family violence, used to describe exclusively male violence against women, actually convey the message that women are as violent as men. (Phillips and Henderson, 1999, p 120)

Documents from international organisations and governments also talk of violence against women and children, but rarely or never of male violence. In Italy a Directive of the President of the Council in 1997[2] talks of 'prevention of violence in personal relationships', 'developing … statistical findings on the phenomena of sexual violence and sexual abuse also in the family environment', 'permanent monitoring of the phenomenon of violence against women and children', 'abuse in the family', 'sexual violence' and 'domestic violence'. At no point does the document talk of male violence. In a more recent document of the European Community, *The protection of women against violence*,[3] which is full of sound analyses and innovative recommendations, we observe a similar tendency. In 50 pages the term 'violence' – against women, sexual, marital, domestic – is mentioned 271 times, rape 36 times, incest and sexual abuse four times each respectively, making a total of 311 code words indicating male violence but without denoting it clearly. Explicit terms are much rarer: male violence/violent men are talked of four times and it is specified five times that violence/rapes are committed by men/husbands/male relatives. The effort to be neutral and also take into account the rare cases where women are the perpetrators of violence and men are the victims is obvious. However, linguistic avoidance of the expression 'male violence' is even more surprising if we think that in ordinary language the tendency has been – and is still – precisely the opposite: in fact, the term 'man' has been used by extension to indicate men and women, the whole of humanity, as in the expression *les droits de l'homme* (man's rights), commonly used in many French-speaking countries instead of 'human rights'. On the other hand, the word humanity itself comes from the Latin *homo*.

Among mechanisms making linguistic avoidance and consequent euphemising possible, Lamb and Keon (1995) describe using neutral terms regarding gender, such as 'abuser' and 'perpetrator', considering the couple inappropriately as the agent and using the passive form; thus the talk is of women or children who have been raped and wives who have been beaten and killed rather than men, boys or husbands who rape, beat and kill. This process is particularly visible when it is interwoven with professional jargon. In an analysis of the clinical records of a first-aid hospital department in the US, Warshaw (1993) observes how both the perpetrator and the context of the violence disappear: women are beaten, but it is not understood by whom, they are killed by some impersonal agent, hit by a fist, a bottle or a chair moving through space just at that time. Often they are also no longer women, but an eye, a jaw, the spleen or the liver. This method, which is typical of medical language, is certainly not used deliberately to hide male violence; but in fact it contributes to making it invisible to the eyes of health staff.

These practices are not connected exclusively with covering up male violence against women. On the contrary, they are used every time there is a desire to hide responsibility for a criminal act, its seriousness or the act itself. The Nazis talked of 'selection' to indicate prisoners to be sent to the gas chambers; civilians killed in war are defined as 'collateral damage' and bombardments of urban areas as 'clean, surgical strikes' (Bandura, 1999; Glover, 2001). During the Anglo–American invasion of Iraq (in 2003) an American newspaper reported news according to which 'Baghdad's hospitals were running out of supplies [of drugs] to treat the burns, shrapnel wounds and spinal injuries caused by the fighting'.[4] Thanks to this euphemistic formulation, not only do those responsible for the suffering, caused by the 'fighting' and not by the fighters, disappear, but also the victims themselves, who become depersonalised and made into things: wounded civilians become burns, shrapnel wounds and spinal injuries.

An example of how words count concerns the extermination of at least 800,000 Tutsis in Rwanda, committed by the Hutu in 1994. The commander of the small intervention force from the United Nations on the spot, General Dellaire, did his utmost to obtain the reinforcements that would have enabled him to protect the population, but without success because of the opposition of various countries, including the US and Britain first and foremost. The conflict between Dellaire and the United Nations materialised around the term 'genocide'. There is in fact an international protocol to be followed in the case of genocide, which obliges the United Nations Office to intervene and this explains why there was a refusal to use this term to define the massacre of almost a million people in a few months solely because of their ethnic origin (Staub, 1999, p 186).

## 3.2 Dehumanising

Dehumanising victims is an essential part of being able to commit acts of cruelty without remorse. While the perception of the other as a human being and therefore similar to yourself brings about empathetic reactions, depriving victims of their humanity allows you to remain indifferent to their suffering. Among the social conditions necessary for evil to surface Staub (1999) describes the cultural devaluation of the other, who is seen as lazy, stupid, inferior and morally deficient. The enemy, oppressed people, prisoners to be tortured or internees to be gassed are defined as 'stupid savages', 'filthy natives', 'demons' or as animals: 'pigs', 'dogs' and 'worms'.

Social psychologists, such as Staub (1999) and Bandura (1999) use various examples, including the Nazi genocide of Jews and gypsies and the Vietnam War, in their investigation into the 'roots of evil' and the various mechanisms for dehumanising. But their analysis applies perfectly well to violence against women. Sexual abuse, torture, abuse and extermination, let us say it simply, of women and children would not have been possible if the killers and witnesses had not belonged to a culture where the female sex was devalued and dehumanised. This systematic devaluation of women, particularly their intellectual and moral capacity, is a constant characteristic of the cultural output of Western philosophers and scientists from Aristotle to Derrida, via Rousseau, Kant, Freud and many others.[5] Like oppressed people, who are to be dominated or exterminated, women are often called by the names of animals in everyday language: cats, kittens, bunnies, fawns, gazelles, geese, hens, snakes, monkeys, cows, bitches, pigs, sows and piglets;[6] or they are defined by their anatomical parts: legs, arse, tits. This is such a frequent and commonplace way of dehumanising that it appears harmless and goes unnoticed. That it represents a demonstration of hostility and discrimination instead becomes immediately obvious in some contexts, as in harassment in the workplace. Even though it seems more innocuous, the expression 'woman-object', which is used currently to denote a very common phenomenon in everyday life and in the media, emphasises precisely this: if the woman is an object, she is not human, she is something else with reference to humanity.

Dehumanising women is a systematic practice in pornography. Andrea Dworkin and Catharine MacKinnon (1988) maintained that one of the damaging effects of pornography consists of presenting the dehumanisation of women as though it were something legitimate and amusing, an 'entertainment'. In fact, according to these scholars the dehumanisation and subordination of women (or other socially weak people), shown in a sexually explicit way, represents the very heart of pornography. According to their formulation this happens when women are presented as sex objects or consumer goods; as dirty or inferior; penetrated by objects or animals; raped, tortured, injured, mutilated and killed; in attitudes or positions of subordination or subservience; as though desiring and enjoying the violence inflicted on them, particularly rape, incest or other sexual abuse; and when parts of their bodies are displayed in such a way that women are reduced to these parts (Graycar and Morgan, 2002).[7] In Italy, since the 1990s, pornography has been particularly brutal and violent. In successful films, women are degraded in all ways, tortured and raped with the clear intention of teaching them to 'stay in their place', which means in a subordinate role. They can be degraded and tortured because they are not considered human. If they then enjoy it, according to the typical plot of the pornography film and myths about rape, this represents subsequent proof of their lack of humanity (Adamo, 2004).

Decades of experimental research in social psychology have shown that exposure to violent pornography alters the perception and behaviour of people, making them less sensitive to the suffering of others, more inclined to find violent and degrading practices acceptable and to believe that rape is an act without negative consequences for the victims (Russell, 1993; Malamuth et al, 2000). Like all laboratory research, it is not taken for granted that the results may also be generalised in the real world. Still, the evidence of many women who have suffered sexual violence as children or as adults confirms the central role of pornography: the abusers used pornographic material to show them what they wanted them to do, particularly if they were violent or humiliating practices, and they were often expected to enjoy situations where they were raped and tortured. Particularly among women abused as children, many revealed that they had been used for pornographic films or photos, intended for home or commercial use.[8]

Not all consumers of pornography are or will be rapists. Still, it is worrying that a degraded and dehumanised image of women is a consumer item for millions of men and perhaps the principal source of reference as regards sexual relationships for some of them. In the US, the hiring of a pornographic video has almost doubled in 10 years: from 400 million a year in 1991 to 759 million in 2001. Those who hire them are men in 78% of cases, 19% are heterosexual couples and 3% are women (Seager, 2003). Pornography also serves as a means of sexual education for many adolescents. Still in the US, boys look at their first pornographic magazine when they are 13 years old on average and see their first pornographic film when they are 14. It is not surprising that the turnover for the pornographic film industry in the US is estimated at about 10 billion dollars a year (Rhode, 1997).

The dehumanising process has been analysed in depth by survivors of extermination camps. The humiliation of the victims was not inflicted casually or due to cruelty that was an end in itself. On the contrary, making them non-human served to justify and legitimise the decision and the final act of killing them and reducing or removing the anguish of the killers (Levi, 1958; Bandura, 1999). We observe the same method of proceeding in violence against women. In domestic violence men humiliate their companions in various ways for a long time; calling them 'whores' often represents the preliminary to physical and sexual violence. Since they are 'whores', you can do what you want with them, they deserve beating, sexual violence and more. In fact, as we have already seen, prostitutes are considered socially less than human (Baldwin, 1992). The same process may occur during rape: the woman is a 'whore', 'bitch', 'cunt' and you can do what you want with her. Then torturing her and the expressions of suffering and agony therefore confirm that the victim was contemptible and deserved what was inflicted on her (Brownmiller, 1975). Particularly cruel practices observed during war or ethnic rape, such as raping a woman in front of her husband or after killing him in front of her or forcing her to lie on his body (Sideris, 2003), seem to pursue the same ends. At the end of the dehumanising process, moral and social codes no longer apply to the victims: killing them becomes the right thing to do (Staub, 1999).

Another aspect of dehumanising is the removal of individuality. Social psychology research has shown how easy it is to commit acts of cruelty when the victim is depersonalised (Bandura et al, 1975). But removing individuality is a social practice affecting women systematically. The expression we may find in our newspapers even today – 'workers, students and women took part in the demonstration' – is an accurate picture of social relationships, in which women are deprived of their individuality and reduced to their sex (Guillaumin, 1992).

It is not by chance that one of the aspects of resisting oppression and violence is the victims wishing to keep their human characteristics (Levi, 1958; Améry, 1996). This effort to rehumanise becomes necessary when dealing with women killed by men. When journalists report the murders of women killed by their ex-partners after separation, they talk less about the victims than their killers. About him they tell us he was alone, desperate, mad with love and grief and, above all, that he had tried to get back together with her several times (*poor thing!*); about her we know little or nothing, if only that she had 'rejected' him repeatedly (*bad woman!*). In the end he is more human than she is and we run the risk of feeling sympathy for the killer rather than his victim (Morgan, 2006). A similar observation was the starting point for Suzanne Laplante-Edward, the mother of Anne-Marie Edward, one of the 14 young women shot down at the Polytechnic of Montreal by a man convinced that feminists had ruined his life, when she started an initiative with the title *Sixth of December 1989: Giving the Victims a Face*. This was a presentation of photos of the young women killed and their history, intended to contrast with the behaviour of the media, which, by giving the killer a name and telling the story of his life, ended up by making him almost a hero, whereas his victims were always presented in a group, depersonalised, without a name and without a face (Laplante-Edward, 1996).[9] The same applied to *NHI – No Humans Involved*, an artistic demonstration that took place in San Diego in the US in 1992. This initiative also had its origins in a massacre of women. Forty-five women were raped and killed in the city between 1985 and 1992, without the killer or killers being identified. As a police officer admitted, these cases are considered using jargon as 'misdemeanour murders of biker women and hookers ... sometimes we'd call them "NHIs" – no humans involved' (Scholder, 1993, p 43). Only in seven cases out of the 45 did the press publish a photo of the victim. The project involved various aspects, including giant posters with the photo of one of the victims, Donna Gentile, and the acronym NHI and an exhibition with the photos and names of all 45 women killed. In cases where it was not possible to find a photo, the artists supplied one of theirs as a sign of solidarity and to show that any woman may be raped and killed. For many relatives of the women killed this was the only occasion when they could commemorate and grieve for their daughters, sisters, mothers and wives (Leigh Butler, 2001).

## 3.3 Blaming the victims

Blaming the victims, attributing responsibility for their condition – poverty, disease, rape – to them represents a powerful mechanism for moral disengagement. William Ryan (1976) recalls how in the American slave-owning society, dehumanising slaves – they were not really human, were they not perhaps some species of domestic animal? – and attributing responsibility for such a condition to them was a process that allowed even noble souls to tolerate slavery and above all enjoy its benefits, without feeling uncomfortable and without having to call into question the good image they had of themselves. A century later the ideology of blaming the victim served to justify and legitimise the poverty and social exclusion of black Americans, attributed from time to time to the 'culture of poverty', the presumed matriarchal structure of the black family or the sexual behaviour of the lower classes, rather than racism and oppression towards them. For Ryan (1976, p 20), blaming the victim has its place in a long series of American ideologies that have rationalised cruelty and injustice; they are hostile acts – one is almost tempted to say acts of war – directed against the disadvantaged, the distressed, the disinherited.

There could be no better definition of blaming women and children who are victims of male violence. It is the abused woman who provokes the beating: she argues, disobeys, cooks badly, is untidy and refuses sex. She is a castrator, but if she stays with him she is a masochist: she likes violence, it meets her deepest needs, or so she has learned, it is her cultural model. Even women killed by their partners are responsible for their own death because, if they had agreed to go back to him, that is if they had not stubbornly wanted to separate at all costs, if they had been better wives and had done more to understand him, to save their marriage, if they had not provoked him by saying they did not love him any more or that they loved someone else ... And the girl who is raped did she, also, not provoke it, dressing like that, going out in the evening, going to a dance, accepting a coffee? How much did she really struggle, how much did she defend herself? Is it not perhaps true that she enjoyed it after all, like the heroines who are raped or blackmailed in famous films from *Gone with the wind* and *Three days of the condor* to *The piano*? And did the child sexually abused by her father not perhaps provoke him and seduce him to some extent, naturally with her childish ways, but ...

Exaggerations, outmoded stereotypes? And yet 'provocation' by the woman still represents a mitigating circumstance in cases of men killing their partners or ex-partners, as we will see later. The idea that women are responsible for the violence men inflict on them is firmly rooted in the beliefs of those who should protect, help or take care of them. Of the health workers interviewed in an Italian study, 58% thought that women are responsible for the violence they suffer from their partners and 32% thought that they suffer it because they are 'masochists'; 40% agreed on the fact that it is women who provoke rape and considered that a woman cannot be raped against her will (Gonzo, 2000). In another Italian study, psychiatrists interviewed also felt that battered women are masochists (Paci and Romito, 2000). Following the Freudian tradition, contemporary psychoanalysts such as the French Françoise Dolto maintain that children abused by their father actually wanted and seduced him and took pleasure not only from the sexual relationship with him, but also from the humiliation of the mother.[10] In the 1980s an American judge defined an 11-year-old girl who had been abused as 'an unusually promiscuous young lady' (Rhode, 1997, p 11). Twenty years later an Italian judge defined a 13-year-old girl who had been abused as a sexual instigator, provocative and cunning. This moral judgement was presented as a mitigating circumstance for the stepfather who had abused her (and perhaps also her little brother). The judge talked of her as 'a young woman', an unusual term for a 13 year old, but one that has the advantage of making her adult and making the image of a seductress wanting to give herself plausible (Moro, 2003).

The way rape trials are conducted leaves you dumbfounded by the cruelty with which judges and lawyers often furiously attack the victim, who is accused of lying or discredited: she has already had sexual relationships, she is unemployed, she lives alone, she has family problems, she shaves her legs. These systematic acts of hostility have been observed in countries that are very different from each other, going beyond differences in the law and how trials are conducted. In Britain the absolute right of lawyers for the defence to dig up the sex life of the woman was only limited in 1976; if they wish to ask questions on the subject, now they must ask permission from the judge, which permission judges tend to give even today, however (Lees, 1997). Suspicion and blame regarding the victims have been written into the laws of some countries for a long time. In Britain and Australia, the *corroboration warning* obliged the judge in a rape trial to remind the jurors of the danger of convicting someone based only on the word of the woman who had reported him. Alhough it was repealed in the 1990s in both countries, it is still in use; in Australia an inquiry by the Senate shows that a percentage of judges, varying from 30% to 45% according to the region, continue to apply it. Even in 1993 a judge had no shame in telling the jurors in a rape trial that in his vast experience he had learned that when women say no, often they actually want to say yes (Graycar and Morgan, 2002), the same words used by the psychoanalyst Dolto in the interview already mentioned:

> [Women] always say no, no, and in the end they say yes ...
> if the man knows how to 'make it yes'. This is why there
> is the proverb: a lady ... when she says no, means perhaps,
> when she says perhaps, means yes, and when she says yes,
> is no lady ... it is the psychology of the girl, whose anxiety
> is connected with the desire to be loved, attained and
> conquered with force.[11]

Dolto makes things worse by adding that women often experience orgasms that are very profound and therefore 'unconscious': they are not aware that they have enjoyed it, but the man is! By the way, the woman enjoying rape after all represents one of the justifications used by rapists and their lawyers (Scully and Marolla, 1984, 1985).

In this context the connections between psychoanalysis and the law are close and their consequences are devastating. The most famous legal text in English *Evidence in trials at common law* by J.H. Wigmore, originally written at the very beginning of the 20th century and commonly known as *Wigmore on evidence*, draws inspiration directly from Freudian theory, according to which accounts of sexual abuse suffered by children do not refer to events that actually happened, but are an expression of the unconscious desires of the children themselves to have sexual relationships with their parents or parental figures. This authoritative text, on which thousands of judges have been trained in English-speaking countries, in the last edition published in 1961 maintains that:

> modern psychiatrists have amply studied the behaviour of errant young girls and women coming before the courts in all sorts of cases. Their psychic complexes are multifarious, distorted partly by inherent defects, partly by diseases, derangement or abnormal instincts, partly by bad social environment, partly by temporary psychological or emotional conditions. One form taken by these complexes is that of contriving false charges of sexual offences by men. No judge should ever let a sex offence charge go to the jury unless the female complainant's social history and mental make-up have been examined and testified by a qualified physician. (Quoted in Graycar and Morgan, 2002, p 355)

That psychological theories, in this case psychoanalysis, and the law are so consistent and unanimous in discrediting the victims of male violence should not surprise us, since both reflect the ideology of blaming the victim and in so doing achieve an important objective: exonerating the aggressor. According to Ryan (1976), ideology is defined as a set of concepts and beliefs, based on a distortion of reality and drawn up, sometimes unconsciously, to defend the interests of the dominant group, in this case the perpetrators of violence. Generically blaming the victims may not be enough to protect these interests: in some cases it is necessary to punish them.

## 3.3.1 Blaming and punishing victims of rape

As we have seen, in Western, so-called developed countries, victims of rape who report the violence – not more than 15% of those who have suffered it[12] – are still denigrated at the trial stage. Where incest is reported, usually it is the children who are taken away from the family and not the man who has raped them. In Italy, taking away the child still represents the most widespread practice, even though the law would allow the person being investigated to be taken away. In the US, these children may end up confined in psychiatric departments, hardly progress from what used to happen at the beginning of the century, when they were shut up in institutions for sexual delinquents.[13] In other countries, women and children who have been raped become pariahs, so weighed down with shame that the only solution provided by the community and the family is to marginalise or kill them. In Palestine, children and adolescents who have been raped, often by relatives, are killed by other members of the family to prevent the shame affecting and penalising the whole family, while the rapist goes unpunished (Bellamy, 2000). In Pakistan, women who report a rape may in turn be reported for adultery, imprisoned and condemned to death. It is estimated that 80% of women held in Pakistani prisons are guilty of 'adultery'. In Mozambique, Somalia, Bosnia, Kosovo and Kurdistan, women who have been raped by enemy soldiers are often expelled from the community, condemned to isolation and civil death and sometimes killed; their children, who were conceived in violence and given birth to in anguish, are almost always abandoned and, again, sometimes even killed (Seager, 2003; Sideris, 2003). The same fate was often reserved for children and women who were raped in the disturbances following the Anglo-American invasion of Iraq; on the other hand, in the US, women soldiers who have been raped or sexually abused by their fellow soldiers are often punished for consuming alcohol or 'fraternising' with soldiers of a different rank, for example, when they dare to report what has happened.[14]

## 3.3.2 Blaming and punishing battered wives

In the area of domestic violence the Freudian or psychodynamic model legitimises an individualistic and psychopathological interpretation, where violence is attributed to the characteristics of the personality of the violent man and the battered woman. The behaviour of the man is the result of deep frustration and anxiety; the woman provokes him with her castrating attitude. The woman also derives masochistic satisfaction from suffering violence; this explains why the victims of abuse do not always leave the violent man.

In the 1980s feminist psychologists and psychiatrists had to fight to oppose the diagnosis of masochism (in fact female masochism) being included in the *Manual for diagnosis of mental illness* (DSMM) (Caplan, 1985). Still, these models remain powerful. In France, according to Marie-France Hirigoyen (2005, p 81): 'When dealing with women and couple relationships, psychoanalysts confuse the causes with the effects and continue to talk of masochism'. In short, whether or not it is in the DSMM, masochism is a recurring category in the discourse of health and social workers

Systemic theory, the principal theoretical reference in family therapy, constructs the responsibility of women for the violence they suffer in a more sophisticated way (Bograd, 1984). In this model, which was inspired by the work of Gregory Bateson, the symptom of one member of the family is read as a means to maintain the stability of the whole system. What happens, including violence, is never linear: the process is interactive, responsibility is diffuse. In systemic family therapy the couple is considered as a problematic unit and the relationship is analysed from a circular perspective; in the systemic approach, too, the victim is responsible for the violence inflicted on her (Dell, 1989; Lamb, 1996). According to this theory incest works to maintain a pathological family balance and the 'pathology' is often connected to the behaviour of the mother, who is cold and distant; it therefore talks of the incestuous family or incestuous mother, and not the incestuous father; paternal sexual abuse was provoked by the child or mother and therefore the father is to some extent excused (Armstrong, 2000). We will see later how family mediation, which draws inspiration to some extent from systemic family therapy, with its emphasis on neutrality of intervention, may actually end up by blaming and punishing women who have suffered domestic violence.

The same conclusions are arrived at by the co-dependency model, according to which, if women stay with their abusive partners, it is because this situation meets their deep needs. The theory of co-dependency sprang up in Anglo-American countries to help alcoholic men assume responsibility for their behaviour. But in view of the difficulty of the task it quickly changed, switching attention from the alcoholics to their wives, seen as *enablers*, that is those who made the alcoholism of their partners possible by their behaviour (Lamb, 1996).

These models represent the quintessence of the social insistence that women take on deviant male behaviour and put them in a paradoxical situation: they are masochists or co-dependants if they stay with the alcoholic and/or violent husband, egoists, irresponsible and vindictive if they leave him. In an Italian study the psychiatrist of an alcohology department frankly admitted putting pressure on the wives of alcoholics not to leave them during treatment and the psychologist of the same department acknowledged that it was better to avoid discussing domestic violence, because otherwise men tended to give up the treatment itself (Paci and Romito, 2000).

### 3.3.3 Victims blaming themselves

In view of what has been said it is not surprising that women attribute responsibility for the violence they have suffered to themselves and feel they are to blame. In a study carried out in Taiwan, interviews with 35 rape victims revealed the feeling of blame as the dominant theme. Women felt ashamed of losing their virginity and felt to blame for destroying the honour of their family; they felt 'dirty' from the abuse; they were afraid and ashamed of reporting it; they attributed male violence to their behaviour; and they were ridiculed, insulted and blamed by members of their family and by the rapists themselves, who always went unpunished. Although some of these reactions may result from the characteristics of Chinese society and particularly the value attributed to female virginity (Luo, 2000; So-Kum Tang et al, 2002), others are similar to what is expressed by Western women. Young women interviewed in the US by Phillips (2000), for example, attributed responsibility for the sexual violence suffered to themselves: they had agreed to go out with this man they had kissed him and so on. For this reason they were also reluctant to call 'rape' rape, thus contributing to the social invisibility of violence.

For some decades social psychologists have been studying how attribution mechanisms work, particularly why and in what circumstances we attribute responsibility for violence to the perpetrator, victim or context respectively. Attributing responsibility to the victim makes us feel less vulnerable: if they suffered violence because they made a mistake, we can keep our belief in a just world or at least a predictable one and we may find security in the fact that, if we behave well, nothing bad will happen to us. Blaming the victim and believing in a just world therefore meet important psychological needs for predictability and control and this may explain why these mechanisms are adopted by the victims themselves (Lerner and Miller, 1978).

In children who have been victims of abuse in the family the very dependence of the child on their parents and their need to feel loved put them in a situation where it is difficult for them to understand what has happened to them and acknowledge the parent as perpetrator of the violence; as a result they may end up by developing the feeling of being to blame for what has happened (Janoff-Bulman and Frieze, 1983).

Whether blaming yourself may represent a protection mechanism in general still remains controversial. While some studies show that in the victims of disabling accidents those who attribute responsibility for them to themselves have a better psychophysical recovery, the opposite seems to be the case for victims of rape: blaming themselves is associated with greater suffering and psychological difficulties. When the reactions of the surroundings are negative, the victims also tend to blame themselves more.[15]

These explanations still overlook the social aspect. If keeping control over reality represents an important psychological need, it is a tragedy that the only possibility of control left to women is that of attributing responsibility for violence inflicted on them by others to themselves. Lamb (1996) formulates the theory according to which women intuitively know the depth of misogyny and prefer to assume the blame for the violence suffered rather than feel at the mercy of such deep hatred.

There is a powerful expectation that from their years in the nursery onwards women will take on male behaviour: from teachers to psychiatrists, all expect women to prevent men from doing stupid things, check their sexuality and violent behaviour, keep them sweet and so on. However, this social demand on women coexists with their lack of authority and power and the lack of means to bring it to a successful conclusion. Reshaping male behaviour and limiting violence would require profound social restructuring, which men as a whole certainly have no interest in carrying out. Individual women are therefore asked to take on an impossible task, thus creating the conditions for those who do not succeed feeling guilty.

### 3.3.4 Blaming mothers

When in doubt, blame mothers. (Morgan, 1992, p 201)

Mothers are considered responsible for everything that happens to their children and, by extension, the evils of the world. This is a powerful idea in common sense ('it's not surprising, with a mother like that!'), which has been taken up and legitimised by various experts. The ubiquitousness of blaming mothers, it being a 'natural' explanation, almost an instinctive reflex, must not deceive us as to what it means and how it works: blaming mothers means obscuring the role of those who are really responsible until they are absolved.

In South Africa during the Boer War (1899-1902), for example, the English interned about half the civil population − 120,000 people − in concentration camps so appalling that 22,000 children died of deprivation. The English newspapers attributed this slaughter 'to the neglect, brutality and ignorance' of the Boer women and their obvious incompetence as mothers (Bianchi, 2001b, p 431). Today, faced with the problems of an affluent society, which cannot ensure good-quality medical care and schools for all, other experts (Murray and Herrnstein, 1994) attribute the fall in the level of intelligence in the US to the sexual behaviour of poor mothers. The criminal behaviour of serial killers is also attributed to the fault of the mother. After the Montreal massacre − 14 young women killed at the Faculty of Engineering − Canadian newspapers were quick to identify the origin of the problem: Marc Lépine, the murderer, had been brought up by his mother alone! What better example of the damage caused by mothers? The person who remained in the shadows was, once again, the father: a violent man, who had terrorised and abused Marc and his mother until she left him and had brought up the family alone by working hard (Morgan, 1992).

Experts − doctors, psychiatrists and psychoanalysts − have contributed to the pervasive ideology of blaming mothers with their specific tools, creating a paradoxical situation, which would be comic if it were not cruel and above all paralysing: whatever they do, mothers are wrong in their eyes (Ehrenreich and English, 1979). They were considered pathogenic, that is responsible for mental illness or behavioural problems in their children, if, still according to various experts, they were egoistic, cold and distant and therefore rejecting. Until the 1970s, for example, the prevailing theory regarding autism attributed its cause to mothers.[16] In these same years, however, other experts and sometimes the same ones stigmatised the opposite behaviour, that is mothers who were too affectionate, quick to sacrifice, overprotective and therefore castrating. According to the psychoanalyst Rheingold, for example:

> We may not say that maternal destructiveness is the prime factor in all pathological states, but the total evidence to hand seems to permit one to say that it enters causatively into a greater range of disorders than any other factor, and that it is the predominant determinant in more individual cases. Even the nurturant mother is not without destructive effect. It is her mutilative impulse in its castrating form which

cannot be separated from the mother's sexual seduction of the child. Here ... one deals with behaviour which is more frequent and more obtrusive than we have allowed ourselves to believe. (Quoted in Armstrong, 2000, p 31)

Along the same track the psychoanalyst Margaret Mahler urged her colleagues to observe how mothers held their children: close to them, 'like a part of them', a symptom of being unable to part, or away from them, 'like an object', a symptom of rejection. Paediatricians have accused mothers of not wanting to breastfeed their children or breastfeeding them too long; psychoanalysts have interpreted sickness during pregnancy as unconscious rejection of the pregnancy, and the absence of sickness as an even more unconscious rejection of the pregnancy and therefore even more damaging for the mental health of the future child. In the 1920s behavioural psychologists saw maternal love as dangerous; according to J. Watson children 'would be better off if they never knew their mothers'. But after the Second World War the psychoanalyst J. Bowlby cautioned women to stay at home and look after their children all the time: even the mother reading a book took away the attention owed to the offspring, ending up jeopardising their mental health. In the same years an American psychiatrist, E. Strecker, listing the categories of 'bad mothers', established the daring comparison between Nazism and 'momism', in which Nazism represented 'a surrogate for the bad mother with a swastika instead of a heart'. B. Bettelheim, another psychiatrist and psychoanalyst, compared autistic children with those interned in Nazi concentration camps and the behaviour of mothers of autistic children with that of the guards.[17] (All the above cited in Ladd-Taylor and Umansky, 1998.)

## The incestuous mother

In this context, the logical consequence is that mothers are also considered responsible for the violence men inflict on their children. Reconstructing the history of incest, Louise Armstrong recalls that in the 1960s, when it was no longer possible to deny its frequency, society found itself faced with a dilemma: whether or not to admit that so many respectable men, pillars of the community, were sexually abusing their children. It was necessary for the experts to find an alternative explanation. 'They visited the Oracle, and the Oracle said: "Mom"' (Armstrong, 2000, p 31). Here was the perfect solution to the problem: the incestuous mother! – mothers complicit in incest or cold, indifferent mothers or frigid wives rejecting their husbands, who had to find comfort in the bed of their five-year-old daughters. According to R. Gardner (1992), psychiatrist, psychoanalyst and inventor of the parental alienation syndrome, as we will see later, the mothers of abused children are passive, masochistic women, who reject their husbands sexually. The role of the therapist is to make them more available, so that the husband will have no need to turn to the daughter again for his sexual gratification (1992, p 585).

The construction of the type of the incestuous mother arises as a direct consequence of the pressing need to exonerate fathers from incest. If it has taken such a hold at a social level, it is because it conforms to the ideology of blaming the mother, the other face of the strong expectation that mothers will take on everything and will be able to protect their little ones in any situation (Humphreys, 1997), an expectation that does not decrease, even when faced with the paradox of asking an individual mother to do more than society as a whole. This is also a plausible interpretation for social and health workers because its model is based on two dominant psychological theories, psychodynamic theory and systemic theory. It is also a model that may find a degree of confirmation among those working in social services, where clients may have serious problems at a social or personal level. But given that only a small minority of cases of interfamilial sexual abuse are reported (Koss, 1992, 1993), the records of social services are not representative of what happens in the general population. In fact epidemiological research outlines a different picture, where the principal risk factors for incest are domestic violence by the father against the mother, the absence of a maternal figure due to death or serious illness (physical or mental) of the biological mother in primis and the fact of living with the father alone. Other research indicates that usually mothers are not aware of the violence committed against their daughters; when they discover it or are informed of it, in spite of the confusion, pain and destruction that incest brings with it, the majority of them believe their daughters and try to support them.[18] It must not be forgotten that separating mother and daughter and setting them against each other ('if you tell, mummy will kill herself, send you away'; 'only you understand me, I prefer you to her' and so on) represent strategies frequently used by the aggressor to protect himself and continue the incestuous behaviour undisturbed (Herman, 1981; Hooper, 1992). It is also possible that the number of mothers who recognise incest and believe their daughters is increasing with the passing of the years in line with greater social awareness on the subject. In one of the first studies (Myer, 1985) more than half the mothers believed their daughters and protected them, while a third stood by their husband, who was often violent towards them as well. Only a minority, all women with serious mental health problems, did not believe it, showing lack of interest rather than hostility towards their daughters. In another inquiry (Sirles and Franke, 1989) almost 80% of mothers believed their child. In more recent work it was not possible to study the effect of any negative maternal reactions, because the majority of mothers believed the daughter and almost all of them considered her not in any way responsible for what had happened (Ruggiero et al, 2000). In another study the mother–daughter relationship was evaluated by the daughter herself: almost all the girls who were victims of abuse described the relationship with their mothers in positive terms, even though only a third had revealed the abuse to her in the first instance (Lovett, 1995). On the other hand, female adolescents interviewed in Italy (Crisma et al, 2004) explained how it was actually the affection they felt for their mothers that prevented them from revealing the violence: they did not want to give her other troubles or were afraid of 'destroying the family' with serious consequences for all, if the aggressor was a man belonging to it.

For a woman, recognising that her own partner has sexually abused her child is terrible. It is a question of deciding whether or not to leave a man perhaps she has loved, perhaps she depends on economically and sometimes she is afraid of; it means fighting against him, if he denies it and counterattacks; running the risk of losing the support of relatives, setting herself against the other children and finding herself in a vacuum; dealing with a child who has been abused and shows her/his suffering in various ways; being regarded with suspicion (collusive, malevolent or simply incapable) by social services; and feeling that somehow she has failed as a woman and mother for not knowing how to prevent incest. It is paradoxical that services and workers that are slow, ambiguous and often completely incapable of protecting the victims of incest (Frenken and Van Stolk, 1990; Gibbons, 1996) are then so quick to condemn mothers when they behave in an uncertain or contradictory way.

Faced with mothers who more and more often believe their children, try to protect them and report their partners, it becomes more difficult to maintain the model of the incestuous, indifferent or collusive mother. But if there is no scapegoat, again there is the risk that incest will be shown for what it is: frequent behaviour by 'normal' men. Admitting this is unbearable to most people, who therefore urgently seek ways to show that the mothers and children are lying.

## The myth of false reports of incest during separation

The time of separation is almost always unbearable for a violent man. He realises that he is losing his hold: in spite of the hardship, humiliation, beating and terror, the woman has found enough courage and enough social support to free herself from the violence together with the children. It is therefore a dangerous time, when the violence tends to become more intense. In this context it may be that a mother reports the sexual abuse committed by the father against the children. There is nothing surprising in this: the decision to separate may have been sparked off by the actual discovery of the abuse; or the child finds the courage to talk after the father no longer lives with the family; or the abuse starts after separation, when the father is alone with the child during visits.

As a reaction to the ever greater capacity of mothers to protect their children from sexual abuse in the last few years the case of so-called false reports of incest during separation has arisen. A loud group of experts – lawyers, judges, psychologists, psychiatrists and social workers with the usual support of the press – protests that (1) there are a great many reports of incest made by mothers during separation; (2) the percentage of false reports is particularly high in this context; and (3) mothers invent or exaggerate abuse because they are frustrated, resentful and want to take revenge on their ex-partners. This tendency is also noted in Italy, as shown by the following passage from a psychiatrist at a child abuse centre in Rome:

> We must emphasise here a dangerous increase in reports of alleged sexual abuse during legal separation cases [no figure is quoted]. Many of these reports which are enclosed here are quite unfounded [no figure is quoted] because they are dictated either by frenzied conditions or by vindictive behaviour which in the psychopathology of the couple fall under 'endless games' of which the child becomes the only victim. Before accepting and reporting them it is desirable to carry out a very accurate psychological investigation. It is considered that the parent or relative who is really 'abusing' is the one making the false report and triggering a long and complex legal mechanism, not to safeguard the child but for their own benefit 'against' the child. Only an accurate physical and psychological preventive diagnosis may prevent useless 'violence' and the 'mourning' caused by separation from the other parent. (Tortolani, 1998, p 163)

These statements are not substantiated. According to various studies, less than 10% of reports of sexual abuse are not sufficiently well founded. Of the research available, the most reliable from the scientific point of view is that carried out on samples which do not come from a single source (the private practice of a single consultant for example) and where transparent criteria are used to decide whether a report is credible or not. The results of this research show that (1) the percentage of reports of sexual abuse during separation is very low, even in cases of conflict-based divorce; (2) there are mothers who report fathers, but also fathers who report the new companion of the mother or reports made by third parties; and (3) the percentage of reports where it is difficult to ascertain the truth (because the child is young for example) is low and that for false reports is even lower (Faller Coulborn et al, 1997). Let us consider in more detail the results of Thoennes and Tjaden (1990), who analysed 9,000 divorce cases involving child custody disputes, relating to 12 different US family courts. In less than 2% of cases one of the parents had made a child sexual abuse report. The authors used the assessment of experts and workers in child protection or mental health services as the basis for deciding whether the reports were well founded. The results show that in the 2% of reports made in the context of conflict-based divorce, half were without doubt well founded; a third were not very likely; in other cases there was not enough information to decide. However, some of the criteria for deciding that a case was not very likely were somewhat questionable: the child was very small, there was only a single episode of abuse and there was a serious dispute between the parents. As Malacrea and Lorenzini (2002) rightly note, the fact that the reliability of a report cannot always be assessed may be more an indication of the professional limits of the workers than a proof of the falseness of the report itself.

The more recent results of Trocmé and Bala (2005), taken from a study on a national level carried out in Canada, are just as clear. Analysing 7,672 cases of 'child maltreatment' referred to the 'child welfare authorities', the authors conclude that only 4% of these cases were made up of false reports. When there was a 'custody or access dispute', this proportion was higher (12%); it must be emphasised that the principal subject of the false reports was neglect and not sexual abuse. Moreover, non-custodial parents, usually fathers, were more likely to make false allegations (15%) than custodial parents (2%), usually mothers. The study documented only two (out of 7,672 cases!) intentionally false allegations made against non-custodial fathers. The authors conclude that 'the problem of deliberate fabrication by non-custodial parents (largely fathers) is more prevalent than deliberate fabrication of abuse by custodial parents (largely mothers) and their children' (Trocmé and Bala, 2005, p 1341).

Still, prejudice relating to false reports of abuse during separation remains strong. An example is the case of an 'exaggerated accusation' of child sexual abuse by a separated mother, taken from research carried out at the Children's Court of Turin in Italy (Roccia and Foti, 1994). An eight-year-old girl recounted to the honorary judge, a psychologist, that when she went on holiday with daddy and the new person he lived with, they played in bed and daddy put 'his finger in her fanny'. According to the report by the psychologist 'the mother is resentful towards the husband who, according to her, before their separation cheated on her, brought prostitutes home and had himself masturbated by her with pornographic films or magazines'. Therefore, 'the accusations represent a way of taking revenge on the husband, taking him away from his children and discrediting him'. In reality, according to the authors of the research, 'something had really happened between father and child ... on the borderline between what may be called play and what instead becomes sexual abuse. The mother had taken advantage of the situation to try and blame the husband'. But 'the judge did not fall into the trap ... emphasising to both parents that there is a limit ...: the mother may not use the children in her personal fight against her partner, the father may not and must not continue with ambiguous physical games with the children' (Roccia and Foti, 1994, p 239). The case was filed, it is therefore likely that no measure was taken to limit visits between father and child. The attempt by the mother to protect her was interpreted as her personal revenge and therefore delegitimised; or rather the protective mother and abusive father were put on the same level.

In short, reports made during separation being false is a myth, in which many workers believe so firmly that a report of incest made by the mother in this situation is more likely to be filed than in any other, thus leaving children without protection.[19]

As John Myers (1997, p 107), professor of law in California, sums up:

> There are cases – many, I fear – where a father sexually abused his child but the child's mother and her lawyer can't prove it in court. If the mother can't prove the abuse, she can't persuade the judge to give her custody. In fact, the law can backfire on her. Not only does she fail to prove the abuse, she is branded a false accuser and a hysterical woman. The judge awards custody to the father! Why? Because the

judge concludes, at the urging of the father's attorney, that the mother made a false charge of abuse and that she is crazy, hysterical, vindictive, unstable, unreliable and utterly unfit for custody

### The parental alienation syndrome

When it is decided to hide the truth, the first thing to do is to feed people a different truth to keep them happy. Otherwise they start to wonder whether perhaps the real truth is not hidden somewhere and this is not good at all. (Le Carré, 2001, p 307 of the Italian translation)

We find another version of the mother reporting the father out of revenge in the 'parental alienation syndrome' (PAS), an invention by R. Gardner (1987), American psychoanalyst and forensic expert, who usually acts as consultant for the defence in the assessment of children who are alleged to be victims of sexual abuse. According to Gardner, reports of sexual abuse made during child custody disputes after a divorce are always false and are attributed to PAS, a condition in which the child hates or denigrates a parent (almost always the father) and refuses to see him, while it idealises the other (almost always the mother). According to this model the child refuses contact with the non-custodial parent not because it has reason to be afraid of him, but because he has been 'alienated'. The false accusation of abuse falls within the strategies of the mother to exclude the father. PAS is a psychiatric condition and a form of violence against the child practised, obviously, by the mother. Gardner also proposes a scale to distinguish between true or false accusations of sexual abuse, the *sex abuse legitimacy scale* (SAL).

PAS and SAL are concepts that have no scientific value: they are based on observations of an unspecified number of cases followed by Gardner, which obviously represent a very particular selection of cases of abuse, also interpreted through his particular convictions on the subject of sex between children and adults, family and social roles of men and women and so on (Myers, 1997). Since 1988 an authoritative expert such as Jon Conte has defined SAL as:

Probably the worst unscientific rubbish I have ever seen in this field in all my career. Basing social policy on something of such flimsiness is dangerous madness. (Myers, 1997, p 138)

In fact, both these 'measures' represent nothing more than the opinions of their inventor who, in spite of presenting himself as the author of more than 250 books and articles, has rarely been published in scientific journals (Sherman, 1993; Myers, 1997). Gardner has created a publishing house, Creative Therapeutics, which publishes his books, audio and videocassettes and has a website where he publicises his material. He has also published some articles in *Issues in Child Abuse Accusations*, the journal of R. Underwager, psychologist, 'expert' in sexual abuse, ex-Lutheran pastor and declared supporter of paedophilia.[20] Gardner himself is a supporter of paedophilia. Apart from the abuse revealed during separation, which he claims is always false, he acknowledges that the majority of reports of incest, about 95%, are true (Gardner, 1991, p 119). Still, this is not violence: Gardner maintains that children have strong sexual needs, they are often the instigators of incest and take great pleasure in it. Any negative consequences come not from the incest itself, but from the social attitude against it. Only for this reason does Gardner recognise that once it has been discovered, it is necessary to prevent the abuse being repeated, but maintains that the therapist must do everything he can not to alienate the abused child from the abusive parent. His therapeutic instructions are illuminating. Any sense of guilt suffered by abused children is assuaged by recalling that in other cultures incest is not considered a problem; to meet their unresolved sexual needs after the incest has stopped, it is suggested that they masturbate (Gardner, 1992, pp 549, 580, 585). The mother is seen as passive, masochistic, often herself a victim of abuse in childhood (something that is not unlikely, by the way, given the endemic frequency of abuse). If she has reacted to the discovery of incest in a 'hysterical' way or used it as an excuse for a denigration campaign against the father, the job of the therapist is to calm the hysteria down and defuse the anger towards the husband and incestuous father (Gardner, 1992, pp 576-7). Gardner does not think it necessary to submit the father to therapy, let alone take him away from home. Intervention may possibly be proposed for him that, far from concentrating on the incest, allows him to improve his self-esteem. It needs to be explained to him that 'there is a certain amount of paedophilia in all of us' and that 'paedophilia has been considered the norm by the vast majority of individuals in the history of the world' (Gardner, 1992, pp 592-3). The father in question only had the misfortune to be born at a time in history when paedophilia is seen in a bad light and it is better not to relapse if he wishes to avoid punishment by moralists (Gardner, 1992, p 593).

In spite of the very serious limits of his work on an ethical and scientific level, Gardner enjoys high esteem, and not only in the US (see Eriksson et al, 2005; Radford and Hester, 2006). It is not clear how much those appraising him know of his thinking, but obviously some of the things he supports sound familiar and are shared by many authors working in the field of child abuse.

### Failure to protect

To sum up, according to these theories, mothers who do not report incest are passive, rejecting, collusive and complicit, those who report it are aggressive, vindictive, hysterical, and lying anyway. Their requests are not listened to, their attempts to protect their children, which are often desperate, backfire against them: showing how wicked and resentful they are and how stubbornly they wish to denigrate the father and separate him from the children. But if at the end of the day physical or sexual abuse is shown, and in some cases the only really convincing way to show it is the death of the child, again it will be the mother who is held responsible. Since the 1980s in many American states mothers have been held legally responsible, civilly and criminally, for the abuse their partners inflict on their children and as such may be accused of 'failure to protect'. These mothers, who have not inflicted abuse, are accused of not protecting the children, tried and convicted.[21] Often the man has also committed violence against the woman, but according to many judges in the US, suffering abuse serves to indicate that the woman knew of the violence of her partner: this may represent an aggravating and not an excusing factor. Another aggravating factor consists of the fact that the woman had thus exposed the children to 'witnessed violence', which is considered as a form of abuse in itself (Mahoney, 1991; Miccio, 1995; Kaufman et al, 2003). Schneider (2000) quotes two cases of women who, after they had separated from violent men, had obtained a removal order against them. Nevertheless, the ex-husbands, in one case armed, had entered the house to attack them and the women had had to run away. In both cases, the judge granted custody of the children to the father, as the mother had 'abandoned' them, although only for a few hours to save her life.

As usual, there is no Italian data on the subject. According to workers in many antiviolence centres, in Italy women who are victims of domestic violence also run the risk of losing custody of their children because they are considered incapable of protecting them from paternal violence. The fact that in many cases these women have repeatedly sought help from institutions – police, doctors, social services – without finding it, and together with the children are paying the price of these institutions not being able or not being willing to act, is not taken into consideration at all.

The fact that a minority of reports of sexual abuse are invented, there are mothers who do not know how to or do not wish to protect their children and there are mothers and fathers who slander the other parent on principle does not detract in any way from the analysis just presented. False reports during separation and the parental alienation syndrome are myths, created to make the children who are victims of abuse keep quiet and exonerate the men who have inflicted it. The trick consists of going beyond accusing the children of lying or seducing and enjoying; what makes these tools really effective is discrediting the mothers trying to protect their children and making them powerless.

## 3.4 Psychologising

As we have seen, some psychological theories may become powerful tools for blaming the victims and reducing them to powerlessness. More generally, psychologising consists of interpreting a problem in individualistic and psychological rather than political, economic or social terms and consequently responding in these terms. At the same time it is a simple cognitive method for categorising and interpreting reality and a powerful social mechanism for defusing awareness of oppression and potential rebellion (Doise et al, 1991). Consider the attribution of certain behaviour to psychiatric pathologies, for example. In the slave-owning US it was inconceivable that black slaves, who were considered little more than animals, could have such dignity and such a desire for freedom as to try repeatedly to run away, risking not only death but also dreadful torture. The psychiatrists of the time therefore 'discovered' two new syndromes, one, 'disathesia aethiopica', characterised by a refusal to work and disobedience towards their masters, the other, 'drapetomania', characterised by an insuppressible need to run away (Tavris, 1992). Closer to home, during the First World War European psychiatrists diagnosed psychiatric disorders for deserting or pacifist officers. In fact, admitting that so many young men were refusing to fight would have been interpreted as too radical a criticism of the war and therefore socially destabilising (Bianchi, 2001a).

Psychologising is therefore essentially a depoliticising tactic for supporting the status quo and dominant power relationships. This works by delegitimising: if the actions of the deviant are attributed to his personal characteristics (psychological or biological, in this last case we talk of naturalising), they lose credibility and are therefore less effective in producing change (Doise et al, 1991); and by decriminalising: if the deserting officer is mad, he will end up in front of a psychiatrist and not a court martial. In the same way, if domestic violence or incest are connected with psychological problems, society will offer violent husbands and incestuous fathers therapy rather than punishment.

### 3.4.1 Psychological responses to domestic violence

We have already seen how common sense and some psychological models interpret domestic violence as a psychological problem for the woman involved – she is aggressive, provocative or masochistic or all of these things together – and for the perpetrator – he is frustrated, depressed, with low self-esteem and unhappy. When women or couples undergo therapy of the psychodynamic or systemic type, domestic violence may remain completely ignored, as it is seen only as an epiphenomenon of underlying disorders; if it is considered, responsibility for the violence is somehow diffused and has nothing to do with the person inflicting it (Bograd, 1984; Dell, 1989).

Even outside these therapeutic contexts psychologising still seems to be a common, immediate response by health and social services and workers. Consider the tendency to send battered women resorting to first aid to a psychiatric department, even in the absence of specific symptoms, which has been observed in various countries. Given that the psychiatrist will rarely face up to the reality of violence, this choice turns into a disadvantage for the woman: she is stuck with a label of mental instability, confirming what the violent man keeps telling her ('you are mad, they will take your children away from you' and so on). A vicious circle is set off, in which her psychological suffering runs the risk of increasing because of the treatment (drugs, psychotherapy) and she is made to fit a psychiatric type, ending up by appearing as the cause and not the consequence of violence (Stark and Flitcraft, 1996; Paci and Romito, 2000; Humphreys and Thiara, 2003).

An Italian study has also shown that, when they intervene in what they define as 'marital disputes', rather than arresting the violent man, as Italian law would allow them to do, police officers prefer to propose psychological intervention, which they are proud of: 'we act like social workers or psychologists, one goes with the wife and the other with the husband, we calm them down, we mediate, we make them talk, they are married after all....' (Bascelli and Romito, 2000, p 174). This response not only does not protect the woman from the risk of further abuse, but once again gives her the idea that she is jointly responsible for the violence that has occurred.

It is not very likely that inappropriate psychologising by first-aid staff and police officers is due to acceptance of theoretical psychodynamic or systemic models, more likely it is based on common sense and represents above all a simple, economic response. The doctor who sends the battered woman to the psychiatric department and the police officer who acts as family mediator have the impression they are doing something good, but above all they are saving time and work and the bother of intervening on other levels: that of listening sympathetically, giving information and social support to the woman and arresting the violent man.

Another example of how psychologising represents a problematic response, even though motivated by good intentions, is the 'battered woman syndrome', formulated in the 1980s by the psychologist Lenore Walker (2000), based on the model of 'learned powerlessness' (Seligman, 1975). According to this theory, when a human being (or another animal) finds itself in a painful situation from which it tries to escape, and there is no relation between its efforts and the results obtained, it will end up by developing a sense of powerlessness, characterised by apathy, loss of hope, incapacity to react and lowering of immunity defences, ending in death. According to Walker, this model allows the psychological reactions of a woman who has been abused for a long time to be explained and demonstrates that some behaviour, such as difficulty in reacting, lack of confidence in change and so on, may be the consequences of violence. Like all psychiatrising models, battered woman syndrome is also socially imposed: mental health specialists liken it to post-traumatic stress disorder and in the US it has become an integral part of the defence of battered women accused of not protecting their children or killing their violent partners (Mahoney, 1991; Ferraro, 2003). Although in some cases this 'diagnosis' may have helped judges to grasp the daily experience of terror, it has done so at the very high price of psychiatrising. On the one hand, lawyers and magistrates expect to find themselves faced with a syndrome, characterised by unmistakable symptoms in a very simplistic way; when they do not recognise a specific picture, particularly when the woman is not shown to be completely powerless, they can no longer accept her actions (Jones, 2000). On the other hand, by interpreting the behaviour of the woman in medical and psychopathological terms, complicity between social agencies, such as the police, and the violent man goes unseen. In fact, if battered women sometimes become as powerless as the syndrome describes them, this is as a consequence of indifference to their repeated requests for help as well as the violence. In the cases examined by Elizabeth Schneider (2000), women who had killed a violent husband, apparently in cold blood, when he was asleep for example,[22] had realistically assessed that this was their only way out and this was the only time to do it. But for society it may be simpler to interpret this behaviour in psychiatric terms and acquit the woman in rare cases, rather than analyse its own incapacity to prevent male violence and protect women from very serious violence.[23]

Psychological programmes for violent men, which sprang up in North America in the 1980s and are very popular today – in Canada there are more than 200 of them – are another aspect of psychologising and decriminalising domestic violence. They represent a response to the problem posed by the increase in reports and court proceedings for domestic violence and the consequent jamming up of the courts (Dankwort and Raush, 2000). Violent men are offered the choice between following treatment or another penalty (fine, prison), usually after they have been convicted; in some cases, following treatment is offered as an alternative to the report and court proceedings. From the start these programmes have been developed along two lines, which are the antithesis of each other. According to the first, which draws inspiration from feminist analysis, male violence is seen as a means of controlling women; this desire to control, which is considered unacceptable, becomes the principal aspect of intervention. Often these programmes are put forward in cooperation with antiviolence centres and refuges for battered women; their prime concern is the safety of women and children. An example of this type is Duluth in Minnesota (Dobash and Emerson Dobash, 1992). The second line draws inspiration from the men's liberation movement instead and is a psychotherapeutic model, which considers men as frustrated and unhappy because of society and promotes men's solidarity. In this context domestic violence is seen as a loss of control, caused by stress, difficult childhood experiences and so on, and men are seen above all as 'victims' of the system, women and feminism. Programmes with a psychotherapeutic approach are much more frequent, rarely have contact with antiviolence centres and do not deal with the problem of the safety of women at all. Assessment of the effectiveness of the programmes is controversial: it is not clear if they work in reducing the violent behaviour and dangerousness of these men (Dobash et al, 1996). There are cases of violent husbands who have killed their ex-wives shortly after attending a programme of this type.[24] Other negative consequences are less tragic but more frequent: the woman is reassured by the fact that her partner is following the programme and decides to give him another chance instead of leaving him; the violence does not decrease, even though sometimes it changes form, because the men have learned more sophisticated psychosocial control techniques from the programme itself.

In short, although there are interventions regarding abusive partners that put the question of male violence and the safety of women and children at the centre of the work, the majority represent diversions from dealing with the aggressors on a legal level instead. Often these programmes, which are financed with public funds even at the cost of financing antiviolence centres, are run by explicitly antifeminist, masculinist groups. Allowing the perpetrators of violence to escape from the penalties provided by the law for criminal acts committed, they do not resolve the problem of male violence and may represent a subsequent risk for women and children (Dufresne, 2002).[25]

## 3.4.2 Family mediation

The Australian jurist Jocelynne Scutt (1988) has drawn attention to how, at a time when various groups experiencing discrimination – such as women, aborigines and workers – became aware of their rights and made claims to obtain justice in the courtrooms, the practice of mediation was invented, a method for managing conflicts that moves them from a legal level to a psychological level and privatises them with the double advantage of making them less visible socially and being more economic.

In the last few years mediation has become one of the principal tools for treating the consequences of divorce, particularly in the case of child custody disputes (Saposnek, 1998; Kurki-Suonio, 2000). From a theoretical point of view, family mediation draws inspiration from the systemic model with its notions of the circularity of processes, diffused responsibility and neutrality of the therapist. From an ideological point of view, the reference model is that of the 'good divorce' or the good separation, where the husband and wife put their disputes to one side for the 'good of the child', and this good is identified a priori as maintaining constant relationships with both parents, often in the form of joint custody (Cresson, 2000). According to the model of amicable divorce, disputes between husband and wife in this phase are a consequence of the tension connected with the event as such, made greater by the legal proceedings, and not the extension or exacerbation of previous disputes that led them to divorce. With this basic assumption (which is not proven and seems strange: why divorce if they got on so well?) the path is already open for denying domestic violence. In fact the practice of mediation requires the ex-husband and wife to concentrate on the present and future without digging up the past and related disputes. Also, and this is also a decisive aspect, any reports or legal proceedings must be suspended. These demands are problematic for the victims of domestic violence: not considering the past is easier and above all more advantageous for the violent man than for the battered woman. If the woman tries to discuss it – pointing out that meeting her ex-husband to 'hand over' the children puts her in a dangerous situation or expressing the fear that he will neglect them or abuse them, for example – she will be reprimanded for not following the rules and treated as a vindictive, resentful woman (Radford and Hester, 2006), the same accusation as already described in the parental alienation syndrome and false reports of abuse during separation. Yet this happens and may represent a deliberate strategy by violent men (Rhoades, 2002). Given that separation limits the possibility of men dominating and controlling their ex-partners, some of them try to get the court to impose family mediation precisely because it provides an opportunity for meeting their ex-wives and continuing to persecute them. A study carried out in California has shown that in more than two thirds of family mediation cases imposed by the court there had previously been domestic violence; in 60% of these cases it was also difficult to ensure the safety of the women: some of them had been killed by their ex-partners while they were going to the mediation sessions (Beck and Sales, 2001). In Japan, where mediation is obligatory if either the husband or the wife does not consent to the divorce, more than a third of cases concern situations where the husband has been violent (Yoshihama, 2002). We do not have accurate data as far as Italy is concerned, but we know that there has been violence in almost half the couples who separate, almost always by the husband against the wife (Barbagli and Saraceno, 1998). It is therefore likely that the practice of mediation in Italy also occurs in cases where it should be avoided.

According to many authors, family mediation should never be used in a case of domestic violence.[26] In a report to the European Parliament, the hon. Marianne Eriksson (1997, p 7) expressed

> concern because the connection between violence inside the family home and protection of the children is often neglected; many women are therefore exposed to continuous abuse because decisions by the courts authorise contact between a violent partner or ex-partner and the children; it appears that in such cases the measures for protecting the children should also protect the parent not responsible for abuse.

Yet it is likely that mediation will be proposed or imposed precisely when there have been serious disputes and violence, because in other cases agreements on handling the children are usually reached by the parents independently.

In spite of the risks, everywhere women are often subject to great pressure to accept mediation rather than start legal proceedings (Radford and Hester, 2006). Just as in the case of so-called false reports of paternal sexual abuse during separation, women run the risk of finding themselves in a highly dangerous situation: if they state their concerns due to past or present violence, they will be accused of not following the rules of mediation and considered as vindictive or paranoid; if they play the game and ignore the risks, they may suffer other abuse and their children may suffer from it.

In this context there must be a better understanding of what the motives and advantages of family mediation are, apart from relieving congestion in the courts. The results of an authoritative review of the literature on the matter, published by the American Psychological Association, are surprising: it is not possible to demonstrate any advantage of mediation compared to the legal handling (lawyers, proceedings and so on) of divorce. In the medium and long term, the ex-husband and wife who have undergone mediation are not less litigious than others, do not respect agreements relating to the children more – visits and financial contributions – and return to court in equal measure to change previous agreements (Beck and Sales, 2001).

It is interesting to consider the opinions of Donald Saposnek (1998), a pioneer of family mediation. Saposnek is the director of the Family Mediation Service of Santa Cruz in California, the state that has expressed a clear preference for joint custody by law since 1979 and where family mediation has been imposed by the court in the case of disputes relating to the children since 1981. In short, Saposnek is a real expert on the subject as well as a witness who is completely in favour of the practice of mediation. He recalls that the purpose of mediation is to increase contact by the children with the non-custodial parent, almost always the father, as much as possible. Still, he recognises that (1) if the father–child relationship was difficult in the years when they lived together, divorce will be a source of relief for the latter and no visit imposed by the court will succeed in building a satisfactory relationship (Saposnek, 1998, pp 27-8); and (2) joint custody does not serve either to make fathers really involved in the care of the children or to make the experience of divorce easier for the latter (Saposnek, 1998, pp 319-20). He also states that in order to proceed in the work of mediation, it is necessary to start from the assumption that both parents are able to ensure adequate care of the children. But what do you do when this is not the case? What do you do, for example, when a father, who is not interested in the children or does not look after them well, insists on having sole custody of them or demands joint custody, openly acknowledging that this is a way of taking revenge on his ex-wife or controlling her? Saposnek presents many cases with these characteristics, admitting that they represent a dilemma for the mediator who, let us remember, must maintain an attitude of neutrality. In spite of his dispassionate analysis of the behaviour and motives of fathers, the expert ends up by proposing compromise solutions, in which mother and father 'meet each other half way'. So where is the advantage for the children? In the hope that, if the father spends more time with them, he will become more responsible, or perhaps if the mother agrees to requests by the father, relations between the ex-husband and wife will improve and this could be advantageous for the children. Surprisingly, Saposnek openly acknowledges that the procedure may penalise women and put the well-being of children at risk. He concludes: 'Is this too great a sacrifice to expect of the children?' (Saposnek, 1998, p 321).

In short, even the supporters of family mediation point out the limits and questionable function of re-establishing paternal authority after divorce, even to the detriment of the well-being of women and children. It is not surprising that in many countries family mediation has been sponsored by separated fathers' movements, in which violent ex-husbands are often active.[27] Analysis of how family mediation works also confirms the conclusions that Scutt (1988) made on the subject of this tactic, which is applied to various situations of conflict: between employer and employee, state and citizen and so on. Members of groups that have been discriminated against or oppressed gain no advantage from privatising justice and decriminalising and psychologising disputes, because these 'disputes' also represent abuse inflicted on them by dominant groups.

### 3.4.3 Psychological prevention of sexual violence against children

Programmes of the psycho-educational type for preventing sexual abuse against children have been set up in the US since the 1980s, and these programmes are directed not at potential abusers but at potential victims. The content of these interventions, which are aimed at children at primary and elementary schools, may be summarised by the 'four Rs': recognise, resist, refer, reassure. The child, having learned to distinguish 'good' contact from 'bad', should be able to say no and therefore defend itself against abuse, or at least seek help if abuse has already occurred. These programmes are very widespread today: in the US it is estimated that about two thirds of children between 10 and 14 years old have followed a programme of this type in their schooling (Finkelhor and Dziuba-Leatherman, 1995). Do they work? In the majority of cases, after the intervention children assessed in the school context are better at discriminating between good and bad contact and reacting in the appropriate way (Déttore, 2002). Still, this tells us nothing about their capacity to protect themselves in the real world, particularly if the abuse is committed by people close to them, such as members of their family or a teacher, whom the children have learned to obey, because these programmes do not always take account of such a possibility. Research into abusers, whether they are members of the family, known or unknown, show that these men use sophisticated strategies to get close to children, get them used to more and more brutal practices, threaten them and blackmail them. These 'instructions for use' are revealed and discussed particularly via the Internet. Even though it is not wrong to teach children to protect themselves and assert their independence and their rights, it is disheartening that so far this is the only strategy for prevention of sexual abuse that society has been able to imagine and put into practice. In fact it is grotesque to ask a five-year-old child to be able to recognise a paedophile and succeed in defending themself against him, something that obviously neither the psychosocial services nor the police have been able to do, given that the majority of men who abuse children do so repeatedly and almost always with impunity (Conte et al, 1989; Itzin, 2000b).

### 3.4.4 Psychologising: a drift

Psychologising represents an easy and almost 'instinctive' method of interpreting reality as well as a type of intervention in social conflicts that has the advantage of being economic and giving the illusion that something is being done, but without putting power relationships up for discussion. If intervention does not have the desired effects, it may become an effective tactic for delegitimising those not playing the game: victims who are no longer passive, opponents and deviants (Doise et al, 1991).[28]

The tendency to make interpretations and carry out interventions of a psychologistic type represents a high risk even in the women's movement. In France the Psychanalyse et Politique group has always maintained that women are not oppressed, they are repressed and that the priority is 'changing their heads' rather than changing the world.

Describing this tendency in the US, Barbara MacDonald (2003, p 157) declares that:

> the 'therapising' of the personal at the cost of the political was devastating: there we were again, trying to change ourselves rather than working to change society.

Reconstructing the recent history of incest, Louise Armstrong has also shown the failures of this process. Thanks to the women's movement, incest came out of hiding and, by revealing the power relationships underlying it, took on a political dimension. The spirit of self-knowledge groups, where so many women discovered that their experience was not isolated, was the antithesis of therapy: the purpose was to analyse the situation of women and not analyse the woman; to change patriarchal society and not make the woman 'change herself'. It was a radical political project that was dangerous for the dominant order and social reaction was to press for a change in the psychological sense: put them all in therapy! This brought about the change from the *survivors movement* to the *recovery movement*, from a political movement to an individualistic, therapeutic movement (Armstrong, 1993, 2000).[29]

Postmodernist feminism for its part, redrawing psychoanalytical thought (Brodribb, 1992), promoted a view of rape that put the blame on the victims, similar to that characterising the dominant culture, reducing anti-rape policies to an exclusively psychological dimension (Mardorossian, 2002).

This drift may also be seen in the practices of refuges and antiviolence centres in Europe and the US. Various factors come into play: on the one hand, public financing often requires a professionalisation of activities in return, which can only go in a psychological direction; on the other hand, the job of the workers is so hard and stressful, with little social recognition and not always rewarding, that it is easier to move the intervention from the political to the psychological level (Thibault et al, 2003). In various countries centres no longer accept women based only on the principle of their needs, but require them to be able to take part in projects or adapt to the methods of the centres themselves; if the woman cannot do so, because she has a mental health problem or because she is an immigrant with language and financial difficulties, she will not be accepted (Crenshaw Williams, 1994). In many centres in Italy, women are routinely offered a meeting with a psychologist, irrespective of whether they actually have psychological problems or whether they want one (Bruckner, 2001); a similar procedure to that of first-aid doctors who send battered women or women who have been raped to a psychiatric department. According to an observer in the US,

> many women's shelters and rape crisis centres no longer function as democratic grass roots organisations working toward ending the social problem of sexual violence but as State-funded liberal agencies ... promoting self-help and personal healing. (Mardorossian, 2002, p 771)

These changes, which are understandable at the level of personal and professional choices by workers and often made with the conviction that they are beneficial for the women accepted, represent nothing less than a denial of the political analysis of violence, as well as the specific methods and expertise of antiviolence centres and the history of feminism itself, which has made the radical criticism of many psychiatric and psychological models one of its starting points (Millett, 1970; Chesler et al, 1995).

Of course, you must be careful not to throw out the baby with the bath water: on the one hand, those suffering violence may need psychological help; on the other hand, not all psychological theories are intrinsically decontextualised, conservative, misogynist and profamily. Psychology, in its awareness of its limits, may provide important tools for understanding reality and acting on it. Still, if we are able to learn from history and experience, an analysis of the past and present of psychologising, its theoretical foundations and actual consequences should impose on us extreme caution in accepting a tendency that is difficult to control.

## 3.5 Naturalising

> Of all the vulgar modes of escaping from the consideration of the effect of moral and social influences upon the human mind, the most vulgar is that of attributing the diversities of conduct and character to inherent natural differences. (J.S. Mill)[30]

Men commit rape because their sexual instincts are raging, uncontrollable and easily unleashed by seeing a beautiful girl or provocative clothing. They commit rape because they are hot blooded, because a man is a man and hormones are hormones. Did a Japanese Member of Parliament not say that perhaps rapists at least have the advantage of still being vigorous males, more virile than those who propose sex instead of impose it?[31] These remarks, which are offensive in their triteness and vulgarity to women who have been raped, but also to all those men who are not rapists, represent common-sense explanations as well as more or less arrogant justifications by rapists and their lawyers.[32] But this is also the view of rape proposed in the 1970s by sociobiology:

> socialization toward a gentler, more humane sexuality entails inhibition of impulses … [that] are part of human nature because they proved adaptive over millions of years…. Given sufficient control over rearing conditions, no doubt males could be produced who would want only the kinds of sexual interactions that women want; but such rearing conditions … might well entail a cure worse than the disease. (Symons, 1979, quoted in Fausto-Sterling, 1992, p 157)

> mallard rape … may have a degree of relevance to human behavior. Perhaps human rapists, in their own criminal misguided way, are doing the best they can to maximise their fitness. (Barash, 1979, quoted in Fausto-Sterling, 1992, p 157)

The same statements reappear in evolutionary psychology (EP), the latest development in sociobiology:[33] 'Rape is … a natural, biological phenomenon, a product of the human evolutionary heritage' (Thornhill and Palmer, 2000, p 30). According to the sociobiologists the preference of men for many, young, beautiful partners, is functional for the greater spreading of their own genes and is therefore necessary in the general design of evolution.

In the same way as for some psychological theories, the agreement between common sense and 'scientific' theory explains the popular success and persistence of these models. It does not really matter whether these are theories based on little proof, inconsistent and often refuted by other data or, even worse, cannot be demonstrated, like the theory of rape drawn up by Thornhill and Palmer (hereafter, T & P). According to T & P, rape represents an adaptive strategy, carried out by a species during its evolution, as it allows the rapist to maximise his *fitness*, that is the capacity to spread his genes; it is therefore an act that is not only sexual but also reproductive. The theory draws inspiration from observations of 'rape' in two animal species: the scorpion fly and a type of mallard duck. Here we find the first problem: how correct is it, or rather how misleading is it, to use such language? In all languages the definition of rape refers to a sexual act committed without the consent or against the will of a woman.[34] How appropriate is it to call copulation between two flies 'rape'? Apart from the question of language, to which we will return, the T & P theory has received severe criticism from the scientific world and from women who are active on the subject of violence (Fausto-Sterling, 1992; Brown Travis, 2003). Without going into details, here are the main points. If rape is adaptive behaviour that is functional to evolution, as it maximises genes being passed on, it would need to be able to be shown that a rape produces more descendants than a consensual sexual relationship. Now, it is estimated that fertilisation occurs only in a small proportion of rapes and it is highly likely that this fertilisation will not lead to the birth of a living child, because the woman may have an abortion voluntarily or as a consequence of trauma; in some cultures she may kill herself, be killed by members of the family or kill the child. The theory is also based on an assumption that T & P have not taken the trouble to verify correctly: they maintain that the majority of rapes concern women of fertile age. But we know that this is not the case: a large percentage of rapes, perhaps the majority, concern children or adolescents who have just entered puberty, where fertilisation is impossible or inappropriate, as they are too young; the victims may also be old women or of the male sex and finally consideration needs to be given to oral and anal rape, rape with objects or vaginal rape without male ejaculation, all quite frequent methods (Koss, 2000, 2003). If being prone to commit rape is passed on genetically and therefore can be inherited, it would also need to be able to be shown not only that children born from a rape have a tendency to be rapists, but that they are so for genetic reasons. Another questionable aspect of the theory concerns the suffering of the victims. According to the evolutionary reading of T & P this suffering, far from representing a reaction to the violence experienced, is also adaptive behaviour, which allows the woman who has been raped to signal her lack of consent to her legitimate companion (the possibility that he and the rapist are the same person is not considered). To 'prove' this hypothesis they state incorrectly that married women of fertile age experience more psychological suffering as a consequence of rape than children and postmenopausal women do.

Although rape is natural behaviour, T & P specify that they consider it reprehensible and propose measures for prevention: explaining to girls it is better to avoid dressing provocatively and going to isolated places alone and expounding the principles of the evolutionist theory of rape to boys so that they can suppress their 'instincts' (Koss, 2003).

According to Jerry Coyne (2003), an evolutionary biologist, supporters of EP tend to put chatter and science on the same level. *A natural history of rape* (Thornhill and Palmer, 2000b) tells a story worthy of an evening at the pub: it cannot call itself science and merits neither interest nor respect from the public. But may we remind you that T & P are two university professors, their book has been published by the Massachusetts Institute of Technology and press and television have given them great prominence in the US, allowing the two authors to present themselves as champions of 'science', as opposed to 'feminists', who are passionate, ideological and obscurantist.

The mixture of scientific inadequacy, arrogance and media success characterises many of the proposals of sociobiology and the more recent evolutionary psychology. These two disciplines have given scientific legitimacy to the naturalising tactic, which we may define as a cognitive, social mechanism, leading first to the origin of complex human behaviour being attributed to 'natural' reason – genes, hormones, evolution, the brain – and second to the conclusion that if that is how it is, that is how it must be. The sociologist Colette Guillaumin (1992, p 49) observes ironically that 'Nature, the latest arrival to take the place of the gods, sets the social rules and ends up organising special genetic programmes for those who are socially dominated'.

Even though all human beings should be equally 'natural', in fact some, such as women and other oppressed groups, are more natural than others. Precisely because they are so close to nature, emotional and impressionable, historically women have been denied access to education and certain professions. In the 19th century it was maintained that the psychology of the woman was dominated by the uterus (hence the term 'hysteria'), but also that her reproductive equipment needed all the energy available in order to function as it should and therefore no energy was to be removed for study, for example. Still, in the 19th century, eminent scientists maintained that women and black people had smaller brains, getting their calculations wrong and a little mixed up, when they were not satisfied with the results (Gould, 1998). Today other scientists continue to believe, wrongly, that women suffer psychological disorders during hormonal changes or that there are significant differences between the sexes in the lateralisation of the brain, such as to legitimise social and professional differences (and salaries as a consequence) between men and women. Another version still explains differences in behaviour between the sexes as genetically programmed and resulting from the success of 'ancestral' adaptation, which took place more or less in the Pleistocene period (Fausto-Sterling, 2000). From such examples it can be seen how resorting to an explanation in naturalistic terms has been and still is one of the simple explanatory methods of common sense, as well as a powerful social tactic for legitimising what exists, systems of oppression in primis. Anna Fausto-Sterling, biologist and science historian, conveniently recalls that the theory of rape as the fruit of natural evolution appeared towards the mid-1970s, when feminists started to denounce sexual violence, defining it as a political act to control and terrorise women and emphasises that 'our debates about the body's biology are always simultaneously moral, ethical and political debates about social and political equality and the possibilities for change. Nothing less is at stake' (Fausto-Sterling, 2000, p 255).

In this social debate on equality and rights, looking at other animals for comparison represents the immediate reaction. But this reaction is problematic, first of all because of the obvious differences between the human animal and other animals, such as language and passing on culture, but also because if we look at nature as a source of proof, we may find everything and its opposite: in the fly the male 'rapist', in the praying mantis the female who eats her 'partner' after copulation. As Robin Morgan (1970, p 558) recalls, 'When faced with the "look at other species" argument, remember: the sex life of spiders is very interesting. He fucks her. She bites his head off. And think of the bees!'.

Let us think of the bees, indeed. In a chapter of *La vie des abeilles* ([1901] 1968) Maurice Maeterlinck described 'The massacre of the males', who are killed by the workers after carrying out the task of fertilising the queen. The males

> satisfied and corpulent, block the paths and clog the passages, hampering work, jostling and being jostled, stunned, boastful, full of stupid, innocent scorn, and scorned in their turn ... without realising the exasperation they are causing around them and the fate that awaits them.... And whilst they do so, they soil the place....They appear to be busy ... as though they were indispensable gods who, rushing riotously to the outside, are going to carry out some magnificent task, unknown to the common herd.... But the patience of bees is still not equal to that of men ... the serene workers change into judges and executioners.[35]

And so on ... The text continues with a detailed description of the massacre of the males who are now useless. The splendid prose of Maeterlinck draws our attention to the humanising language he uses to describe the bees and reminds us that when the human observer (traditionally a male) studies the world of other animals, inevitably he does so through the lens of his own experience and culture, using the concepts and language he uses to describe himself and those like him. In short, observing animals and describing them and then concluding that human beings behave like them and therefore human behaviour is natural and in some way unchangeable, is a not very convincing circular process, which became threadbare when female scientists started to work in fields only occupied by males of their species until then.

Primatology, the science that studies non–human primates, provides a particularly illuminating example. Where male primatologists had seen only ardent, dominant and aggressive males and timid, shy females, female primatologists also observed active females, who took the sexual initiative also with males of another group and even when they had already been fertilised. These discoveries also allowed it to be shown how misleading the language used previously had been: the behaviour of primates was described in such a way as to evoke courtship by a socially dominant male (a university professor?) of a female of lower status (a student or a secretary?) rather than copulation between monkeys (Blaffer Hrdy, 1999). Scientists of the female sex entering these fields of research have doubtless made the picture observed more complete and the science more objective (Fausto-Sterling, 2000; Gowaty, 2003), showing the unspoken intention in much of this work.

Darwin was a man of his time when he wrote that 'the man is more courageous, pugnacious and energetic than the woman and has greater inventive genius'.[36] This does not detract from the theory of evolution, which remains a fascinating and complex construction, the only one that allows us to explain the evolution of the species. Sociobiology and evolutionary psychology even more so represent only rather rough and often instrumental versions of this theory that are full of faults and impossible to verify. In short, these contemporary and apparently sophisticated forms of naturalising are great illusions that, like psychoanalysis, seem to meet the need to provide a global explanation of human existence, but without bothering about either scientific proof or moral, ethical or political concerns.[37]

## 3.6 Distinguishing, separating

Another formidable technique for hiding is separating. In fact, presenting various forms of violence as distinct from each other and giving different names to them, prevents us from seeing their continuity and that they are perpetrated by the same category of people to a large extent. Robin Morgan (1992, p 238) expresses it effectively when she states:

> If I had to name a single quality characteristic of patriarchy, it would be compartmentalisation, the capacity for institutionalising disconnection. Intellect severed from emotion. Thought separated from action ... if I had to name a single quality characteristic of global feminism, it would be connectivity – a capacity dangerous to every status quo, because of its insistence on noticing.

So, although between 30% and 60% of the children of battered women are also abused by the father, and although one of the principal risk factors in paternal sexual abuse is violence against the mother (Fleming et al, 1997; Edleson, 1999), violence against children is presented as distinct from violence against wives. Not seeing the continuity between the two phenomena represents a serious risk for children who are entrusted to fathers who have been violent husbands.

So although about 70% of murders of wives or ex-wives are preceded by domestic violence from their partners (Campbell et al, 2003), these murders are presented as separate, something different from abuse: the first attributable to 'too much love', 'passion' or 'raptus' by the man, the second to 'marital disputes'. In this case not seeing the continuity between the two phenomena is also mortally dangerous for the women involved.

So although rape is rape, various types are presented as separate from each other, studied by different experts: marital rape, rape by people who are known, rape by people who are unknown, date rape, rape by priests, child rape, war rape and ethnic rape. This compartmentalisation hides the dreadful evidence that any of us may be raped by one or several men in the course of our lives.

So although at the heart of prostitution there is always a situation where the woman is dominated and made into a thing, 'free' prostitution is considered as separate from 'forced' prostitution and prostitution involving adults is separate from prostitution involving children. When it occurs in Western countries, child prostitution is also treated as something separate from interfamilial sexual abuse, ignoring cases where the child who has been a victim of incest is then loaned or sold to other men. Along the same lines the paedophile is separate from the so-called normal man and the organiser of a child pornography and prostitution network is made to fall into a different category from the incestuous father, even if they are sometimes the same person (Kelly et al, 2000).

The concept of paedophilia is a good example of two tactics working together: psychologising and separating. By defining those who use children sexually as different and sick and distinguishing them from normal men, we reassure ourselves with the fact that child sexual abuse is confined to a group of perverts. In reality the concept of paedophilia itself – having or fantasising about sexual activity with children/ prepubescents as the preferred or exclusive method of achieving sexual stimulation – is highly controversial and only a small proportion of men who abuse children present any psychiatric pathology and have sexual relationships only with children (Itzin, 2000b). There is also an overlap between various types of aggressors: often incestuous fathers also abuse other children apart from their daughters, use or produce pornographic material and are members of networks for the sexual exchange of children (Abel et al, 1988; Eldridge, 2000). Still, the construction of separate categories and the emphasis on the paedophile serves to obscure a fact that is difficult to digest, that is that sexual violence against children is not only pervasive, but it also carried out first and foremost by normal men. As Louise Armstrong reminds us, it is 'what ordinary men do routinely and regularly in their own homes as a matter of right' (quoted in Itzin, 2000a, p 3).

Another example of putting these mechanisms into operation is represented by the so-called scandal of sexual abuse committed by priests against girls and boys. The scandal assumed enormous proportions in the US, where there were more than 11,000 reports of child sexual abuse against more than 4,000 priests between 1950 and 2002 (US Conference of Catholic Bishops, 2004), bishops were removed from their posts and one of the largest and richest dioceses – Boston – had to sell a large part of its property to pay for legal costs and damages to the victims. The social effects of this scandal are still controversial. Although, on the one hand, it was useful to confirm the frequency of sexual violence against children, its devastating consequences and, in particular, the fact that children do not lie, on the other hand, it has contributed to reinforcing a misleading message, that is that child sexual abuse is the work of perverts, paedophiles or homosexuals (Wolfe et al, 2003). Just as misleading is the emphasis on sexual abuse, which instead usually occurs together with physical and psychological abuse. In fact, these two types of violence are probably much more frequent in religious institutions also, but have remained in the shade, as though they were completely separate from sexual violence (Finkelhor, 2003). The emphasis on sexual abuse and the presumed homosexuality and/or paedophilia of the aggressors has also ended up by leaving some crucial aspects of this tragedy in the background. Little has been made of the fact that situations where, on the one hand, uncontrolled power is legitimised and, on the other hand, there is unquestioned obedience inevitably presage abuse and violence. The role of the institution with reference to the individual has been just as little discussed: the superiors of the priests involved, reaching as far as the upper echelons of the Catholic Church, were perfectly aware of what was going on: when reports and protests built up, the usual practice to prevent the 'scandal' breaking consisted of moving the priest to another parish, a strategy effectively summed up by the expression 'passing the trash' (Berry, 1992). Carol Delaney (1998, p 240) concludes that 'the glacially slow reaction of the church has shown that the church's primary objective was to protect the priests, not the children'.

Separating also works on a more general level, as the majority of people see social and professional discrimination against women and violence against them as two separate phenomena. Deborah Rhode (1997, pp 95-6) observes that 'we cannot see sexual abuse as a strategy for domination, exclusion, control and retaliation, as a way of keeping women in their place and away from the place men consider theirs'.

Analysing this type of compartmentalisation in a specific professional context, such as the university, Annette Kolodny (1996) shows how we refuse to see the connections between different facts: sexual harassment and abuse towards female lecturers and students, actions to disrupt feminist conferences and endless obstacles to the career of feminist scholars. Her conclusion is:

> Those who do not want the larger problem accurately named and understood ... actively encourage this perception that each event is isolated, *sui generis*, and without aim or method connected to anything else. But the real problem may be just here, in the institutional habit of uncritically accepting 'problems' as *only* discrete events, rather than probing for larger patterns. (1996, p 7)

Faced with this tendency feminist scholars have tried to show continuity between various forms of oppression and violence. Since the 1970s, for example, Mary Daly has shown the connections between spatially distant, historically oppressive practices, such as witch hunting in Europe and *suttee* (suicide, often forced, of widows) in India, foot binding in China, genital mutilation in Africa and psychological and surgical castration in the US and Europe (Daly, 1978; French, 1992).

More specifically on the subject of violence, we are indebted to Liz Kelly (1988) for the concept of the continuum of violence, according to which apparently separate events are characterised by common elements, so that they can easily change from one into another. This concept gives us a better understanding of the experiences of some women, which cannot be fitted into a single category. Harassment at work, for example, includes a continuum ranging from looks, gestures, allusions and proposals to sexual abuse pure and simple. Twenty years later the jurists Regina Graycar and Jenny Morgan (2002) show the continuity between phenomena such as forced sterilisation, the use of untested drugs on women, experiments in the gynaecological field without the consent of patients and sexual violence, having in common the fact that they cause physical injury to women as women.

The effectiveness of separating as a tactic for hiding seems clear from these examples, as well as the need to reveal these mechanisms to be able to combat them. There is still a risk in doing so. Keeping various types of violence and various types of perpetrators separate, thus obscuring the crucial conclusion that the principal people responsible are men, ordinary men, presents an advantage that cannot be overlooked and that is the possibility of forming alliances on some aspects of the question with men who are not involved in violence, or at least not in that specific type of violence.[38] Many men consider the crimes of paedophiles horrible, even though some of them visit pornographic paedophilia sites on the Internet or are not worried about knowing whether the prostitutes they see on the streets, and perhaps even use, are children.[39] Many find domestic violence and rape unacceptable, but consider it normal to be served at home, control their companion or comment 'jokingly' on the physical characteristics of their colleagues in the workplace.

More generally, reporting male violence, laying out the facts, showing the continuity and all the tactics and strategies for hiding, presents such a terrible and disheartening situation that many prefer to close their eyes and avoid confronting it.

The philosopher Michèle Le Doeuff expresses it well when she talks of the

> perception of social 'dysfunction' we have in shreds (when we have it): one day we agree to see domestic violence, one day incestuous rape, one day the greater unemployment of women, one day sexism in text books or language, one day the inadequate number and quality of nurseries, one day the situation of single mothers, one day prostitution circuits, one

day pornographic posters, one day genital mutilation, one day the lack of independence of immigrant women ... and then, as all this is painful, we hasten to see nothing more. And at most we see those who suffer, not those causing the problem. Two million women abused in France makes two million abusive men among us. (Le Doeuff, 1998, p 342)

## Notes

[1] The term 'strategy' comes from the Greek and means military comand. According to the dictionary, its first meaning is 'branch of the art of war to do with the conduct of war'; broadly speaking, it indicates 'prearrangement and coordination of the means necessary to achieve a certain objective'. 'Tactics' also means 'branch of the art of war to do with general principles, criteria and methods for using units and means in combat'; broadly speaking, a 'set of actions, tricks and manoeuvres directed towards achieving a goal' (Zingarelli, 2004). When I started to use the terms 'strategies' and 'tactics' in this context, I did so without being aware of their military etymology.

[2] *Actions taken to encourage the attribution of power and responsibility to women and recognise and ensure freedom of choice and social quality for men and women*, dated 27 March 1997, section 9, 'Prevention and suppression of violence, strategic objectives D1-3'.

[3] Recommendation Rec(2002)5 by the Commission of Ministers to the member states on the protection of women against violence, adopted on 30 April 2002 and explanation of reasons. The analysis was made using the Italian translation.

[4] *The Daily Times*, Farmington, New Mexico, 9 April 2003.

[5] See, for example, the work of Spender, 1980; Russ, 1983; Gould, 1998; Le Doeuff, 1998; Tavris, 1992.

[6] People who love animals and do not consider them at all inferior to human beings do not agree with this analysis. I found the observation that Barbara Katz Rothman (2005) makes in her book on 'transracial adoptions' on the fact that small children are called 'monkeys' or other similar names illuminating. Rothman says that the context is crucial: 'Within race, the use of pet or animal terms is affectionate ... Across race, in a society in which animal imagery has been used as an epithet – or more – for people of color, pet imagery is something else' (2005, p 121).

[7] Dworkin and MacKinnon prepared a draft order in 1988, in which they maintained that pornography should be treated as a form of sex discrimination (Dworkin and MacKinnon, 1988). The order became the basis for legislation on pornography in Canada (Graycar and Morgan, 2002). Conceptualising pornography as sex discrimination rather than 'obscenity' represents an excellent example of an epistemological break.

[8] See, for example, Russell, 1997, and Rachel Pearce interviewed by Catherine Itzin, 2000.

[9] Through political pressure and information work Mrs Laplante-Edward also contributed to having a law approved in Canada imposing greater control on the sale of weapons (Laplante-Edward, 1996).

[10] 'Le plaisir absolu', Interview by C. Rihoit with F. Dolto, *Marie Claire*, April 1984, pp 101–5.

[11] 'Le plaisir absolu', Interview by C. Rihoit with F. Dolto, *Marie Claire*, April 1984, pp 101–5.

[12] According to ABS Women's Safety Australia (December 1996) only 14.9% of women sexually attacked in the previous 12 months reported the fact to the police (Graycar and Morgan, 2002, p 256).

[13] Gordon, 1988; Armstrong, 1996; Lezin Jones and Kaufman, 2003.

[14] Banerjee, N. (2003), 'Rape (and silence about it) haunts Bagdad', *The New York Times*, 16 April; Schemo, D.J. (2003), 'Women at West Point face tough choices on assault', *The New York Times*, 22 May, p A16.

[15] See the work of Bulman and Wortman, 1977; Furnham, 2003; Hart et al, 2003; Feinauer and Stuart, 1996; Ullman, 1996; Arata, 1999; and Kahn et al, 2003.

[16] Autism is a congenital condition with a strong neurological component and is not caused by the behaviour of the parents (Schopler, 1985). The mothers observed by the 'experts' in question, rather than being severe and distant, were desperate and terrified of being judged negatively by them. For their part, the experts felt uncomfortable faced with a mysterious condition like autism, which they could not treat and which made them face up to their professional limits (Taylor McDonnell, 1998).

[17] For criticism, see Ehrenreich and English, 1979; Gianini Belotti, 1983; Romito, 1990; Caplan, 1998; Ladd–Taylor and Umansky, 1998.

[18] Finkelhor et al, 1990; Hooper, 1992; Fleming et al, 1997.

[19] See the research by Humphreys, 1997; Saposnek, 1998; Moro, 2003.

[20] In an interview in *Paidika: The Journal of Paedophilia* (1993, 3, pp 2-13), Underwager maintains that 'paedophiles need to become more positive and make the claim that paedophilia is an acceptable expression of God's will for love and unity among human beings'.

[21] For example, some years ago a woman was sentenced to 36 years in prison because, while she was asleep, the man she was living with killed her daughter. According to a journalist there are hundreds of similar cases in the US and none the other way round, that is fathers being considered responsible for the fact that the mother has killed the children (Liptak, A. (2002), 'Judging a mother for someone else's crime', *The New York Times*, 27 November).

[22] Even in the US, women who kill their husbands are in a minority. It is calculated that less than one battered woman in 100,000 kills her violent partner and that between 70% and 90% of those who do so act to defend themselves against an imminent attack (Rhode, 1997, p 291). In the US about half the women killed are killed by their partners or ex-partners, whereas not more than 6% of men killed are killed by their partners or ex-partners (Campbell et al, 2003).

[23] See also the consequences of trauma theory when the social services take charge of battered women in Finland (Keskinen, 2005).

[24] Like O.J. Simpson. See also the section on crimes of honour in Chapter Four, p 96.

[25] For a critical analysis, see the work of Martin Dufresne (www.mincava.umn.edu/papers/limits.asp).

[26] See the analyses of Brophy, 1989; Smart, 1989; Biletta and Mariller, 1997; and Kurki-Suonio, 2000, relating to different countries.

[27] See the analyses by Babu et al, 1997; Peled, 1997; Dufresne, 1998; and Rhoades, 2002.

[28] It is interesting to note that psychologising has a delegitimising function even when it characterises people in a positive way. For example, M. Yunus, the Indian economist who invented the microloan and winner of the Nobel peace prize in 2006, recalls that one of the ways of discrediting his programme and denying it the funds necessary was to attribute its success to his personality and not the qualities of the programme itself (Yunus, 1997).

[29] See the 'Recent history of sexual violence against boys and girls' section in Chapter Four, p 127.

[30] English philosopher (1806–73), husband of the feminist philosopher Harriet Taylor, quoted by Fausto-Sterling, 1992, p 123.

[31] 'At least gang rapists are still vigorous', according to Seichi Ota, liberal-democrat Member of Parliament, in a debate on the fall in the birth rate in Japan, reported in McAvoy, A. (2003) 'A bad week for women in Japan', *San Francisco Chronicle*, 5 July.

[32] Curiously, nobody seems to reflect on the contradiction between the existence of these so-called powerful and uncontrollable sexual instincts and the frequency of impotence problems in men, which is made obvious by the enormous consumption of drugs to treat erectile dysfunction, such as Viagra. According to the data reported by Ims Health, one billion of these pills are consumed worldwide; in Italy 27 million of them have been consumed since 1998 ('Viagra, Italians among the major European consumers', *Il Piccolo*, 18 November 2003). According to American research, 10% of men between 19 and 59 years old do not succeed in having an erection and many more acknowledge lesser disorders (Déttore, 2001).

[33] The advocates of evolutionary psychology, often animal behaviour psychologists, maintain that 'universal' aspects may be found in human behaviour, that is behaviour our predecessors developed in the Neolithic period, which has been shown to be adaptive from the evolutionary point of view and has therefore been passed on genetically. As can be imagined from similar statements, EP is a theory that cannot be tested in fact. For a criticism, see Rose and Rose (2000).

[34] More recently the criminal codes of many countries have taken account of the fact that the victims of rape may also be of the male sex.

[35] Maeterlinck, M., *The life of bees*, Italian translation by M. Buzzi, Newton Compton, Rome, 1991, pp 132-3.

[36] C. Darwin, *The origins of the species by means of natural selection*, 1876, quoted by Rose and Rose, 2000, p 132.

[37] Two scholars belonging to different traditions, the evolutionary biologist Jerry Coyne (2003) and the feminist sociologist Ann Oakley (2002), consider both psychoanalysis and sociobiology to be on the same level as 'major delusional systems', even though now psychoanalysis has lost a lot of its sheen, at least in Anglo-Saxon countries. Coyne (2003,

p 183) writes: 'Freud is no longer the preferred behavioural paradigm. Darwin is the emerging model. Blame your genes, not your mother'.

[38] I owe this idea to Karen Messing, to whom I am grateful.

[39] In 1996 350,000 people went to Brussels to demonstrate their horror at Marc Dutroux, who was guilty of torturing and killing at least four little girls (Papitto, F. (2004), 'Sabine face to face with the monster', *La Repubblica*, 20 April). It is statistically impossible that there were no violent men (or women) among them.

# FOUR

# Hiding strategies

Two principal strategies emerge from analysing male violence in recent history: legitimising and denying. In legitimising, male violence is not hidden in any way: it is visible, but as it is legitimate, it is not defined as violence. When men commit it in the context of the family against those people (women and children) that they consider their property, these actions and toleration of them are often codified in laws. Outside the family some male behaviour, such as using people in prostitution, is accepted by society, even when it takes the most hateful forms.

Denying is necessary, when struggle and social development have made legitimising extreme forms of violence unacceptable and other methods are sought to hide it or not take a position on the subject. We can identify various forms of denying. The most direct form consists simply of not seeing the violence and its consequences. It has been and still is widely practised by those close to the victims: members of the family, acquaintances, health and social workers, police officers and magistrates. Another method consists of attributing another meaning to what has happened: something has happened, but it is not violence. Thus rape is not violence but seduction, passion, hot sex and so on. Denying may take even more complex and sophisticated forms, particularly in socio-historical contexts like the present, where it becomes difficult to avoid seeing the violence or consider it legitimate or distort its meaning systematically with impunity. It comes into operation when the victims recognise what has been inflicted on them as violence, find allies and may thus ask for protection, compensation and justice. As we have already seen, various tactics take over in these cases in order to discredit the victims and those supporting them, hide the identity of the abusers or at least their responsibility, shift responsibility from the abusers to the victims or their supporters and finally rehabilitate the abusers and show them in a good light.

Legitimising and denying are different strategies, each of which seems prominent in different socio-historical contexts. Still, as we have just mentioned, these strategies may also coexist and often are part of a continuum: when legitimising is no longer possible, denying is put into operation. For this reason some examples, such as exercising patriarchal rights over children, ending in incest and murder, will be discussed within both strategies.

## 4.1 Legitimising male violence in the family

According to the prevailing ideology the traditional family, that is the patriarchal family, is the place for the affections, a safe, protected place, a 'refuge in a world without a heart' (Lasch, 1982). The reality is the opposite: for women and children the family and the home are dangerous places, where there is a great risk of suffering violence, ending in death. In peacetime in the US and Italy the majority of women killed are killed by their partners or ex-partners in their own homes or relatives' homes (Campbell, 1992; Barbagli and Colombo, 1996).

This may also be because behaviour, which is considered criminal when it happens outside the family, is considered legitimate instead and therefore not as violence when it happens in the family environment. Let us consider rape. The so-called conjugal exemption, that is the exception made for rape committed by the husband against the wife not being considered a crime, remained in force until 1980 in France, until 1991 in the Netherlands, until 1994 in England and until 1997 in Germany. In the US the conjugal exemption still remains in force in 33 states out of 50. In Italy the criminal code has never explicitly provided the conjugal exemption, but convictions for the rape of a wife have always been very rare and until the 1960s judges recognised the obligation of a wife to supply sexual services as *remedium concupiscentiae* (remedy against lust) for the benefit of the husband or in the name of continuity of the race. Even in 1993 the Appeal Court gave a judgment in favour of an abusive husband who beat and raped his wife. The same logic of 'conjugal duty' also underpinned traditional Catholic doctrine and made the idea of rape committed by the husband inconceivable.[1]

### 4.1.1 Crimes of honour and other violence

When the honour of a man or the whole family lies in the behaviour of the women (wives, daughters and sisters), if this honour has been sullied by their behaviour, the legitimate way of washing away the shame is to kill them. The law sanctions the killer or killers being acquitted or given minimum sentences or not even being tried. In fact, as the community legitimises the behaviour of the killers, many of these murders are not reported. It is therefore not possible to know precisely how many women and girls have been killed for this reason. In Turkey, a NATO country eager to enter Europe, dozens of cases have been reported of women and girls killed by fathers or brothers to safeguard the good reputation of the family. In some countries with an Islamic tradition it is the state or community that absolves these acts: in Iran and Nigeria, a woman considered to be an adulteress or of doubtful morals may be buried from the waist down and publicly stoned. In short, the crime of honour is a crime by the state in defence of the patriarchal family.[2]

Crimes of honour are recognised in the criminal codes of the majority of countries in the Middle East, India, Pakistan and Afghanistan. The codes talk of 'adultery' in general, but in fact any behaviour a man (father or brother) considers of doubtful morality – a girl chatting to a man, going to the cinema without permission, having a fiancé who is unwelcome to the family – already gives him the right to kill her and becomes a reason for acquitting him or drastically reducing his sentence. A family is also dishonoured when one of its female members suffers rape; if it is not possible to resolve the problem otherwise (if the rapist refuses marriage, for example), it is lawful to kill the victim to restore the family's good name, as happened in Kosovo and still happens in Palestine. In some of these countries there was a vain attempt to put the crime of honour up for discussion. In Jordan in 1999 repealing the relevant article of the criminal code was rejected resoundingly in Parliament.[3]

There is a great desire to stand back from these cultures. And yet there is more continuity than break between Western and Middle Eastern cultures on the subject: legislators in Islamic countries took the idea of legally sanctioning crimes of honour from the Napoleonic code in force in France in the 19th century, the same code that inspired legislation in many European countries (Spatz, 1991).

In the Anglo-Saxon legal and cultural tradition the crime of honour does not exist as a category in itself. And yet, even in these countries there is understanding and solidarity for men who kill unfaithful wives in a moment of anger. What seems to be at stake here is not so much the concept of 'family honour' to be preserved, but the idea that the wife belongs to the husband, who may therefore do what he wants with her. If his wife belongs to him, it may be understood how adultery offends him and makes him angry to the point of justifying an act of violence (Spatz, 1991). In 1992 the Supreme Court of Ohio had to answer what one commentator defined without any irony as 'a difficult question': 'How much provocation is reasonably sufficient to reduce a murder charge to voluntary manslaughter?' (Biggerman, 1993, p 977). The answer is that 'reasonably sufficient provocation' usually consists of discovering the wife *in flagrante delicto*, whereas a verbal confession of adultery is not. However, the nature of the connection with the woman in question plays a part. If the adulteress is his wife, the provocation for the man is greater than if she is his fiancée or living with him; the state of anger and the murder resulting from it are more legitimate and mitigation of the sentence is more justified. These distinctions may seem and are convoluted and recall the distinctions of the French criminal code, which until 1975 considered adultery committed by the wife in the marital home more serious and therefore the crime of honour more excusable (Alemany, 2000). Even in Italy, until 1968 adultery was a crime punishable by imprisonment according to different criteria for men and women. The husband was punished (article 560 of the criminal code) only if he made his lover into his concubine, bringing her into the marital home or keeping her 'elsewhere to general knowledge' (Boneschi, 1998).

Still, there are many judges who have no embarrassment in supporting these theories. In 1994 a judge in the US sentenced a man who had killed his unfaithful wife to 18 months in prison on the basis that his homicidal behaviour was an understandable reaction after all: 'I seriously wonder how many married men would have the strength to walk away without inflicting some corporal punishment' (Rhode, 1997, p 111). In Britain, where at least two women are killed by their partners or ex-partners every week (Seager, 2003), many killers are not convicted of murder, which involves life imprisonment, but for the lesser crime of manslaughter. In this case the duration of the sentence is at the complete discretion of the judge. The most frequent reason for changing murder into manslaughter is 'diminished responsibility': the accused must show that at the time of the murder he was suffering from a mental problem that reduced his responsibility. This 'diagnosis' must be confirmed by two psychiatrists. Even when the murder happens after a history of marital violence and death threats, many judges show sympathy towards these men and tend to pardon them: it is not really murder after all, but rather a family dispute that ended badly (Lees, 1997; Morgan, 2006).

We also find similar tendencies in Italy. In 1994 a man, U.G., killed his ex-fiancée: after he had attacked and hit her, he forced the car into a canal and let her drown. In the hours that followed he made every effort to cover the traces of the crime. Some years later the judges reduced his sentence in the appeal court, making allowances for the mitigating circumstances of provocation: U.G. had acted 'in a state of anger caused by unjust action by others'. The provocation, the 'unjust action' committed by others, consisted of the woman refusing to go back with him because she was in love with someone else.[4]

In some cases men who kill women are not acquitted, but become heroes. This is what happened in the US to O.J. Simpson, a famous sportsman, accused of knifing to death his ex-wife, Nicole Brown, and a friend of hers. In spite of a history of abuse and serious death threats against Nicole and irrefutable evidence, Simpson was acquitted in the criminal proceedings in a trial staked entirely on accusations of racism by the American police, where marital violence was ignored. He also obtained custody of the two children he had had with Nicole. However, in the civil proceedings Simpson was recognised as being responsible for the two deaths and sentenced to pay a huge sum as compensation to their families (Schneider, 2000). A few years after the murder Simpson is rich (he ran away to another state so as not to pay the compensation), he lives with his children, he is stacking up reports of abuse by his fiancées and is welcomed as a hero every time he takes part in a sporting event.[5]

If murdering wives is considered a minor crime or even lawful behaviour, it is obvious that battering is treated as a problem that is not only private, but even completely irrelevant. Trivialising violence by husbands against wives and the idea this may be a right is still expressed by many with absolute candour. Battered women asking for help from the police or health workers, who are interviewed in various countries, may hear the response: 'if a woman's beaten, she must have deserved it' or 'if my wife behaved like that, I'd beat her, too'. It is not easy for a woman to report her partner, when faced with this attitude, never mind the shame, hope for change, pressure by relatives and threats of more and worse violence. When they decide to do it, they may be discouraged and sometimes intimidated by the police (Romito, 2000). In spite of these obstacles, many women go through with it. It is an admirable act of courage, determination and faith in institutions, which often still turns out to be useless. In Italy, out of 20,000 reports of abuse in the family made in the 1980s, 14% resulted in convictions and sentences were minimal (Stefanizzi and Terragni, 1993). In London more recently, out of 512 cases of domestic abuse, only 20% of the men were arrested; only in 4% of cases (19 out of 512) did it go to court; and only 3% of the men (13 out of 512) were convicted (Lees, 1997). In Belgium, out of 535 cases of domestic abuse reported to the police in Huy in the 1990s, only in 12% of them was a report made to the public prosecutor's office and only a fifth of the reports (that is 2% of the original reports) reached the examining magistrate; the others were filed, although the women also showed signs of serious violence and injury (Romito, 1999a).

It is obvious that police officers and magistrates often do not consider marital violence as real violence. Sometimes they are violent husbands themselves and therefore think it right to abuse a wife, punish her and so on. In 1994 an American judge ignored reports of abuse by a woman, K.C., against her ex-husband three times; on the fourth report he sentenced the man to follow a programme for violent husbands, that is a course of eight hours for 'anger management'. At the end of the course the man killed his wife and committed suicide. The judge, Ronald Kunz, defended his decision to the hilt, maintaining that after going through the experience of divorce himself he understood the feelings of separated husbands and sympathised with them (Rhode, 1997). Many subscribe to the idea that the family as it is, that is the patriarchal family, represents a fundamental social institution and are reluctant to intervene in situations of domestic violence, fearing that this will lead to the breakdown of the family tie. Thus they tend to trivialise violence, do not arrest the violent man and discourage women from making reports. Paradoxically, if the women, who continue to suffer beatings and threats in the meantime, then withdraw the reports, they will be discredited and held to be to blame for this reason (Mullender, 1996; Temkin, 1997; Bascelli and Romito, 2000).

After analysing the laws and practices of courts in different countries from the Middle East to the US, the jurist Melissa Spatz (1991, p 597) concludes as follows:

> Throughout the world, men who murder their wives encounter legal systems that are lenient toward their crimes and treat the murder of a wife as a less serious crime than the murder of a stranger. Such systems permit men who kill their wives to avoid punishment or receive mitigated sentences through a variety of techniques, including the creation of statutory and common law defences to criminal charges and non-enforcement of criminal laws.... By such legal devices, countries around the world have in effect sanctioned these murders.

### 4.1.2 The struggle by fathers to control their children

The anthropologist Carole Delaney (1998) draws our attention to the myth of Abraham, a myth common to all three monotheistic religions, where a father agrees to sacrifice his son, submitting himself to the will of another man, God the father in the Christian tradition, whom he recognises as more powerful and authoritative. In the myth it is taken for granted that the son belongs to the father, who may therefore sacrifice him, and obedience to a superior authority is valued; the fact that killing the son in the name of these values is a dutiful and legitimate act is also sanctioned.

Paternal violence against children, from psychological abuse to beating and incest, ending in death, is frequent. As we have seen, although fathers spend little time with their children, much less time than their mothers in particular, they inflict abuse and violence on them more often and it is always more serious abuse. After what has been said in previous sections, particularly after analysing the mechanisms used to keep children who are victims of incest and their mothers quiet, it is reasonable to ask again how socially legitimate paternal violence is. In other words, to what extent does society today recognise that fathers own their children and have the right to do what they want with them, use them sexually and kill them?

Far from being provocative, the question springs from observation of the facts, particularly cases of fathers killing their children after separation or divorce (Pennington and Woods, 1990; Dufresne, 1998; Saunders, 2004). Let us consider a case that happened in San Francisco. Kevin S. shot dead his eight-year-old son, who had spent the morning with him, in front of his mother, who had come to collect him, and then committed suicide. The husband and wife had been separated for a short time and there was a documented history of violence by the man against the woman. A few weeks before, the mother had requested an emergency protective order because the ex-husband had attacked her and she was afraid for herself and the child. However, the court had denied the request: the domestic violence had not been judged sufficiently serious and above all the order would have had the effect of preventing Kevin from seeing his son. That was precisely what the mother was asking for, but the magistrate considered it unacceptable. The fact that there was a 'child custody dispute' was considered a reason for not granting a protective order in fact. According to the magistrate responsible for the decision, the protective order may 'tear a family apart': 'The suspect also has rights, and this amounts to banning them – a lot of the time it amounts to kicking them out of their home. You have to take that into account'.[6]

Two observations: the protective order and not paternal violence tears a family apart; the break-up of a family is considered more serious than the possibility of a woman or child being killed.

We can identify similar elements in a case that happened in Quebec in 1993. D.R. was serving a prison sentence for violence inflicted on his ex-companion. The man, a 30-year-old psychology student, had not accepted separation. To convince her to change her mind, he had persecuted, abused and attacked her physically and sexually. He had also threatened to kill her and kill their child, even from prison. In spite of this, he succeeded in obtaining permission to see his son unsupervised at Christmas. He was granted bail thanks to the evidence of a psychiatrist, according to whom D.R. 'did not present any risk to society'. The request for bail presented by his lawyer was supported by the public prosecutor's office. The decision to grant him permission was made by the same judge, who a year previously had released a man convicted for violence towards his ex-wife, who was killed by him as soon as he was out of prison, as he had threatened to do repeatedly. To conclude, D.R. strangled his child and when his mother came to collect him, he held her prisoner for hours, torturing and raping her. He then tried to commit suicide, without success, and told the police he had killed his son 'to spare him the anguish of divorce' (Dufresne, 1998).

Similar cases are frequent in various countries (Saunders, 2004). It is therefore urgent to try to understand the reasons why judges, psychiatrists and other professionals or representatives of institutions support requests by men for access to their children, who explicitly say they want to kill and have already committed serious and repeated violence.

To understand the logic of these decisions, they need to be put into their historical context, a context where the social changes of the last decades have been put up for discussion and in some case limited traditional patriarchal rights, although inequality between men and women remains deep. Let us consider custody of the children after divorce. Until the middle of the 19th century the children belonged to the husband and stayed with him, when there was a divorce, even if they were very small (Smart, 1989). This practice represented a valid means of dissuading women who wanted to leave their husbands because they were violent, for example. In 1828 during a debate in the English Parliament a Member of Parliament declared:

> It is notorious that one of the strongest hindrances in all cases ... to prevent wives from lightly separating from their husbands is that knowledge that they will thereby lose their maternal rights. This at all times has been a safeguard to preserve the institution of marriage! (Smart, 1989, p 4)

The same tendency also prevailed in Italy, where even at the beginning of the 20th century fathers were given custody of more than a third of children after separation (Barbagli and Saraceno, 1998). Even in the 1960s, any child born from an extra-marital relationship by the wife belonged to the legitimate husband, who could remove it from the mother, even if it was to shut it up in an institution (Boneschi, 1998).

Towards the middle of the 20th century the so-called 'tender years doctrine' began to gain ground in Western countries, according to which small children needed their mother. Practices relating to custody after divorce started to change and mothers were given custody of the children more and more often. Around 1970, particularly in Nordic countries and those of Anglo-Saxon tradition, another model took hold, based on gender neutrality, according to which both parents were able to bring up the children after divorce (Smart and Sevenhuijsen, 1989; Kurki-Suonio, 2000).

The current situation in industrialised countries shows an increase in divorce, a general tendency to give custody of the children to mothers by joint agreement between the parents and material and psychological estrangement between fathers and children. According to research conducted in various countries, after divorce only a minority of fathers see their children regularly and contribute to their maintenance, whereas the majority of divorced mothers would like fathers to be there more. In Italy, two years after separation about a third of children never receive telephone calls from their father and about a quarter see him less than once a month; 30% of fathers do not pay maintenance for their children or only pay part of it. This information is particularly worrying, because the situation usually becomes worse as time passes (Smart and Sevenhuijsen, 1989; Barbagli and Saraceno, 1998).

The lack of investment by fathers creates many problems, like the financial one: if non-custodial fathers do not pay an allowance for their children, many mothers have to be financially supported by the state with enormous costs for the community. There is also concern about the psychological consequences of growing up without a father, even though scientific evidence on the subject is contradictory, whereas instead there is no doubt about the serious consequences that witnessing domestic violence and growing up close to a violent father have on the development of the child (Jaffee et al, 2003; Kitzmann et al, 2003). There are also different interpretations of the fact that many fathers become estranged from their children after separation or divorce: for some it is a more emphatic continuation of men not being involved in their care, which was already obvious when they were living together, for others it is instead a reaction caused by the 'alienation' fathers suffer in the courts.

Debate has been sparked in industrialised countries in the last 20 years. Apart from concern about the effects on the children of the father being estranged, there is also explicit concern about undermining the foundations of the traditional family, based on paternal authority: divorced or unmarried mothers, lesbian mothers, mothers who work and have a career or, on the other hand, mothers supported by welfare appear as dangerous forerunners of the attack on patriarchal society. Child custody cases where there is conflict, which are quite rare all considered, are therefore overemphasised and publicised and become the test bench, where opposing practices and principles are confronted (Kurki-Suonio, 2000).

As things stand, awarding joint custody of the children to both parents and therefore sharing responsibility after divorce, which is formulated in different ways in different countries, is presented as the remedy for involving fathers more on a psychological and financial level, but in practice serves to maintain paternal control over the children and the ex-wife. The State of California expressed a preference for joint custody back in 1979, Sweden and Finland in 1983, Britain in 1989 and Germany in 1998 (Kurki-Suonio, 2000). In Italy joint custody became the principal, ordinary solution from 2006 .

It is noted that when talking of joint custody, this is often understood as legal custody and not material custody: this may mean that the mother continues to look after the children on a daily basis, but the father has the right to intervene at any time and therefore interfere in the day-to-day life not only of the children, but also the ex-wife. This interference is always problematic for women, since the purpose of divorce is actually to break up an unsatisfactory or difficult relationship, but may become tragic when there is a dominating or violent man. In fact, social services and the court may force a woman, who has moved towns or taken refuge in a secret home, to leave it or make her address known in order to facilitate contact between father and child, exposing her to the risk of being attacked on these occasions. According to the same logic, a father may oppose specialist examinations of the children aimed at verifying (or ruling out, obviously) any sexual abuse.[7]

At least three ideologies and various policies are involved in supporting joint custody (or sharing parental responsibility, according to the term in use in Britain): the liberal ideology of equal opportunities between men and women, mothers and fathers; that of the New Right with its emphasis on the need to restore the traditional family and paternal authority; that of separated fathers' movements, of which there are now many in Western countries, which are tough and more and more politically influential (see Box 1 in the Appendix).[8]

These ideologies are supported by the common contemporary psychology of the importance of fathers or 'new fathers'. Let us consider the Canadian Guy Corneau, a Jungian psychoanalyst and representative of the masculinist movement for fathers' rights, who is listened to a lot in Quebec and France. In his book *Père manquant, fils manqué* (Corneau, 1998), which is considered an ideological bible for the movement, he maintains that the paternal presence is necessary, particularly in the first two years of life, in order to allow the 'young male to have access to aggressiveness ... sexuality, a sense of exploration, but also logos, which is understood as an aptitude for abstraction and objectification' (Corneau, 1998, p 23).[9] And on the other hand, 'all children without a father systematically show a deficiency on a social, sexual, moral or cognitive level.... Being without a father is like being without a backbone' (Corneau, 1998, pp 26, 39).

But fathers need not worry: nobody is asking them to be involved in an equitable way or at least partly in the day-to-day care of the child, what is important is that 'the child is in contact with the father's smell, hears the deeper sound of his voice and jumps into his arms' (Corneau, 1998, p 32).

Corneau is not hampered by references to scientific work; his dreams or those of his patients are quite sufficient to prove his theories. Obviously what he maintains is in keeping with the values and beliefs of many, another example of the closeness between the discourse of some experts, those most supported by the press, and the most vulgar common sense.[10] The problem arises when judges draw inspiration from his theories to decide on the custody of the children in cases where there is conflict (Dufresne, 1998).

Fathers' rights movements protest that they are discriminated against in decisions by the courts relating to custody of the children (Boyd, 2002). However, the information available gives the lie to their accusations. Research in various countries shows that there is conflict regarding custody of the children in not more than 10% of divorce cases and fathers are given custody of the children in about half the cases; in only one study were mothers slightly favoured. In Australia, if there is a dispute, the family courts give custody to fathers twice as often compared with what happens in cases where there is consent, even when there is domestic violence.[11]

According to various observers, judges use a double standard when assessing parental capacity. To be considered good mothers, mothers must show that they put the interest of the child before their own, to the point of sacrificing all their interests. Often judges ask them to give up studying or pursuing a career to stay at home all the time, thus pinning them down in a situation where they cannot win: if they do not have any training or a good job, they cannot maintain their children and custody of them will be given to their father for this reason. Whereas,

> virtually any involvement by fathers with their children constitutes 'good enough fathering'; regardless of their previous pattern of behaviour, most fathers are deemed able to offer some benefit to their children. (Eriksson and Hester, 2001, p 791)

Who are these fathers who come to court to have custody of their children or joint custody? One theory is that they are loving fathers who are interested in their children and have always been involved in their care. Still, the information available suggests that at least some of them belong to the opposite type. Often they are men who previously had absolutely no interest in their children on an emotional and material level, and they are often dominating or violent men. It is precisely the latter who are most likely to start proceedings to obtain custody and tragically are also those most likely to obtain it. A case by way of an example in the US concerns the decision by a judge to give custody of the children to the violent husband after he had visited the refuge where the woman and children had hidden to escape the violence, and had found it 'inadequate': better the father's home.[12]

We observe the same tendency in Britain. In a study 53 women who were separated from a violent husband were studied for some years. A good 50 of them were attacked repeatedly when they met their ex-partners to 'exchange' the children, and half the children suffered physical or sexual abuse by the father during visits. When the women confirmed the need for protection, they were labelled as egotistical, uncooperative and hostile, running the risk of losing custody of their children (Radford et al, 1997).

There is no research on the subject in Italy, but the results of some qualitative studies essentially lead in the same direction: when women oppose indiscriminate access to their children by their violent ex-partners and try to protect themselves and their children, they are often punished by social services and the court (Romito, 2000) (see Box 2 in the Appendix).

In Australia files relating to 100 custody cases where there was conflict were analysed, which were selected from those where there was apparently no violence by the partner (Rhoades, 2002). The analysis showed that in 17% of cases the father deliberately used contact with the children to control and persecute the ex-wife and that in 55% of cases contact was an occasion to inflict subsequent violence (death threats, attacks, rape). Two mothers suspected paternal sexual abuse, but the judges decided in favour of the father: one woman was judged 'paranoid', the other accused of not understanding that the highly sexualised behaviour of the child represented only a demand for attention. In line with the model of the parental alienation syndrome, deciding to give custody of the children to the father, the judge had considered the maternal concerns a form of psychological abuse of the children (Rhoades, 2002). In fact, in the *sex abuse legitimacy scale* (SAL) one of the criteria for deciding that abuse is invented is the fact that the mother has turned to a lawyer or a doctor (Sherman, 1993) (see Box 3 in the Appendix).

When deciding on contact between fathers and children after separation or divorce in cases where there is conflict, magistrates and psychosocial workers seem to proceed by a succession of denials: they deny the frequency and seriousness of abuse against women in the couple and paternal abuse against children; they deny that men who abuse women and children are the same; they deny the continuation of male violence even after separation; and they deny the risk of very serious violence during meetings between fathers and children.

These denials work to maintain patriarchal logic: fathers own their children and have the right to do what they want with them, including incest, an idea many continue to support, even though not at all consciously. Today the patriarchal discourse pure and simple and the model of the owner father have become unpresentable and are dressed up with more modern and acceptable discourse, such as the language of equal opportunities between men and women and mothers and fathers, and psychological discourse in particular. Thus the ideology of new fatherhood is flourishing where, on the one hand, it is taken for granted that there is an equitable division of work in the couple (false, see Seager, 2003) and, on the other hand, it draws its inspiration by taking psychodynamic models here and there – from Jung to Lacan – to maintain the importance of the symbolic paternal function. For Corneau only the presence of the father allows the child to have access to logos, for example. As Geneviève Cresson (2000) points out, it is a little curious that there is never any mention of a symbolic maternal function: perhaps women and mothers are denied the symbolic? To men the symbolic, to women ... what? The trivial? The material? And Cresson (2000, p 132) adds:

> Few ask themselves what this 'symbolic function' becomes in the hands of a man who abuses his wife; is there not perhaps a need to protect children from symbols like this?

> But mostly this expression seems to work like a charm: once
> it has been pronounced, everything has been said, there is
> no need to discuss anything further.

In short, it is easy for these violent fathers and ex-husbands to continue
to dominate their wives and children. Given the continued financial
inequality between the sexes, men also have greater financial resources
and may therefore engage tougher and more effective lawyers (Sherman,
1993). In countries like the US the lawyers of mothers running away
with their children, in order not to hand them over to their fathers, run
the risk of being struck off the register and financial ruin if they refuse
to reveal to the court where mother and child are hiding; certainly not
an incentive to stand by these women (Pennington and Woods, 1990).
If this were not enough, there may be physical violence. In Australia
from the 1980s onwards numerous terrorist attacks have been carried
out with bombs being thrown at the staff of family courts, where child
custody cases are decided: a judge and an adviser were killed and there
are connections between these crimes and some of the most aggressive
representatives of fathers' rights movements, particularly the Men
Confraternity (Graycar, 1989).

From his observation post in Quebec – more than 500 women and
children killed in nine years by men, almost always ex-partners or
fathers (Dufresne, 1998) – Martin Dufresne, who is active in a group
of men against sexism, notes that the choice of encouraging contact
between a child and the violent father is explained

> by the importance these people (psychiatrists, psychologists,
> social workers, judges) say they attribute to the 'place of the
> Father', which is often disguised as the 'interest of the child',
> not its real interest in being protected from a violent adult,
> but its symbolic interest in remaining within the sphere of
> paternal authority.... For these people the theoretical risk
> of abuse is far lower than the real risk that the child may
> become adult outside symbolic male power. If the worst
> comes to the worst, I have the impression that for them the
> power and threat the father brings to bear represent useful
> or even essential training for a child of the male sex or that
> it must learn to respect the male somehow. Paradoxically, the
> more the father lacks interest in or threatens the child with
> his behaviour, the more the risk of discrediting the paternal
> figure feeds the ardour of the system to protect this 'place
> of the Father', therefore guaranteeing the prerogatives of a

violent or negligent father at any price. (Martin Dufresne, personal communication, November 2002)

In short, the risk of a child being killed is taken into account and weighed up against the possibility of growing up without a father, using psychological language, against the possibility of the father losing his rights over it, according to a more objective analysis. The result is that today in many industrialised countries denying or even only restricting contact between father and children is considered more serious than exposing the child and the woman to the risk of violence and death (Rhoades, 2002).

In this discourse men, the fathers, thus change status from oppressors to victims: discriminated against in courts, thrown out of their homes, separated from their children, desperate. It is a discourse that finds no confirmation in the data available, but is repeated loudly and aggressively by separated fathers' and men's movements and taken up obligingly and uncritically by the press, in the titles of articles relating to cases of men killing their children and wives, for example. Of course the suffering of these men should not be undervalued, since some of them took their own lives after taking the lives of others. But the mistake is in interpreting it as the product of divorce and the so-called alienation suffered by men because of legal proceedings, ignoring the aspect of domination and possession, which formed elements of their violence even before separation. Proposals to avoid tragedies and deaths resulting from this interpretation – the right of access to the children, joint custody – thus end up by legitimising precisely those demands for control and possession that lie behind the violence and are never put up for discussion.

In short, these data indicate that on many occasions institutions support the claims of violent men to exercise their patriarchal rights, even though this means putting at risk the well-being, health and sometimes even the life of women and children. Although violence by fathers against their children is no longer legitimate in any way or even valued by society, as in the myth of Abraham, it still seems to be accepted as a by-product that is unpleasant perhaps, terrible in some cases, but is inevitable to achieve what many still consider to be a higher purpose, that is maintaining male authority over wives and children.

Recent events have accustomed us to the concept of just war and humanitarian bombs, where collateral damage (that is civilians killed) is an unpleasant but inevitable event. The evidence discussed in this section suggests that women and children killed by ex-husbands or fathers represent collateral damage, the price society is prepared to pay to keep patriarchal rights intact or re-establish them, when necessary.

## 4.2 Legitimising outside the family: prostitution

> Prostitution is buying the right to rape. (Evelina Giobbe, 1990, p 67)

The violence of prostitution may be denied only through multiple distinctions and separation – between free prostitution and forced prostitution, the prostitution of adult women and child prostitution, war brothels and war rape – where the first term indicates a socially legitimate and sometimes legal practice and the second a practice recognised as reprehensible and illegal. The purpose of this section is to discuss the relevance of these distinctions and reveal continuity where the prevailing ideology imposes separation. Only in this way will it be possible to show that 'ordinary' prostitution, which is not practised by children or by women who have been trafficked, does not happen in war, and does not involve the torture and death of the prostitute, is intrinsically violence, and to show through what psychosocial mechanisms this may remain hidden.

### 4.2.1 Continuity between sexual abuse against children and prostitution

A lot of research has shown the relationship between a history of early sexual abuse and violence in the family and prostitution. According to studies carried out in Canada and England, between 80% and 90% of women or girl prostitutes have suffered serious violence in the family and about half have suffered incest. Transvestites or homosexual boys, who become prostitutes, often have similar stories behind them. According to Evelina Giobbe (1990), who became a prostitute and then founded the WHISPER association (Women Hurt in the Systems of Prostitution Engaged in Revolt) in the US, prostitution is taught and learnt at home. There are many roads leading from sexual violence in the family to prostitution:

- children abused by their father or other members of the family are exchanged or sold to other men;

- they grow up identifying themselves with what their father has done to them, learning to use sex as goods for trade, even to get affection and attention, convinced 'that's all they're good for';
- they run away from home to escape abuse and end up on the prostitution market, because there is no other way for a runaway child to survive;
- or they even learn prostitution in the institutions or homes/families where social services have put them in order to remove them from a violent father or family.

Swann (2000) described the process by which children who have become vulnerable from histories of violence and neglect are seduced by adult men they fall in love with, who induce them to become prostitutes. When the deception connected to the pretence of romantic love is not enough to keep them in prostitution, violence may become extreme (Nixon et al, 2002; Williamson and Cluse-Tolar, 2002).

This information is confirmed by the age of the prostitutes: in Western countries at least a third of street prostitutes are children. The average age for going into prostitution is between 13 and 15, which means that many are younger, like the 11-year-old Albanian girl or her compatriot, who was not much older, carrying her soft toy bear behind her as she worked, both prostitutes on the Italian streets.[13] All this is highly disturbing and indicates, on the one hand, the persistence of child prostitution even in the West and, on the other hand, the closeness between industrialised countries and developing countries: in India the average age for going into prostitution is between 10 and 13 (Raymond, 2002). Another separation also fades, between sex tourism, which it is generally known involves adolescents and children in particular, and 'ordinary' prostitution, which is consumed at home: in both cases the men buying sex, the so-called clients, often buy children.

In the light of these data terms such as 'juvenile prostitute', 'protector' and 'client', giving an idea of free choice in a free market, with reference to girls who have often run away from home because of maltreatment or abuse, are more than inappropriate and misleading, they are obscene. It needs to be said clearly that these are children who are being raped and men who are doing the raping (Swann, 2000).

### 4.2.2 Soldiers, peacekeepers and sex tourists

Wherever an army arrives, brothels are organised; the condition of the women exploited may range from maximum to minimum coercion in these cases. From 1928 to 1945 the Japanese government forced thousands of women, particularly Koreans and Philippinos, to serve the Japanese army as sex slaves. Like women who are trafficked today, some were led to believe they had got a good job, others were sold by their poor families, many were simply abducted. Up to 200,000 women were confined for years in these military brothels, held in slavery and raped dozens of times a day. The daily horror was such that almost all the survivors came out of it devastated. The expression 'comfort women', which is often used to denote them, is tragic, because it suggests that many men feel 'comforted' by being able to use a woman sexually in a state of slavery (Dolgopal, 1995).

In Thailand, prostitution, which is illegal, made its name in the 1970s to meet the demand for 'rest and recreation' by the American troops in Vietnam: in 1981 there were 300,000 prostitutes in Bangkok alone and 70% were infected by venereal disease, which represented almost half the women working in the city. Today in Thailand children become HIV positive after they have spent about six months in a brothel. In the Philippines, sexual exploitation, carried out to meet the demand of the servicemen at the US naval bases, is concentrated in the towns of Olongapo and Angeles City. Thousands of men – owners of brothels, bars, porn cinemas and massage parlours, a third of them soldiers or ex-soldiers, as well as corrupt Phillipino officials – share the profits from such exploitation, which are estimated at about 500 million dollars a year. There are at least 100,000 child prostitutes, many of them children and grandchildren of women who have become prostitutes, who have never had another world as reference other than prostitution. Although prostitution is illegal in the Philippines, there are frequent health checks: if a girl is found positive for the Aids virus, the owner of the bar or brothel is informed, as well as the Navy; a photo of the girl is often put on the notice board, so that every sailor knows her. Nobody informs the girl, she will work it out for herself from the ostracism and poverty that gradually surround her. In Belize, an ex-colony accommodating an English military base, when a soldier is found positive in a test for HIV or venereal disease, he must inform his superior of the name of the prostitute he thinks infected him. With the first of these 'mistakes', the girl receives a reprimand from the owner of the brothel; with the second mistake, she is fined; with the third, she is sent away. Nobody asks who infected her.[14]

It is pointed out that although part of this business is run by the underworld, it is thought out and organised at the highest institutional levels (Unesco, 1986). In 1967 the organisation of 'rest and recreation' areas for American soldiers staying in Vietnam was contracted between the government of the US and the government of Thailand. In

1971 the World Bank, then under the presidency of R. McNamara, recommended the promotion of sex tourism in the latter country with thinly veiled words. Today the profits from the prostitution market represent 14% of the Gross National Product in Thailand (Robinson, 1997; Seager, 2003).

In the last few years the peacekeeping forces of the United Nations have been responsible for very serious actions against women and children in the civilian population they should have been protecting. In Cambodia the arrival of 100,000 peacekeepers and officials from the United Nations in 1991 sparked off considerable trafficking of girls and children from the country to the town: in Phnom Penh alone, the number of girls becoming prostitutes rose from 6,000 in 1991 to 20,000 a year later. Peacekeepers were prepared to pay up to 500 dollars for a child who was a virgin, who was not worth more than 10 dollars after the first time (Fetherston, 1995; Grandits et al, 1999).

In Mozambique, soldiers, particularly those from the Italian contingent, took part in sexual violence and organised sexual trafficking of children and adolescents. According to a Norwegian observer, 'adolescents were considered as sexual prey by thousands of peacekeepers who went through Mozambique between the 1992 peace agreement and the 1994 elections' (Grandits et al, 1999). In Somalia in 1993-94, Italians in the peace contingent were accused of raping young Somali women and in 1996 of organising the trafficking of children for sexual exploitation in Sarajevo. In spite of strong evidence, high command denied it. In Bosnia, peacekeepers of various nationalities were accused of frequenting a brothel run by Serbs, where Croatian and Muslim women were held prisoner, as well as organising the trafficking of drugs and women. In Liberia, Guinea and Sierra Leone, dozens of officials from the United Nations and some non-governmental organisations (NGOs) sexually exploited women and children: sex in exchange for food or accommodation in a camp. While the international community reacted with horror at the rape and torture committed by militias and armies in the last wars in Bosnia, Kosovo and Rwanda, it was much more reluctant to act and punish soldiers and officials from the United Nations and NATO, who were responsible for similar crimes.[15]

The biologising and naturalist ideology, according to which male sexual behaviour is guided by uncontrollable instincts, contributes to keeping these practices alive, presenting them as necessary and inevitable and hiding their violence.[16] Defending the institution of brothels for soldiers and at the same time sexual violence outside brothels, Yasushi Akashi, head of the United Nations mission in Cambodia and then head of the 'peace' mission in ex-Yugoslavia, declared that 'hot-blooded,

18-year-old soldiers have a right to have a couple of beers and chase local young beauties' and accused his critics of being 'puritans' (Grandits et al, 1999).

Sexual crimes by United Nations Office peace contingents bring us face to face with evidence of how neutral concepts, such as peace, have traditionally excluded women, their bodies, experiences and pain. How is it possible not to see the contradiction between the sexual use of women in a country worn out by war and the idea of peace? Trafficking, abduction and rape of girls and children are the norm. But in a context of poverty and desperation the contradiction also exists, if they are adult women, who decide to become prostitutes.

According to the prevailing ideology, male desire is peremptory: brothels and prostitutes are therefore necessary to satisfy men and prevent rape. However, as we have already seen, men and soldiers use prostitutes and commit rape. Again, according to the prevailing ideology, a prostitute is 'rapable': and as she is a prostitute, what is done to her may not even be considered rape (as rape within marriage is not considered as such in a lot of legislation). It is also possible that the sexual use and abuse of a prostitute becomes a model for the sexual use of other women. Brothels and rapes, even of children, have increased around the US base of Okinawa in Japan: from 1988 to 1995, 169 soldiers ended up in front of a court martial for rape (Johnson, 2000). In Japanese culture, where a woman who has been raped is overwhelmed by shame, blamed and marginalised by her family and society, this number represents a very small proportion of the rapes that actually happened.

Naturalising male behaviour makes it possible to avoid asking how and why male desire is expressed in such a way that a man finds satisfaction, 'recreation' or comfort in using a woman or child sexually, an act that at best constitutes masturbation in the body of another and at worst is rape. The idea that male desire is uncontrollable also leads to a dehumanised view not only of the woman, who is simply a receptacle for male relief, but also of the man, who is inevitably prey to the instinct to use violence.

When the soldiers leave, because the war or peace mission has ended, other men arrive, the sex tourists. At least 13,000 Australians with an average age of 30-35, who are largely professionals, judges, lawyers and teachers, arrive on holiday in the Philippines every year to make the most of the party. The same happened in Cambodia and Thailand, where many multinational companies organise sex tours for their male employees as company bonus holidays (Sturdevant and Stoltzfus, 1992).

The context and justifications of sex tourism are different to some extent. All those men who fill charter flights for the South of the world individually or in groups rarely see what they are doing as violence or sexual abuse against children. But as they usually come from countries where having sex with a child is prohibited or at least not well thought of, justifications are constructed that allow them to avoid facing up to the troublesome idea of behaving immorally. These justifications correspond to the model of moral disengagement proposed by Albert Bandura (1999). When sex tourists are interviewed, they maintain that it is better for these little girls to earn a living as prostitutes than die of hunger (advantageous comparisons); on the other hand, it is not prostitution, but rather an amorous adventure where men are giving some kind of present (euphemistic labelling); everybody does it anyway (diffusion and displacement of responsibility); there are no negative consequences for the girls (distortion of the consequences); it is also the girls themselves who are looking for clients and hooking tourists (attribution of blame to the victim); in these countries children mature earlier and are more sensual (dehumanising) (O'Connell Davidson and Sanchez Taylor, 1996a, 1996b).

### 4.2.3 Ordinary prostitution and trafficking

Few could dispute the fact that Korean women held in slavery by the Japanese army or Philippino children thrown onto the sex tourism market do not suffer violence. It is calculated that about half a million women and children are trafficked every year in Western Europe for the purpose of sexual exploitation; nobody doubts the existence of forced prostitution or the conditions of extreme violence and discrimination to which these women are subject (Hughes, 2000; *Stop Trafficking*, 2002). Still, many maintain that some prostitutes have chosen to do it, it is a job like any other or even better, where the woman can express herself and her sexuality. For some of them it is an independent choice and disputing this independence means not respecting their capacity for self-determination. After all, as the famous scientist, Stephen Hawking (1993, p 16), declared: 'scientists and prostitutes get paid for doing what they enjoy'.

And yet, if we look closely at the information available, the theory of choice is questionable. We have already pointed out that a sizeable proportion of prostitutes went onto the 'market', when they were still children. As far as trafficking is concerned, it is estimated that more than 75% of women trafficked by European and Eastern countries are not aware that they will become prostitutes. Those who are aware of it never imagine the extreme levels of coercion, bordering on slavery, and violence, ending in death, to which they will be subject. A Russian girl thought being a prostitute consisted of being kept by a rich, handsome man, like in the film *Pretty woman*, for example (Hughes, 2000). Trafficking women, which is extremely profitable, is run by organised crime, it is therefore obvious that the media in the countries involved are reticent about the actual 'working' conditions women may expect, when they arrive at their destination (Hughes, 2000). When the deception is no longer enough to ensure an influx of women allowing demand for the sex market to be met, the traffickers may buy girls from their families or simply abduct them. In countries where the value of female virginity is supreme, another strategy is to rape the girl so as to make her 'damaged goods'. At this point there is no other road except prostitution (Miller, 2002).

In a study carried out in France (Mathieu, 2002), although none of the women or men interviewed had been trafficked or held in slavery, going into prostitution was the result of direct or indirect coercion. For adolescents running away from home, young homosexuals rejected by homophobic families or drug addicts it was financial coercion; in other cases women became prostitutes because they were induced to do so by a lover/pimp, sometimes with violence, at other times with emotional blackmail. For some transsexuals prostitution seemed the only way of being able to be part of an environment characterised by extravagant styles of consumption. As for it being contrary to an approach to the question in terms of 'extreme poverty', Mathieu (2002, p 64) concludes that 'going into prostitution is always the result of coercion, therefore the distinction between free and forced prostitution is irrelevant'. In this French research and research carried out in Oslo (Hoigrad and Finstad, 1992) most of the prostitutes came from the proletariat or subproletariat and many had suffered violence in the family. The decision to become a prostitute could represent a form of resistance, a way of reacting to something that perhaps was even worse than prostitution: poverty or abusive family situations.

Although the rhetoric about choice is difficult to sustain from what has been said, is it legitimate to declare instead that prostitution represents a 'job like any other'? Women prostitutes describe the mechanisms put into operation to bear the physical and psychological intrusion of men that normally they could not even bear to have near them: dissociation, mental escape, numbing (Nixon et al, 2002), mechanisms that are also similar to those put into operation by sexually abused children. They also express the sense of horror and betrayal when occasionally they have an orgasm with a client, also in this case a feeling shared with the victims of sexual abuse and rape (Giobbe, 1990). And just like victims of rape, women prostitutes show high levels of psychological suffering, particularly post-traumatic stress syndrome. A study has shown that these reactions – panic attacks, nightmares, dissociation – are more frequent among women prostitutes than Vietnam veterans (Farley, 2003). Other violence is added to these characteristics that are intrinsic to prostitution and also exist in less extreme situations: rape and physical abuse by clients, pimps or police officers, abuse and insults from passers-by, torture and death (Williamson and Cluse-Tolar, 2002) (see Box 4 in the Appendix). Serial killers kill prostitutes in particular, perhaps out of misogyny or because they know that these deaths are of no interest to anyone and they may get away with them with impunity. In Italy the bodies of 186 foreign women were discovered in 1999 alone, almost all of them prostitutes, who were victims of the racket and killed because they had tried to escape or killed by a client for 'fun' (in the US these crimes are called 'recreational murders') (Monzini, 2002).

According to many people, this violence could be eliminated or reduced if prostitution were legalised, as in Holland or Germany, where women prostitutes work in brothels or organise themselves in cooperatives. There are obviously enormous financial interests behind this position: for the organisers and exploiters, prostitution and pornography represent earnings of billions of dollars a year (Hughes, 2000). Not to mention the interests of a great many men, the 'clients', who do not want to give up a sexual interaction that satisfies and gratifies them (Jeffreys, 1997). Even some prostitutes still declare that prostitution is, or may become, a job like any other, even more advantageous than others on a financial level, as well as sexually liberating. These are not frequent positions, but the media have been an echo chamber for them, making them visible and almost more legitimate than the voices of those women who have escaped from prostitution instead and consider it a devastating experience (Leidholdt and Raymond, 1990). In Italy some women confirm that they have chosen this occupation without being forced by anyone, declaring they have control of the sexual transaction with the client and do not mention, or only occasionally mention, violence. This is the position of Pia Covre, representative of the Committee for the civil rights of prostitutes: 'when I was a prostitute ... I enjoyed myself, I liked it very much; if I had to go back I would do it again and would start earlier' (Covre, 1999, p 50). This is a position that contrasts with that of another woman prostitute, Toby Summer: 'A prostitute is a person turning off her emotions, being psychically somewhere else while someone who despises her is making love to her' (Jeffreys, 1997, p 211).

## 4.2.4 The controversy surrounding prostitution

Prostitution is intrinsically violence, even if it is practised in 'good conditions', which rarely happens, however. Its essence is making the woman a thing, an object, so that she is no longer a person and often not even a body, but parts of a body. It is a dangerous process because each sexual act making her a thing takes place in a continuum of dehumanisation, which may also end in acts of extreme male violence (Stoltenberg, 1993). It is a model of sexuality based on the disparity between the sexes and reinforces it, where men not only have no need to establish an egalitarian relationship, but do not even need to make the effort to establish a relationship, much less negotiate sexuality giving pleasure to both. Using children or people in conditions of poverty or desperation reduces even further the demands that a woman who is not a prostitute or not dominated in any way could face him with, until they are removed altogether. Prostitution is therefore not the inevitable response to the alleged boundless and unbridled sexual needs of men, as the prevailing ideology would like it to be. First, it is debatable whether these needs are boundless or greater than those of women.[17] Second, the lie is given to them being uncontrollable by the very way prostitution is organised and practised: men of all social classes often go in groups, perhaps to have a good time at the end of the evening (the so-called 'whore tour', Cutrufelli, 1996); when they travel for work reasons, they are guaranteed an 'escort' and conclude business in brothels (Jeffreys, 1997). Prostitution is instead a solution constructed by society to meet the inability of many men to interact with a woman on equal and intimate terms, a solution to their crippled emotional and sexual lives, and would be inconceivable in a context where women were not dominated.

As Kate Millett observed in the 1970s, at the heart of prostitution is not sex, or not only sex, but power:

> it is not sex that the prostitute is really made to sell, it is degradation. And the buyer, the 'john',[18] is not buying sexuality, but power, power over another human being, the dizzy ambition of being lord of another's will for a stated period of time. (in Jeffreys, 1997, p 66)

Prostitution also represents a perfect example of that separating or compartmentalising, which, according to Robin Morgan (1992), is a characteristic of patriarchy: intellect severed from emotion, thought separated from action, feelings divided from the body and the Madonna or mother separated from the whore.

And yet conceptualising prostitution as a job like any other and therefore denying the violence represent a constant in recent history. In the 1950s the United Nations Convention for the suppression of people trafficking and exploitation of prostitution led to the closure of brothels in many countries but also revolt by the 'johns' with various lobbies organised in support of prostitution and pornography (Jeffreys, 1997).[19] This controversy is revealed repeatedly in the work of the new Convention on trafficking, signed in Palermo in 2000. Countries such as the Netherlands and Germany, where brothels are legal, and some NGOs wanted to exclude people who 'consent' to being moved from the definition of 'trafficking'. According to these lobbies, with a wider definition there is the risk of preventing some women from choosing to immigrate to work on the sex market, putting the blame on clients and not guaranteeing the presumption of innocence of the organisers of the market/pimps. On the other hand, the supporters of the need to use a wider definition, where consent is not a determining factor, emphasise the difficulty for the victim of proving the absence of consent in legal proceedings. This line prevailed in the end. There was also opposition to using expressions such as 'sexual exploitation' and 'victim', which were considered too emotive. On the other hand, in recent documents from the United Nations and the International Labour Organisation the expressions 'sex work' or 'forced prostitution' are used uncritically and pimps are defined as 'third party business agents or brokers' (Raymond, 2002).

The financial aspect certainly explains the intensity and effectiveness of the pressure exercised by various lobbies to make prostitution and pornography legal or normalise it: the profits are enormous after all. Still, it does not explain why many people adopt this position, who are not exploiters. The controversy also exists in the feminist world. In France in the *Dictionnaire critique du féminisme* (Hirata et al, 2000) prostitution is the only heading to have a double entry, one written by C. Legardinier, which defines it as violence according to the feminist approach, the other by G. Pheterson, which conceptualises it as a job according to the postmodernist neoliberalist approach.

In fact the neoliberalist ideology is one of the tools allowing the extent of the violence inherent in prostitution to be obscured. From the moment the woman has chosen or consented, there is nothing to worry about. Still others maintain that in certain contexts the existence of a 'contract' not only does not represent clearance for any action, but is immoral in itself (Pateman, 1988). Therefore it is not or should not be morally acceptable to sell parts of your own body, rent your own uterus for reproductive purposes or your own body for sexual purposes. The buyer is always wrong, even if he pays, because he is reducing another human being to consumer goods.

A central and revolutionary aspect of the feminist method has been, and still is, to listen to women, believe them and legitimise their point of view. It is understandable that many feminist scholars experience their own evaluation of prostitution as opposed to that expressed by some ex-prostitutes as a dilemma. What right have I to maintain that prostitution is oppression, exploitation and violence, when instead some women prostitutes support an interpretation in terms of independence, choice and profession? This dilemma is not peculiar to the analysis of prostitution. Some feminist scholars have established how much their interpretation of reality – defining housewives as relatively oppressed women in a situation of dependency, for example – conflicts with that of the women themselves, who instead asserted that they have chosen their condition and saw themselves as independent (Acker et al, 1983; Romito, 1990). Mott and Condor (1997, p 83), analysing sexual harassment experienced by secretaries and resistance to recognising it as such, concluded:

> we have time and again found ourselves involved not in a cosy epistemological partnership with the women whose voices we listen to, but a bitter hermeneutic struggle as we assert our feminist visions over versions of the world in which sexual harassment is 'just a joke', in which women are 'not oppressed', in which our respondents have 'never experienced discrimination', in which 'feminists are wrong'.

In the 1970s a central idea in feminism was recognising that many of our choices were conditioned by patriarchal society, without this meaning women were passive, on the contrary the purpose of feminism was to act to change the world. Today feminist respect for women and their subjectivity has been decanted into the postmodernist discourse by distorting it, where nobody may say anything beyond their own legitimate but extremely limited point of view. Particularly in contemporary Anglo-American feminist discourse, the concept of *agency* has also become central and is seen in opposition to the loathed concept of passivity, associated with the concept of victim. In the apolitical, but in fact neoliberalist, context of postmodernism, where all analysis is carried out exclusively on an individual level, there are no tools to understand that it is possible to be active and oppressed at the same time. The fact that women are considered as a race apart interferes with our understanding of reality. It is very useful instead to analyse what also happens to other dominated groups at the same time. Let us consider the case of men and women migrating from the Southern countries of the world to richer countries, where they carry out the worst work, which the indigenous people do not want to do any more. They choose to do it, preferring very hard, dangerous and underpaid work to more awful poverty. They are active, but this does not detract from the fact that they are also horribly exploited. A woman may assess her situation and decide to become a prostitute, but what is done to her in prostitution remains a reification and abusing her humanity. In short, the fact that a situation of exploitation and abuse has been chosen does not change either the exploitation or the abuse.

The way the social world works is not generally accessible only from people's everyday experience. Still, as scholars, we have technologies, such as statistical research, and conceptual tools to understand the reasons why the dominated do not always recognise what is being done to them. The absence or minimisation of experiences of violence in the accounts of some women who are prostitutes is read with the same conceptual tools as we use to understand the denial of other forms of violence by women who are not prostitutes. There is no practical or moral advantage in recognising the violence and degradation suffered, if the person does not see a way out, does not have the tools to give a political reading to what has happened to them and if these processes do not happen in a context of emotional and material support. In the absence of these conditions, recognising that you are a victim is too painful and humiliating and perhaps useless (Thomas and Kitzinger, 1997).

Toby Summer explains why she claimed prostitution as an independent choice, refusing to define her experience as violence. It made her feel better to tell herself: 'I chose what happened (even the rapes), that I felt OK about what was done to my body (even against my will) ... the nausea-alienation-bruises-humiliation-STDs ... poverty-abortion, were all somehow fixable' (Jeffreys, 1997, p 254).

With this mystification she tried to 'transform her degradation into something else, something more human', or construct another representation of reality, as she could not change it. Summer maintained this version for a certain time, even after she had left prostitution, although she could not give a reason for choosing to work in an industrial laundry for a few dollars an hour rather than going with a man. And she concludes: 'Confronting how I've been hurt is the hardest thing that I've had to do in my life' (Jeffreys, 1997, p 150).

To sum up, the rhetoric of choice protects women who are prostitutes, their self-esteem and sense of independence, and others who are not prostitutes, who may thus avoid facing the objective misery of sexuality of many men and their contempt for women.

To understand the logic of this restructuring of reality does not mean legitimising it: although the women who subscribe to it may gain an advantage from it in the short term, in the long term it is in the interest of the class of men and represents another contribution to legitimising and hiding their violence.


## 4.3 The strategy par excellence: denial

> [T]here remains the problem of denial. Even the community of decent people finds society's inability to quell the tide of violence against women is too horrific to accept. The reality of life for a battered woman is indeed beyond the knowledge of the average person and ... denying the truth of the battered woman's story can be easier than confronting it. (Michael Dowd, quoted in French et al, 1998, p 582)

Denial is the principal social strategy to hide male violence, which always seems to work, uses all the tactics and also involves the other strategy described. Denial involves many people and works in many ways. The perpetrators of the violence deny it; their friends, relatives and accomplices deny it; the witnesses deny it, because they share fundamental values, because they are ignorant and because they are cowardly; sometimes even the victims deny it.

Denial takes direct, glaring or more insidious forms. One glaring method materialises in health and social services: even the most serious signs of violence go unobserved. The stories women sometimes tell ('I fell downstairs') are believed, even when there are signs of strangulation, burns and bruises in various stages of healing (Romito, 2000). Nobody asks anything of other women with less obvious signs but chronic problems, often to do with mental health, or who are admitted repeatedly for unexplained reasons; and yet, when they are asked and people are prepared to listen to them, the relieved women recount the violence suffered (Romito et al, 2004b). Other women, who recount what has happened to them and ask for help, are faced with embarrassment, incredulity or attitudes putting the blame on them by health workers (Frenken and Van Stolk, 1990). The greater the blindness of the workers, the more they feel confirmed in it. They do not look, they do not ask, they do not listen, they do not reason, so they may continue to consider violence a rare phenomenon. In the mid-1990s Lucia Gonzo interviewed a sample of health workers in Bologna. Almost half the first-aid doctors maintained that they had never had professional contact with victims of abuse, whereas the *Casa delle Donne* (Women's Centre) in Bologna had received 1,246 new cases during those years (from 1992 to 1995) and the majority of these women had gone through first aid, often more than once (Creazzo, 2000, 2003; Gonzo, 2000). Women pay a very high price for this ignorance in terms of suffering and bad health, but above all their problems cannot be confronted and cured if the cause remains ignored (Krug et al, 2002; Koss et al, 2003). Research carried out in France shows that suffering physical violence, almost always by their partner, increases the risk of women committing suicide in the following 12 months by 19 times; suffering sexual violence increases the risk of suicide by 26 times (Jaspard et al, 2003). Research conducted in Italy reveals that suffering physical, sexual or 'only' psychological abuse by their partner at any age increases the risk of depression by six times (Romito et al, 2005). And yet the connection between violence and mental health is ignored by many psychiatrists, who attribute acute and chronic suffering by the woman to other causes according to their theoretical approach: unconscious conflicts, a badly resolved Oedipus complex, hormones or simply being a woman and therefore unstable or hysterical by definition. In the index of an Italian manual on psychiatry[20] there are no entries for 'maltreatment', 'abuse', 'rape', 'incest' or 'violence'. On the other hand, there is an entry for 'mother' with two subcategories: overprotective and schizophrenogenic, and an entry for 'menopause' with the empty nest syndrome.

Since the 1970s some research carried out in the US has shown that, when first-aid patients are asked if they have suffered violence, a third (excluding victims of car accidents) reveal that they have been victims of it (McLeer and Anwar, 1989). In spite of this, even today violence is rarely confronted by the staff of these services. In Kansas City all recent cases of women killed by their partners or ex-partners have been investigated: in half of the cases the victim had made repeated visits to first aid with injuries and after-effects of rape or suicide attempts. Although the clinical files referred to domestic violence, nobody intervened until the women had been killed (Wadman and Muelleman, 1999).

In short, there is now extensive documentation, published in medical journals, showing how frequent physical, sexual and psychological violence against women is; it proves the connections between suffering violence and various health problems; it describes how a sizeable proportion of patients in first-aid, drug addiction and psychiatric departments have suffered serious and often repeated violence; it emphasises how the majority of patients, whether victims or not, agree to be asked systematically if they have suffered violence (Resnick et al, 1997). And yet, even the latest reviews of the literature relating to the US, where work on the subject has been impressive, conclude that male violence against women remains invisible in health services and only rarely do women receive the necessary care and attention (Koss et al, 2003).

A less explicit form of denying violence lies in the methods society uses to deny inequality between the sexes. Deborah Rhode (1997) identifies three principal methods: denying inequality, denying injustice and denying responsibility. Denying inequality involves: selective perception, allowing part of the problem to be ignored and only isolated incidents to be seen, where there is a strategy; and self-deception for self-protection: if we cannot avoid inequality, we avoid recognising it. Denying injustice comes into play when it becomes impossible not to see inequality, but it is interpreted as difference and not injustice. Here naturalistic tactics come into operation, according to which the inequality in pay between men and women and exclusion of women from positions of power are attributed to presumed biological differences in the skills and motivation of the two sexes. In short, in cases where it becomes really difficult to ignore inequality and injustice, the tactic of denying responsibility comes into operation: there is no collective responsibility, these are individual problems, requiring individual and not social solutions. Rhode shows how these mechanisms worked in a famous case of sexual harassment, involving the jurist Anita Hill as plaintiff and the judge Clarence Thomas as defendant, in the US some years ago. Analysing the reactions of commentators and the media, Rhode highlighted various ways of denying: denying that there is a serious problem of sexual harassment; that women are harmed by it; that men are responsible for harassment and therefore attributing responsibility to the victims; and that legal sanctions represent an answer to the problem. There may also be no limit or reasonableness to denial. Rhode (1997) reports numerous cases where federal judges have denied the validity of accusations of sexual harassment made by women suffering very serious abuse in the workplace: one woman was forced to witness the masturbation of her colleagues; another was regularly called 'whore, cunt, pussy, tits and fat ass'; another still was handcuffed to a lavatory and her colleagues pushed her head under water (Rhode, 1997; Faludi, 1991).

Denial may also be more insidious. It is only recently that I realised, and only because somebody drew my attention to it, the true nature of an ornament – a sculpture about 30 centimetres high – in the house of some relatives. It is a naked woman being carried off by force by a wild man, the prelude to rape, perhaps a copy of the *Rape of the Sabine women* by Giovanni da Bologna. The sculpture is in the place of honour in the entrance. It is difficult not to see it, so that it seems difficult for the energetic, old woman who carefully dusts it not to see what she is dusting. And yet, how aware is she of it? And how aware are art enthusiasts and visitors to museums of the content and significance of what they are looking at and appreciating? What does it take to call rape 'rape'?

The painting by Rubens, *The rape of the daughters of Leucippus* by the twins Castor and Pollux, depicts precisely rape. In the Sala delle Aquile in the Palazzo del Tè in Mantua three pieces of stuccowork represent the abduction of non-consenting women for sexual purposes, which is precisely the premise of rape: Jupiter taking Europa by force, Neptune raping Amione and Pluto carrying off Proserpina (Carroll, 1989). To these examples may be added artistic representations of the myth of Daphne, the nymph who asked to be changed into laurel to escape from Apollo. Clearly she prefers to die rather than be raped. And yet Kerény (1994, pp 121-2) describes the myth of Daphne in this way: 'The first love of Apollo it was said was for Daphne.... Not only Apollo was in love with Daphne....'. Love, in love?[21] In fact, Apollo and Daphne are depicted as two young people in love in the painting by Pollaiolo: the god tenderly embraces the maiden, who is already starting to change into a tree. In the same way in *The rape of the daughters of Leucippus* mentioned above:

> Rubens' depiction of the abduction is marked by some striking ambiguities: an equivocation between violence and solicitude in the demeanour of the brothers, and an equivocation between resistance and gratification in the response of the sisters. The spirited ebullience and sensual appeal of the group work to override our darker reflections about the coercive nature of the abduction.... The effect is to suggest to the viewer the violence and pleasurability of rape at the same time. (Carroll, 1989, p 3)

The question is: for whom does rape represent pleasure and for whom does it represent violence instead? Observing the facts, we would say that for the rapist it represents pleasure, for the victim it represents violence: women and children may die of rape and even those who do not die of it remain marked by it. And yet it is the view of the rapist that predominates in society: it was not really rape, she liked it after all, she was looking for it, she enjoyed it in the end. And it is this that makes the pornographic content exciting and enjoyable at the same time without embarrassment, therefore psychologically and socially acceptable (Russell, 1993). It is a view close to that shared by many psychoanalysts. According to Helene Deutsch (1945), 'female sexuality may blossom only thanks to an act of rape', a position also maintained by Françoise Dolto, as we have seen.[22]

### 4.3.1 Denying sexual abuse against children and incest

> It is very tempting to take the side of the perpetrator. All the perpetrator asks is that the bystander do nothing. He thus appeals to the universal desire to see, hear, and speak no evil. The victim, on the contrary, asks the bystander to share the burden of pain. The victim demands action, engagement, and remembering. ...
>
> In order to escape accountability for his crimes, the perpetrator does everything in his power to promote forgetting. Secrecy and silence are the perpetrator's first line of defense. If secrecy fails, the perpetrator attacks the credibility of his victim. If he cannot silence her absolutely, he tries to make sure that no one listens. To this end, he marshals an impressive array of arguments, from the most blatant denial to the most sophisticated and elegant rationalization. After every atrocity one can expect to hear the same predictable apologies: it never happened; the victim lies; the victim exaggerates; the victim brought it upon herself; and in any case it is time to forget the past and move on. The more powerful the perpetrator, the greater is his prerogative to name and define reality, and the more completely his arguments prevail.
>
> The perpetrator's arguments prove irresistible when the bystander faces them in isolation. Without a supportive social environment, the bystander usually succumbs to the temptation to look the other way. (Herman, 1992, pp 7-8)

Various forms of denial are intertwined when denying sexual violence against girls and boys. We have adopted current terminology in the title, partly to simplify and partly to cause reflection. Still, this terminology is problematic. In fact, the expression child sexual abuse is questionable, because talking of 'abuse' implies that use is acceptable instead and because the term 'child' is generic: in fact, the victims of sexual violence are girls in particular in a proportion estimated at 3 to 1 (Bolen et al, 2000). Even the term 'incest' (from the Latin *incestus, a, um*, which means unchaste or impure) is inappropriate. Its first meaning is legal: 'crime committed by whoever has sexual relations with a descendant or ascendant or relative in a direct line or a brother or sister in a way that becomes a public scandal', according to the Italian dictionary (Zingarelli, 2004). In short, the term 'incest' does not imply domination or coercion or violence, but rather social unacceptability: completely consensual sexual relations between mother-in-law or father-in-law and daughter-in-law or son-in-law are incestuous, for example.

As Valentina Pisanty (1998) says on the subject of denying the extermination of the Jews in the Nazi camps, the temptation to deny the existence of a phenomenon is in proportion to the extent of the phenomenon itself. Sexual violence against girls and boys is so wicked and destructive and at the same time so widespread and pervasive that historically mechanisms for denial have had to be increased, developed and refined to maintain the status quo.

## Recent history of sexual violence against boys and girls

The social visibility of sexual violence against boys and girls has been compared to a karst river, which in its course sometimes appears turbulent and violent and then disappears completely from view. Thus abuse becomes visible at certain times in history, attracts the attention of the public and professionals and then disappears again. Here we summarise only the most recent history, where the key event was recognition and subsequent retraction by Freud. In fact, a historical perspective is valuable, because it widens our outlook, giving more reasons for concern.

In the 18th and 19th century European legal statistics suggest that sexual abuse against children was socially visible for a certain period. In London in the second half of the 19th century a quarter of executions for rape involved cases where the victims were less than 18 years old. In the same period in France, Tardieu, a professor of medicine, had shown that, out of almost 12,000 men accused of rape or attempted rape in a decade, more than 9,000 had raped children.[23] This type of violence also often occurred in middle-class families: the perpetrators were fathers or older brothers. Unfortunately his work was ignored: until mid–1970 standard psychoanalytical-type texts on child psychiatry maintained that incest did not concern more than one case in a million (Olafson et al, 1993).[24] On the other hand, besides the medical tradition connected to Tardieu that recognised the frequency of violence against children, there was another that denied it in the most direct way: by saying that children are lying. According to another French doctor of the time, Brouardel, between 60% and 80% of reports of sexual abuse were false, caused by the hysteria of the child or the mother, 'genital hallucinations' or the licentiousness of the children, who were pretending to be victims. A case by way of an example is that of a girl, Camille, who accused her father, defined as an 'homme fort honorable', of incest. But the doctor said that 'the enormity of the accusations destroys their plausibility' (Masson, 1984). Since Camille persisted in accusing her father and revealed other abuse by relatives, in the end she was shut away in a psychiatric hospital.[25]

Freud, who had spent some years in Paris working with Charcot, was acquainted with this work and familiar with both tendencies. On returning to Vienna, based on his clinical work, he drew up an innovative theory of psychological suffering, which he published in three essays in 1896. According to this model, early sexual abuse was the basis for various pathologies such as hysteria, obsession, paranoia and other 'functional psychosis'. He was convinced he had made an important discovery and described it in his writings as a 'solution to an age-old problem: a source of the Nile'. He expected strong reactions from his colleagues, but perhaps he was not at all prepared for the icy reception of his speech on *The aetiology of hysteria* in April 1896 at the Society for Psychiatry and Neurology of Vienna. In a letter to a friend he wrote that his lecture had met with a freezing reception and as a result the word was going round to desert him: he was finding himself in a vacuum (Masson, 1984). Freud was quite explicit in the lecture and essay: although he also mentioned the term seduction, he spoke above all of rape, abuse, attack, aggression and traumatism. In no part of the text is there the slightest reference to the theory that this violence was only imagined and not really experienced. He also went into anatomical details, explaining that the physical immaturity of the child rarely allowed complete vaginal or anal penetration, for example. Although he had discovered that the majority of abusers were fathers, Freud deliberately hid this fact, talking more generically of 'uncles' or even of nurses, governesses and mothers.[26] In spite of this camouflage, it was still a head-on attack against the middle-class family: since the patients belonged to the upper middle class, there was not even the scapegoat of attributing violence and incest to the lower classes.

Some years later Freud publicly retracted this theory without any trace of scientific reasons that could have induced him to change his mind in any one of his writings, public or private.[27] Analysing the unedited letters and manuscripts of Freud almost a century later, Jeffrey Masson (1984) formulated the theory that the professional isolation, to which his colleagues had banished him, and perhaps the fear of discovering that his own father had attempted abusive behaviour had convinced him to retract. The new theory of hysteria was much more acceptable: trauma no longer consisted of real sexual abuse by an adult, but the projection of the same masturbation fantasies of girls and boys. The Oedipus complex, according to which every child wishes to have a sexual relationship with the parent of the opposite sex, the exact opposite of the original theory on the aetiology of hysteria, became the unshakeable foundation of psychoanalysis. In the course of his career from then on Freud would always talk of 'fantasies', declaring that accounts of sexual violence suffered by patients are false or imagined. The denial by Freud was total and final.[28] To complete the matter, it is recalled that Jeffrey Masson was dismissed from his post as director of the Freud Archives and brutally ostracised by his ex-colleagues and a good part of the American press for revealing and discussing all the behind-the-scenes action to the retraction. It was not the authenticity of the proof they objected to, but the fact that he had revealed its existence.

In short, it is probable that Freud retracted through cowardice, to defend his privileges and protect the hope of a brilliant future. His action has weighed heavily and still does so in the denial of incest and betrayal of children who are its victims, offering those working in the field powerful interpretative categories, which in turn are in keeping with the immediate reaction of anyone facing an unbearable, unspeakable fact: it cannot be true, therefore it is not true. Without making light of the personal responsibility of Freud, still Judith Herman (1992) recalls that, even if he had been more courageous, his discovery would have been difficult to accept in the absence of a social and political context that could support it and support the victims. This context did not exist in Vienna and was quickly disappearing even in France.

Analysing the documents of child protection agencies in Boston, Linda Gordon (1988) arrived at the same conclusions on the connection between individual behaviour and social context. In the period between 1880 and 1910 incest was visible and abusers were often reported and convicted. Even though it was certainly not a golden age for the victims, who often ended up in the care of other families or institutions, incest was not denied and its meaning was not distorted. According to Gordon, this was possible for two reasons: on the one hand, the presence of a feminist movement, which was highly critical of the patriarchal family model and capable of influencing the work of social services with a reforming approach; on the other hand, the fact that social workers of the time saw incest as 'a vice of the poor', particularly immigrant Catholics. It was this sense of distance and superiority that allowed them to recognise what they would have denied instead in other contexts.

Still, after 1910 a different interpretative model prevailed due to the influence of Freudian ideas and the weakening of the feminist movement. What became visible to the eyes of the social services was no longer incest, but the problem of 'sexual delinquents', girls who lived on the street, sometimes even becoming prostitutes only for a bit of food. Yesterday, like today, the majority of these adolescents had run away from home to escape from physical and sexual violence; although it was contained in the clinical records, the information remained in the background, obviously considered of secondary importance (Rush, 1980). Between 1910 and 1960 the figure of the child or adolescent victim of abuse was reconstructed as provocative, lascivious and corrupt and at the same time attention was moved from incestuous fathers and stepfathers to 'dirty old men', a popular version of current paedophiles. Moving attention from abuse within the family home to what happened outside on the street allowed not only fathers to be left in the background, but also the finger to be pointed at mothers. What had been defined before as 'incest' or 'carnal abuse' was reconceptualised as 'moral neglect', a maternal crime by definition. Until the beginning of the century the approach of the services had been moralist and reforming: male behaviour such as drinking, squandering wages, beating wives and children, was considered reprehensible and attempts were made to change it. After this the approach became more psychological; for incest in particular, when it could not be maintained that the child was lying, an interpretation gained ground that attributed responsibility for paternal behaviour to the mother – frigid, castrating and so on. Linda Gordon (1988) concludes that psychologising is a method that prevails at times in history, when hopes of social change are frustrated, and represents a great sign of social powerlessness.

Another lens through which to view the period bridging the two centuries is professionalising. During these years psychiatrists, psychologists and sexologists tried to become established as professions and gain ground from the authority of groups and institutions presented as reactionary: healers, monks and nuns and feminists (Ehrenreich and

English, 1979). In the US the view of moralists and feminists, according to whom abusers were men taking advantage of their privileges, was opposed by the psychological interpretation, which saw them as radically different from normal men and therefore the responsibility of specialists. At the same time this discourse was useful in justifying the existence of new professions and silencing the feminists with their tiresome analysis relating to the female question, family and sexuality. We should not forget that in many countries in those years the women's movement was strong and combative with a utopian ambition and many men felt their privileges under threat. Another way of devaluing feminist demands and keeping women quiet on the question of incest, among other things, was to accuse them of being moralists wanting to desexualise society, man-hating, frigid or lesbians (Showalter, 1985).

The development of sexology and the discourse on 'sexual modernism' contributed to the social reformulation of sexual abuse to a great extent (Jeffreys, 1990). At the beginning of the 20th century there were frequently eroticised images of girls and boys in art exhibitions. An idea of the child as a precociously sexual being gained ground and the negative effects of sexual repression were emphasised, another legacy of Freudian thought. Karl Abraham, a disciple of Freud, insinuated that perhaps sex between adults and children was harmless, sometimes sought by children themselves. Two authoritative American psychoanalysts, Bender and Blau, wrote in 1937:'We often thought that perhaps the child was not an innocent, who had been seduced, but the real seducer' (Olafson et al, 1993, p 14). Albert Kinsey discovered in the 1950s that more than a quarter of the thousands of women interviewed had been sexually abused when they were small. Although the great majority of them, 80%, declared the experience had profoundly disturbed them, Kinsey judged these reactions to be exaggerated and remained convinced that there was no reason for a child

> to be disturbed by the fact that someone had touched its genitals or be disturbed by seeing the genitals of other people or be disturbed by even more specific sexual contact ... the emotional reactions of parents, policemen or other adults discovering that the child has had this contact may disturb the child much more than the sexual contact itself. (Olafson et al, 1993, p 15)

Kinsey showed concern for the fate of the men who, according to him, ran the risk of being unjustly accused by girls or 'old maids', rather than for the little victims. However, while the results by Kinsey on pre-marital and extra-marital relationships caused a sensation and are still quoted, the information on sexual abuse against girls and boys was almost completely ignored.

### The contemporary epoch and the false memory syndrome

The contemporary epoch is characterised by the recurrence of issues that have already been mentioned and by some peculiarities. Public concern and interest in sexual abuse against children perhaps do not have historical precedents for the intensity, duration and involvement of various people in society. It is to the women's movement, particularly the feminist practices of self-knowledge and self-help, that we owe the rediscovery of incest, a rediscovery that is accompanied by a radical criticism of the experts, particularly psychiatrists and psychoanalysts, and their knowledge (Rush, 1980; Chesler et al, 1995). This force succeeded partly in joining up with the desire for action by many professionals, who still consider that sexual abuse against children is frequent, has serious consequences and represents an unacceptable crime, although they do not identify themselves with feminism in any way. The contemporary feminist movement is strong, widespread and for the first time really international; this has also made and still makes a certain influence possible on social institutions, governments and international organisations. The United Nations Office, the World Health Organization, Unicef and Amnesty International have recognised repeatedly that violence against women and children is an endemic phenomenon, infringes human rights and hinders development. Even though 'male violence' is talked of only rarely, references to sexual abuse and maltreatment are explicit. In a report by Unicef (2003) it is recognised that between 40% and 70% of violent husbands are also violent to their children and that, in spite of mothers spending much more time with their offspring than fathers, the latter are the perpetrators of physical abuse against the children, particularly serious abuse, in at least half the cases. These declarations go against the flow of prevailing opinion, according to which there is no contradiction between being a violent husband and a good father and according to which mothers are abusive more often than fathers.

Even though they are not systematic, these convergences between feminist practices and analysis and initiatives and analysis by enlightened professionals, officials and administrators perhaps represent something new historically and certainly an objective threat to safeguarding patriarchal rights, one of which, perhaps the fundamental one, is to have control over the children. It is therefore not surprising that in the

1980s a formidable counterattack emerged in the courts, health and social services and media, some elements of which have already been discussed in the previous sections (Faludi, 1991; Armstrong, 1996).

The so-called 'false memory syndrome' is typical of the counterattack. It is presented as a 'psychiatric pathology', consisting of believing you have suffered sexual abuse in childhood, when instead this did not happen. In the same way as in false accusations during separation and the parental alienation syndrome, in the false memory syndrome the fact of reporting abuse becomes a sign of pathology.

The syndrome appeared in the 1990s in the US when cases started to occur of women who during therapy recalled abuse that was suffered in childhood but then forgotten or repressed for a long time. They then reported the abuser, often the father. In 1992 the False Memory Syndrome Foundation (FMSF) sprang up, a private association funded by parents accused of incest by their adult daughters, the scientific committee of which includes various experts, psychologists and psychiatrists. The British False Memory Society with similar characteristics sprang up in England during these same years. According to the FMSF there is an epidemic of cases, where false memories of abuse have been 'implanted' by dishonest or unscrupulous therapists; all 'recovered memories' – that is all memories of child abuse, which are repressed and then rediscovered by adults, are false; it is also very easy to induce small children to believe that they have suffered abuse, which instead never happened. The Foundation welcomes upper-middle-class families in particular, who have a lot of money to refute accusations of incest, and has found disturbing allies in the world of paedophilia and child pornography, including the psychologist R. Underwager, who is a founder member of its scientific committee.

Still, the evidence gathered by the Foundation in support of the epidemic of false memories is inconsistent; in some heavily publicised cases false memories were then revealed to be real, that is verified, memories of abuse; and scientific research shows how the greater risk is of forgetting traumatic events that actually happened rather than inducing false memories.[29] As an example, Linda Meyer Williams (1994) interviewed a sample of young women who had suffered serious and proven sexual abuse (confession by the abuser, medical reports and so on) when they were small. At the time of the interview 38% of the women did not remember the abuse. Of those who remembered it, 16% declared that they had forgotten it for long periods of their life. The polemic on 'recovered memories' also wrongly includes cases of people who have suffered sexual abuse as children and have reported it only many years later, without ever having forgotten it. A lot of abuse committed by priests or other authoritative figures falls into this category, for example.[30]

It is possible that in the North American context, characterised by ravenous lawyers, enormous claims for compensation and the increase in offers of therapy, there are cases where a patient has been induced by the therapist to attribute a current state of suffering to child sexual abuse that did not happen (Russell, 1999). Still, it is enough to recall the statistics on sexual violence against children to realise that this is not the main problem: although the risk of false reports exists, it is infinitely smaller than the risk, even the certainty, that very many cases have happened and have never been reported (see Box 5 in the Appendix).

It is regrettable to note how mental health professionals are often in the first line in strategies for discrediting sexually abused children and those supporting them: the child is lying, inventing, has not understood properly, is histrionic or hysterical; even if it is true, it is the fault of the mother, who is frigid, rejecting, hostile or malicious; however, there is no need to make a drama out of it and above all there is no need to talk of punishing or reporting the perpetrator of the abuse. It is the model used by Giaretto in the US, which involves a systemic approach where everyone – father, daughter, mother, other brothers and sisters – goes into therapy with the declared aim of 'keeping the family together'; the abusive father is not prosecuted criminally, everyone recognises his faults and forgiveness is encouraged. The treatment is called the Giaretto Model of Parents United (Armstrong, 2000). Parents united? The father who has sexually abused the child and the mother who has tried in vain to protect her? United against what? Against 'incest', an act without material existence that no longer has perpetrators or people responsible. In the US the great majority of workers in child protection services adhere to this model (Kelley, 1990; Deblinger et al, 1994). We may observe a similar tendency in Italy. For the psychiatrist Montecchi (1994), when there is intrafamilial sexual abuse against children, working practice is to assess whether the family can be treated and therefore to propose family therapy. For Tortolani (1998, p 233), 'if the therapeutic contract is accepted, no report is made'. Apart from not reporting the abuser to the legal authorities, as required by the obligations of the law, on the other hand, no measures are taken to protect the child, as 'the fact of accepting to be cured is a guarantee of safety for the child' (Tortolani, 1998, p 277).

The strategy of discrediting is widely practised: discrediting abused children and protective mothers, but also discrediting witnesses and professionals – health and social workers or magistrates – who try to protect them. In the US Gardner describes a large proportion of judges as opportunist and incompetent, sometimes motivated by 'repressed paedophile impulses' (Myers, 1994). In Italy Gulotta (1997, p 155) insinuates that the judges in 'some areas of Italy, such as Lombardy and Piedmont' fabricate abusers of children.

Although professionals usually use relatively cautious and socially acceptable formulations, these obstacles do not limit the message of various separated fathers' associations, of which there are now many in all industrialised countries (see Box 1 in the Appendix).[31] It is possible that some of their members are men of good faith, who have been unjustly deprived of the right to continue to see their children; still, we know that these groups are often led by violent fathers and ex-husbands, some of whom have already been convicted. Separated fathers' associations have Internet sites giving useful information for refuting accusations of incest and getting round the law more generally and seem to have considerable financial means and important contacts, particularly among politicians and in the media world (Graycar, 1989; Dufresne, 1998).

In Italy the Separated Fathers' Movement publishes the bulletin *New Fatherhood*, which talks of the 'myth of the abused child' and the 'usual lie of fathers who are violent and mothers who are victims'; in reality the real victims are fathers, whereas 'women are like the Vietnamese. You can bomb them as much as you like. When you have finished, they come out from underground and win the war'.[32] In a document drawn up by another, very visible group, Gesef (parents separated from children), it is maintained, obviously without any proof, that 'more than 90% of reports of sexual abuse against children are unfounded'. On the site of another association, Growing Together, we find the grotesque syndrome of the 'malicious mother in divorce cases' drawn up.[33] On all these sites the words of Gardner and his inventions, such as the parental alienation syndrome, are taken as gospel and repeated ad nauseam.

The sites of separated fathers' associations (sometimes presented rather as 'parents') also overflow with attacks and insults against services, organisations and workers dealing with violence against children, who are accused of destroying the life of innocent men, wasting public money and so on. In spite of the misogyny, vulgar tone and scientific inconsistency of their arguments, which sometimes touch on the grotesque, these associations are succeeding in applying pressure at a political level. In many industrialised countries it is separated fathers' associations that have sponsored the use of family mediation in so-called difficult separations and have applied pressure to impose joint custody (Babu et al, 1997; Peled, 1997; Rhoades, 2002). This is also happening in Italy, as we will see later. 'Fathers' rights' have become an important social question, with reference to which the violence these men have committed and continue to commit against their wives and children is completely denied once again. We recall that violent fathers are the ones most likely to fight to have custody of the children and the ones most likely to obtain it; when a judge has to choose between the safety of an abused woman and the right of a violent man to see his children, it is usually the latter who has priority. This means putting at risk the safety and sometimes even the life of women and children and in all cases compelling them to a living hell for years.[34]

An analysis of the media makes it possible to grasp the progress of the counterattack. In the US Beckett (1996) identified three principal tendencies relating to child sexual abuse in the press: articles in support of paedophilia, the problem of 'social denial of abuse' (which includes the secondary matters of denial, male prerogatives and evidence of the survivors) and finally the subject of false accusations (which includes errors by workers and false memories). In the period under consideration, from 1980 to 1994, articles in favour of paedophilia, which were always in a minority, decreased from 7% to 0%, whereas the proportion of articles dedicated to the other two categories was inverted. The space dedicated to the problem of social denial was halved, decreasing from 85% of articles in the 1980–84 period to 41% in the following years, whereas that dedicated to the subject of false accusations increased, rising from 7% to 59%. Among the reasons that may encourage such choices by the media, Beckett quotes the need for something new and for dramatising events, as well as direct and indirect pressure and campaigns by groups such as the FMSF and Victims of Child Abuse Laws. To this picture must also be added the fact that the press is once again a male preserve. At the end of the 1990s in the US 90% of newspaper editors and 90% of television directors were men; in Italy 83% of publishing house directors, 96% of daily newspaper directors and 63% of weekly newspaper directors (a good share of which was represented by women's weeklies) were men (Rhode, 1997; Ingrao and Scoppa, 2001). Perhaps it is not surprising that many of these men in a position of power are more in tune with the claims of violent husbands or fathers accused of incest than with the claims of the victims; on the other hand, the former have greater means of persuasion or pressure than the latter, whether financial, political, social or even constituting actual threats (Kitzinger, 1998).

Concluding their article, Olafson et al (1993) ask whether the current reaction will succeed in suppressing awareness of sexual abuse once again. And they add:

If this occurs, it will not happen because child sexual abuse is peripheral to major social interests, but because it is so central that as a society we choose to reject our knowledge of it rather than make the changes in our thinking, in our institutions and our daily lives that sustained awareness of child sexual victimisation demands. (Olafson et al, 1993, p 19)

### Denying incest in practice

In a book that is probably autobiographical the French writer, Christiane Rochefort, makes an incestuous father talk to his adolescent daughter, who is resisting him and trying to escape, like this:

'And who will believe you? Nobody believes children', as he told her then and this has not changed: always on the job, the guard dogs continue to bark at children caught in the paternal trap. 'They all consent!' And this is what kills, the coup de grâce in fact. (Rochefort, 1988, p 163)

A real example of what Rochefort evoked is represented by an Italian case described by the lawyer Tina Lagostena Bassi (1991). For years in a village a man had beaten up members of his family, raped his daughters and killed the child of one of them, a 13 year old he had made pregnant, as soon as it was born. From the trial it emerged that, in spite of the terror, beating and humiliation, one of the girls had found the courage to run away from home; still, she had been caught again and the chief police officer had warned her not to try it again or she would be sent to a reformatory.

Awareness of incest has probably become greater from the 1980s to date, for example the training of health and social services to recognise it, deal with it and to protect the victim. Various patterns of incest are therefore starting to become visible in society with much younger and often male victims and protective mothers and services divided in their behaviour in response. Many cases of reports of paternal abuse during the separation of the parents fall into this category, some examples of which we have given relating to the US (see Box 3 in the Appendix). In France, some of these cases have been documented in research by the Collectif Féministe Contre le Viol (CFCV, 1999), carried out in cooperation with the Délégation Régionale aux Droits des Femmes d'Île de France, this last an organisation of government origin. In two and a half years (from 1996 to 1998) the service got to know of

67 cases of 'incestuous sexual abuse in a context of separation of the parents' with a total of 94 children involved. Seventy-eight per cent of the victims were girls and 22% were boys; 88% were less than seven years old, 22% less than three years old. In 77% of cases the children described the abuse explicitly and named the abuser. Fifty-one reports had been made at the time the research report was drawn up in 1999. In more than half the cases these reports were filed without any preliminary investigation; in 22% of cases the mother did not know what was happening, because she could not obtain information; 9% of cases concluded without giving rise to legal proceedings; one abuser was convicted; in other cases the enquiry or proceedings were still in progress. In 20% of cases the mothers, the protective parent, were reported in turn for not handing over the child to the father and a third of them were convicted (see Box 6 in the Appendix).

Still, some of these cases attracted the attention of the Human Rights Commission of the United Nations, which sent Juan Miguel Petit to France as 'special rapporteur'. In his report (Petit, 2004) he recognises the legitimacy of the concerns expressed by feminist associations and emphasises that in France anyone suspecting or reporting abuse against children, particularly if they are the mothers, encounters enormous difficulties and runs the risk of being accused of lying or manipulating the children in turn and he quotes the situation of divorced mothers forced to run away and leave the country rather than hand over the children to their husbands, who are suspected of being abusers. Regarding the fact that accusations of paternal sexual abuse are less credible when made in the context of divorce proceedings, he declared instead that:

> a detailed examination of some of the reasons why the parents were getting divorced revealed a pattern of domestic violence in the family, including domestic violence committed against the mother. As a result the question of sexual abuse against a child should be seen more accurately as one of the reasons, if not the principal reason, for the divorce. (Petit, 2004, p 14)

Petit received an appeal signed by 157 doctors and paediatricians, who said that they were subject to disciplinary sanctions by their Association when they reported suspected sexual abuse against children to the authorities and, in fact, were put in a position where it was impossible to help these children. On conclusion of his investigation the 'special rapporteur' has the impression that many individuals in a position of responsibility as regards the protection of children's rights, particularly in the magistrature, still deny the existence and scale of this phenomenon to a large extent, unable to accept that many of the accusations of sexual abuse may be true and accusing those making them of having political aims. (Petit, 2004, p 20)

He concludes by asserting the need to carry out 'complete and impartial' investigations of those suspected of sexual abuse against children and recommends 'that an independent body carries out an urgent investigation into the lack of justice for children who are the victims of sexual abuse and those who try to protect them' (Petit, 2004, p 21).

The cases described in the French research represent tragic examples of the denial of incest by society and the more resolute it is in its ferocity, the more children talk and mothers support them, in fact, the more the victims rebel and seek and find help. Still, these cases are also instructive for another reason: some of the workers involved have refused to collude with violent fathers. These choices are not easy or taken for granted. American research shows that 40% of professionals interviewed admit failing to make at least one child sexual abuse report, knowing full well it was their legal duty to do so (Limber, 1995). These failures are due to various reasons: lack of knowledge, uncertainty of what to do, sharing social prejudice regarding the victims of abuse or patriarchal values and fear of retaliation by the abusers. There may be a whole series of retaliations: transfers, dismissals, threats and physical abuse (Campbell, 1988; Bacon and Richardson, 2000; Nelson, 2000). To these reasons must be added the fact that child protection services are understaffed and overworked in various countries. The turnover of workers is high: this proves how hard work is in the front line, but also means that people leave more or less when they have become qualified (Myers, 1994; Malacrea and Lorenzini, 2002). In the US the results of the National Incidence Study show that in 1993 only 44% of child sexual abuse cases reported 'in which harm occurred' were investigated, whereas this was 75% in 1986 (Bolen et al, 2000). A similar tendency has been observed in Stockholm, in Sweden (Nordborg, 2005).

Workers, professionals and magistrates dealing with incestuous sexual abuse are under fire today. Social workers, psychologists and educationalists in particular sometimes find themselves sharing the fate of the mothers: given enormous responsibility but deprived of means and often authority, easy to blackmail and criticise, and criticised if they act and if they do not act, often discredited and demonised by the media, still they manage to stand up to the abusers and their guard dogs, a heroic achievement, although sometimes terribly fragile.

## The paedophile discourse

The concept of paedophilia is problematic. It reassures because it introduces a separation between normal men and others, who are 'perverts' or monsters, but it reassures wrongly, since there is continuity between the normal and the 'perverts' as well as between the various categories of abuse and abusers instead (Kelly et al, 2000).

In this section we will deal with those who define themselves as paedophiles, claiming the right to have sexual relations with children, and more precisely claiming the right for children to have sexual relations with adult men, presenting themselves as an oppressed sexual minority (Jeffreys, 1990).

Interest in studying the claims of paedophiles is twofold: on the one hand, it is instructive to analyse the methods that paedophiles use to misrepresent their behaviour, allowing them to deny the violence committed; on the other hand, it is crucial to highlight the more or less hidden convergence between the paedophile discourse and other social discourses that are much more presentable in relation to abuse against children.

Various authors also interpret the many associations in defence of the rights of paedophiles springing up in Europe and the US in the 1980s as a reaction to the massive feminist awareness campaigns on the subject of sexual violence and the possibility of introducing legislative changes, such as raising the age of consent (de Young, 1988; Jeffreys, 1990). The Paedophile Information Exchange (PIE) and North American Man/Boy Love Association (NAMBLA), for example, have carried out lobbying and cultural activities to publicise the idea that sex between adults and children is a positive act that corresponds to the moral and sexual liberation of children and it is therefore necessary to lower or abolish completely the age of consent, that is the age when a child can decide freely to have sex with an adult. According to the slogan of another association, founded in the US by René Guyon, jurist and Freudian psychoanalyst: 'Sex by year eight or else it's too late'; according to the Gay Activists Alliance, the age of consent should be lowered to six years old and according to the PIE, to four years old (de Young, 1988; Jeffreys, 1990). Lowering the age of consent means decriminalising all abusive behaviour not involving physical violence, in which the adult may compel or entice a child with all the means that age, authority, experience, social and financial means, in short power, place at his disposal. In France Michel Foucault ardently supported decriminalising 'soft paedophilia'. In his book *The desire to know* he describes sympathetically the case of a peasant in the 19th century who was caught molesting a girl ('I only got a caress', probably a euphemism for saying he had himself masturbated), and regrets what followed: report and legal action (Schinaia, 2001, p 44). Two Italian authors, Roccia and Foti (1994) rightly point out how Foucault, who is normally careful of the 'microphysics of power', instead completely ignores the conflict and abuse of power between adults and children that occurs in paedophilia.[35]

When it is explicit and direct, the discourse of paedophiles is intolerable to the majority of people, as well as being illegal. For this reason paedophile organisations have drawn up 'neutralising techniques', rhetorical tools enabling them to reformulate their requests and behaviour, presenting them as innocent or even beneficial. Mary de Young (1988) has identified the following techniques: denying harm, denying the victim, condemning the condemners and appealing to higher purposes.

Denying harm consists of recognising that a certain act has been committed, but without the child being harmed by it. In fact the bulletins of NAMBLA are full of evidence, which cannot be verified, that children and adolescents maintain that they want and value sex with adult men, a position supported by psychoanalysts such as Abraham since the 1920s, as we have seen. Today the theory that paedophilia is beneficial for children, as it works for evolutionist purposes, has been expressed by Gardner (1993, p 115), the inventor of the parental alienation syndrome:

> The child, who is attracted into sexual encounters early, is very likely to become intensely sexualised and go in search of sexual experience in the prepubertal period. A child 'charged' in this way will most probably become sexually active after puberty and therefore will be more likely to pass on his genes to his children at an early age.

Another variation consists of not denying harm, but reattributing responsibility for it: it is not sex with an adult man that traumatises the child, but the reaction of society to it, a theory already expressed by the sexologist Kinsey and the psychoanalyst Gardner, as we have seen. Thus a NAMBLA bulletin maintains: 'the trauma that the police so quickly point out as connected to such relationships [man/boy] are not caused by the relationship, but by what the police themselves subject the boy to' (quoted in de Young, 1988, p 585). This position is supported in Italy today by some separated fathers' associations. In a Gesef document, for example, it says that 'no "expert" called in to carry out expert reports ever thinks it appropriate to check whether the abuse does not consist of the report of abuse itself and the intervention methods the "system" uses to check that it exists. However, someone has also started to report through media channels how the real and more serious abuse is perpetrated instead by the very SYSTEM in charge of child protection'.[36]

The second technique of neutralising is denying the victim as such. Children are 'sexy from birth' and may be conscious partners in a sexual relationship with an adult or even seducers from the most tender age. In the documents of paedophile associations the discussion of the ability of the child to give informed consent is mixed up with details on the possibility of an adult penis penetrating the anus or vagina of a small boy or girl. Although these anatomical references are unbearable to most, much more acceptable instead are references to boys and girls as being seductive: on the other hand, it is this that the psychoanalyst Dolto declared in France[37] and some judges confirm in trials even today (Rhode, 1997).

Condemning the condemners and discrediting them represents another technique frequently used in the writings of paedophile associations. In a paedophile publication from the 1980s we read that 'the "protectors" of children are the real perverts, the real abusers, the real molesters' (de Young, 1988, p 588), a position shared by Gardner in the 1990s. According to a NAMBLA bulletin in 1983, those who deal with child sexual abuse and oppose 'man/boy love' are:

> Police departments suffering from a bad public image due to internal corruption ... District Attorneys needing a dramatic case for the voters to remember and psychiatrists needing public funds to build a private practice. ... Demagogues in state and federal legislation have also found the anti-'boy-love' hysteria tailor-made for raising campaign funds ... (quoted in de Young, 1988, p 588)

It is worth comparing this text to what is maintained in the Gesef document already mentioned, where it is stated that 'the task is aimed only at constructing theories attributing blame and looking for the raw material to feed the welfare machine ... the media business circuit of professional abusologists ... magistrates craving publicity ... activists in the political/administrative bureaucracy'. There is also 'no control over the billions of public funds spent by anti-abuse centres'; in conclusion it asks 'who may ever compensate them (the children involved) and in what way for their childhood and the affection snatched by a scandalous web of financial interests and power'.

Similar concepts are confirmed in the bulletin of the Italian Separated Fathers' Association: 'there are quite specific professionals who make their fortune ... advising mothers to invent episodes of psychological and physical violence. There are "eminent scholars" who have invented "financial violence" and are all on the payroll of great powers that can be identified'.[38]

As de Young (1988) recalls, if those who condemn abuse are reconceptualised as being even more abusive than paedophiles are accused of being, then their accusations are at best irrelevant, at worst hypocritical and conceal personal interests in some way. Thus social condemnation of those abusing children is neutralised.

The last of these tactics is appealing to higher purposes. Paedophile associations claim high aims in their writings: the liberation not only of children, but also gays and lesbians and women in general from a sexophobic and repressive society. In fact, these associations have sought alliances with the women's movement and with left-wing libertarian movements, not finding a great hearing by the first, but sometimes a certain solidarity and ideological convergence with the second (Jeffreys, 1990; Leidholdt and Raymond, 1990).

As far as the documents of separated fathers' associations are concerned, nobody defends abuse as such or sex between children and adults. What emerges more generally is the defence of the patriarchal family from meddling by the state in the form of social services and professionals such as doctors, psychologists and magistrates. Still, the existence of intrafamilial sexual abuse is systematically denied. The arguments contained in the writings examined, which have been amplified by the Internet, contribute to creating the confusion that has already been reported by Louise Armstrong (1996, 2000), where children, who are the victims of sexual violence and particularly the victims of incest, may be reduced to silence once again, while the abusers go unpunished.

### Methods and misdeeds: how the perpetrators of violence disappear from research

This section would not be complete without mentioning the specific role of research. The majority of contemporary work in the medical or psychological field does not deny in any way the frequency of sexual abuse against children and its devastating consequences in the medium and long term. There is more ambiguity about who is responsible for the violence instead: thus generally when the father commits incest, it talks of the incestuous family or mother; when the father is physically violent, it talks of abusive families or parents (Romito et al, 2001). These are euphemisms that often find support in a simplified version of the Bowlby theory of attachment, according to which any event in the life of the child may be attributed to problems of attachment to the mother and then, with further leaps of logic, to her unconscious motives and feelings. For example, in the 1960s the paediatricians Henry and Ruth Kempe used the theory of bonding, still drawing inspiration from the theory of attachment,[39] as the basis for proposing a list of 'early risk factors' in abuse. This list includes the fact that the woman is concerned about the increase in weight during pregnancy, her passive or hostile behaviour towards the child in the labour room and the fact that she considers the child too demanding at feeding time (Breines and Gordon, 1983). Along the same lines in Italy the psychiatrist Montecchi writes in a section in his book entitled 'Where the abusive parent and abused child come from':

> In its nascent state abuse can be seen as a disturbance to the empathy in the first relationship between mother and child, which is understood as a disturbance to the parental function that is lacking. The histories of abused children have shown that the problem does not arise at the time the abuse is revealed, but has ancient origins that can be taken back to the first phases of development and sometimes it is possible to identify the conditions for possible future abuse even in pregnancy. (Montecchi, 1994, p 31)

These authors do not explain what the relationships are between the discomfort expressed by a mother when she is pregnant or giving birth and the fact that her child is abused by the father, uncle or teacher and, indeed, it would be difficult to do so. Perhaps because it is difficult to show these connections, the theories of attachment or bonding are rarely mentioned explicitly in research, even when they obviously form the reference context. As a result these articles appear vaguely surreal, when they are read critically. An example is made of two studies of the risk factors in abuse, which were published in the most prestigious journal in this field (Brown et al, 1998; Kotch et al, 1999). The samples used are enormous and the design of the research is sophisticated. Still, only the mothers are interviewed and above all the perpetrators of the abuse are not identified. The authors choose to consider the risk factors connected with the mother in particular, such as her young age, lack of education and lack of self-esteem, depression, separation from her own mother and infrequent attendance at religious services. Given these methodological choices, which are never discussed, it is not surprising that the results show an association between some maternal characteristics and abuse against the child. In short, even if the abuser is the father or another male figure, it is the mother who ends up in the limelight, a tendency also found in the work of social services (Humphreys, 1999). The reluctance to name the person responsible for the abuse is still more obvious in another study of the risk factors in sexual abuse where, apart from interviewing only the mothers, the only indication in the whole article of the fact that the perpetrators of the violence are of the male sex is deduced from the admission that a lot of abuse consists of 'penetration by the penis'. Even in this case it concludes, unsurprisingly, that some maternal characteristics are responsible for sexual abuse against children; the fathers are not even mentioned, even though it can be deduced by some turns of phrase that some of them are the perpetrators of the violence (Stern, 1995).

The research mentioned represents only examples of a more general tendency. In an analysis of the specialist literature on abuse against children Haskett et al (1996) show that adult men only rarely appear in this research, although they are the principal abusers (Unicef, 2003). Belsky (1993) recognises that, although fathers are the abusive parent more often than mothers, an amazing fact considering the little time men spend with their children, almost all the research concentrates instead on maternal abuse. The authors of a Canadian report (Clément et al, 2000) also arrive at the same conclusion.

Among the sins of researchers, those of omission must then be added to the tendency to obscure paternal responsibility for abuse. Malacrea and Lorenzini (2002) rightly point out how many more resources have been invested to study the risk of 'false positives' in child sexual abuse reports, whereas the real problem, which has still not been studied much, is represented by 'false negatives': all those cases, which are the majority, where there has been abuse, but the child cannot express it, does not talk about it or talks about it and then, blackmailed and frightened, retracts.

Naturally, with such prejudices there is bad research. It is paradoxical that instead it is research showing the frequency of male violence that is criticised as being partial. This research is usually very rigorous, because the researchers also know they must face severe criticism, although often more of a 'political' than a scientific nature (Schwartz, 1997; Romito, 2003).

### 4.3.2 Legislation on joint custody: the final act

> Violence towards women comes from a desire to overpower
> ... that is the figure of the pater familias, the house is mine,
> the animals are mine, the woman is mine and the children
> are mine so I possess them ... in certain cases the man said:
> 'Yes, but what's here is mine. It's all mine here ... I'll do
> what I want with it'.[40]

In a society with a patriarchal tradition women and children belong to the father. In this context the sexual use of children has been, and continues to be, a male prerogative and is obviously a central prerogative, in view of the doggedness with which many deny it and compel the victims to silence. This model of society and these rights have been put up for discussion by the women's movement with ups and downs but with a certain continuity in the last two centuries; there have been substantial changes as a result, against which patriarchal society has put up strong resistance. Only if we keep this context in mind, and the scale of what is at stake, can we understand what is happening today.

Let us consider, for example, the legislative changes that have occurred in various countries relating to domestic violence, the separation of husband and wife and the custody of the children, which have already been partly discussed in previous sections. These changes do not always directly concern the subject of sexual abuse against children. Still, they have their place in this section, as they create the conditions in which abuse, particularly intrafamilial abuse, may continue to be practised or may be prevented or hindered instead.

In Italy the law on taking the abuser away from the family home, which was wanted very much by women who are active in the field of domestic violence, has been formulated so as to make it difficult to apply in practice. A legal gem consists of the fact that the judge may also decide to send the couple to a family mediation centre. In short, a woman asks for her violent husband to be taken away as a matter of urgency, because he has a knife between her shoulder blades, metaphorically or literally, and the judge sends her to undergo mediation together with the man she hoped desperately would be taken away!

In Spain the law on taking the violent husband away has been approved by a right-wing government under pressure from the protests and wave of emotion following dramatic cases of women killed by their husbands; still, today separated fathers' associations are applying pressure for judges to recognise the right of grandparents to see their grandchildren by law, an indirect method to allow violent fathers free access to their children.[41]

In England substantial progress in favour of battered women and their children, such as priority in obtaining social housing after running away from their violent husbands (Morley, 2000), goes hand in hand with the recognition of greater and greater rights by fathers, even if they are violent, after separation. The New Labour government of Tony Blair put concern for the 'social exclusion' of these men at the centre of many measures, thus accepting the point of view of separated fathers' associations that they are victims (Eriksson and Hester, 2001). It also drew up new coercive measures to oblige mothers to guarantee the relationship between father and child, considering the presence of the father to be 'vital', even if he is abusive or manifestly incapable of looking after the children. Even today mothers who refuse to hand over the children to their fathers run the risk of imprisonment, but this measure has had no deterrent effect: mothers prefer to go to prison rather than give custody of their children to a violent man (Radford and Hester, 2006). Also under pressure from powerful associations, such as Families Need Fathers,[42] in 2002 the Children Act Sub-Committee proposed that these mothers, who are described as implacably hostile, egotistical and manipulative according to the theory of the parental alienation syndrome, must follow courses in parenting and undergo psychiatric treatment. If they do not submit to injunctions by the court, they will be accused and sentenced to the same kind of penalties as those applied to men who perpetrate domestic violence or sexual abuse. If they still do not submit, they will be given a prison sentence and custody of the children will be given to their fathers; but the mothers will have to contribute to their maintenance (Harne, 2002).[43]

In France the government of the socialist Jospin approved a law in 2001 that imposed alternate custody (*garde alternée*) between the parents after divorce, irrespective of the reasons for the divorce itself – physical or sexual violence by the man against his wife and children, for example – and the real involvement of the father in the care of the children when they were living together. Alternate residence, which was banned in France until now as it was considered against the interest of the child, may now be requested even by one parent without the consent of the other and imposed by the judge (Delphy, 2002). French law also seems to presume that, if the child divides its time between one home and the other, the payment of an allowance is no longer necessary; in other countries this vagueness in the law has led to the mother taking on maintenance of the child alone. Under pressure from the divorced fathers' lobby the new law also allows the order of the judge in charge of family matters to be replaced by simple confirmation of amicable agreements between parents; to 'facilitate the consensual exercise of parental authority', it also promotes family mediation, which may be imposed by the judge even against the wish of the parents and when there is violence that has been verified. Refusing to hand over the child to the other parent, even if the decision is motivated by a high risk of violence, becomes subject to serious penalties: up to three years in prison and a fine of 45,000 Euros (Dufresne and Palma, 2002) (see also Box 6 in the Appendix).

As in other countries, in Italy Bills on joint custody have also been drawn up by all the political parties, including those on the Left, and have been heavily sponsored by separated fathers' associations. The Bills presented in the course of the 14th legislature include one (No. 1558) based on ideas from the association Growing Together and another (No. 453) on ideas from Gesef. In the majority of these Bills, domestic violence and sexual abuse against children are completely ignored or denied and the idea is accepted that male violence after separation, ending in murder, is the result of suffering and frustration by fathers deprived of their children and not an extreme act of possession by men who, after years of violence, cannot bear to lose control. It is also taken for granted that following separation there is 'a very high percentage of maladjusted children, who need psychotherapeutic treatment in less serious cases, because they have developed a condition of dependency on the mother and rejection of the father' (Bill No. 643). In short, an epidemic: children with parental alienation syndrome and mothers with malicious mother syndrome. And these are only the less serious cases! Of course, things are not like that: children suffer and are disturbed, even seriously, not so much and not only by the separation as such but by disputes between the parents, and even more so by being involved in violence, which is almost always violence by the father against the mother, before, during or after separation (Graham–Bermann and Edleson, 2001; Kitzmann et al, 2003; Walker et al, 2004).

Control over wives and children is too central a prerogative in patriarchy to be given up without resistance. It is therefore difficult to anticipate the outcome of the battle being waged today. On one side this battle sees many women drawn up who are victims of violence and feminist activists, some workers and professionals who consider male violence to be an unacceptable crime inside and outside the family, irrespective of their gender and whether or not they agree with feminist analysis; on the other side there are the abusers, their allies and fellow travellers and their guard dogs. In the middle there is the majority of people, who are little and ill-informed and through laziness and fear of getting involved refuse to see a horrible reality, deny male violence and in the end find it easier to maintain the status quo, which means the patriarchal model, than oppose it. Between 5% and 10% of girls suffer incestuous sexual abuse, without considering other types of violence and without considering little boys: this means that in every group – class, scout association, music school or group of children playing in a yard – at least one or two children are subject to incest. This means that every teacher, sports instructor, educationalist, doctor, psychologist and social worker has an abused child in their class or among their clients. Some of this abuse will reach the police and the courts; some will be dealt with by the media. How to find ways of informing these people, making them more aware and convincing them to embark on a course that may turn out to be difficult and risky for some? How to prevent them from being fearful and cowardly, how to give them courage? The outcome of the confrontation in progress depends on their awareness and support and therefore our ability to persuade them to be on the side of the victim and not the torturer.

### 4.3.3 The victims denying violence

> Taking that step would have helped them. If only they had been able to slip on the tragic hood of the victim, even temporarily. Then they would have been able to face the thing openly and kindle rage at what had happened inside them. Or seek compensation. And perhaps in the end exorcise the memories that persecuted them. But rage was not within their reach.... (Roy, 2001, p 205 of the Italian translation)

The perpetrator of a crime, his accomplices and indifferent witnesses all have good reasons to deny the violence or distort its meaning. But what are the motives of the victims instead? Denying or distorting the meaning of what has happened precludes the possibility of them escaping from the situation and protecting themselves; it makes it impossible to identify the person who is to blame and prevent him from doing more harm; it frustrates any attempt to prevent future crimes. And yet, it is not unusual for victims to minimise or deny the violence suffered. Let us consider research carried out in the US where university students were interviewed on their experience of sexual violence. Of those who had suffered vaginal, anal or oral penetration against their will, that is an act legally qualified as rape, at least half gave a negative reply to a more general question with reference to suffering sexual violence (Koss, 1985; Cortina et al, 1998). The same tendency was found among workers who, although they had experienced various behaviour that could be defined as 'sexual harassment', replied in the negative to a question on suffering harassment in the workplace (Ducret, 1993). This is a striking contradiction that quantitative methods for collecting information, such as the questionnaire, cannot explain. Research with a qualitative type of approach, which was also carried out on university students in the US, provides hints on understanding instead. Out of 30 girls interviewed by Phillips (2000), 27 had suffered at least one experience corresponding to the legal definitions of rape, harassment or abuse; and yet, although they were able to describe the shock, humiliation and fear experienced, only two used these terms to describe what had happened. The others preferred formulations of the type 'things went wrong' and often attributed some of the responsibility to themselves: 'I shouldn't have gone out with him', 'I should have expected it' and so on.

Recognising yourself as the subject of violence may be painful and humiliating and it is not surprising that many people shy away from this awareness. Still, this was not the only issue that emerged from the interviews with the young women in the research mentioned above. What also emerged was a great feeling of uncertainty and confusion. How can I call it rape, if he was my boyfriend, if I agreed to kiss him? And how can I call it violence if I still went out with him, in spite of what happened? The further away what happened was from the social stereotype of rape – an unknown assailant at night in an isolated place – the more difficult it was for the girls to recognise it as such (Kahn et al, 2003).

Now to keep the victim, the dominated person, in a state of confusion represents a winning strategy for the torturer, the dominating person. This is what happens to children sexually abused by an adult. The child experiences confusion about what is happening: it does not have the means to understand or the words to explain; confusion because of the reactions of its body; confusion because of the physical pain and fear caused by acts it must keep secret, often carried out by an adult they loved and trusted and who said he loved them (Déttore and Fuligni, 1999). This confusion induces uncertainty about what really happened and its meaning, as well as feelings of joint responsibility and shame. The victim is paralysed and may continue to suffer violence, sometimes without saying anything or expressing her/himself in such a confused way as to be unintelligible (Bacon and Richardson, 2000).

This state of confusion is increased in the child due to its objective biological immaturity and social subordination. Although they are adults, women and girls who are subject to abuse and violence often share these feelings of confusion, which are made worse by the paradoxical demands connected with the female sexual role of being at the same time sexy and respectable, good company but not of easy virtue, active, determined, perhaps even a little feminist, but always feminine. The girl who has caught the eye of the head of department or the student who is courted by the professor or sexually attacked by her fellow student does not know if the man desires her or despises her, because it is also difficult to accept what is sometimes the reality: being desired and despised both together and being chosen precisely because you can be despised.

For Simone de Beauvoir (quoted in Bartky, 1990, p 14) also, the psychology of women in the patriarchy consists of 'an inner uncertainty and confusion' due to the fact that they are trying to live under the aegis of 'a double ontological shock: first, the realisation that what is really happening is very different from what appears to be happening, and second, the frequent inability to tell what is really happening at all'. Confused, hurt, demoralised, full of shame and repressed anger, according to the concise and bitter definition by the philosopher Susan Bartky (1990, p 14), women are 'eager to please, worried about their weight'. Kathleen Cairns (1997, p 98) talks of the 'fragmented self' of women. She recalls that a woman:

> has been taught to apologize, to distrust and deny her own experiences, thoughts and feelings and put men's needs ahead of her own. Often she either does not know, or cannot say, what she wants, because for a woman to have serious personal wants is selfish, and to announce them is often dangerous. Her not knowing is, of course, then attributed to her natural deficiency and inadequacy, her femininity. It is proof that she needs to be told what she 'really' needs and wants by a male partner and male experts.

Nicole-Claude Mathieu (1991) has shown how women tend to feel blame and apologise for what has happened to them and excuse the perpetrator of the abuse. Many girls who have suffered sexual violence and many wives who suffer abuse from their partners do this: 'if I had not provoked him', 'if I had been a good wife', 'if I had been able to understand him', 'he was too excited', 'he'd been drinking', 'he's tired', 'he's stressed', 'he's not well'. Women who are faced with the unequal division of domestic work also do this: 'it's my fault', 'I'm too demanding', 'I didn't encourage him', 'he's tired, he needs to relax, he's no patience with the child, he doesn't see the dirt'. Paradoxically, the young women interviewed in research into post-natal depression used the term 'poor thing' repeatedly to refer to their partners in a context where there was no division of domestic work: 'poor thing, he would, if he could'; 'poor thing, he tries, but he doesn't know'. In the ideal model of the 'modern' couple care of the children and domestic duties are divided in an equitable way. But women are expected to construct this model in a harmonious way, because obtaining equality is their responsibility, not obtaining it is their failure. As a result many waste considerable energy cognitively restructuring reality in order to minimise and then deny inequality, overvaluing the small contribution by their partners and undervaluing their work, for example (Romito, 1990; Romito and Cresson, 1994).

Many workers seem to put similar strategies into operation in order not to see the various forms of sexual harassment by colleagues or superiors. In the case of traditionally male occupations, they want to feel part of the group and it becomes a point of honour to be 'one of the boys' (Conley, 1998). In the case of traditionally female occupations, it may be a source of pride to put into practice with grace the qualities expected of women: facing a thousand difficulties with a smile on your face, absorbing the stress of others, making men look good (Cline and Spender, 1988). These demands conflict not so much with admitting the existence of comments on your physical appearance and private life, persistent suggestions and unwelcome physical contact, but with recognising it as 'sexual harassment', acts of hostility and contempt towards you (Fitzgerald, 1993). Better then to consider it as 'jokes' as far as possible. Given this premise, it is not surprising that the most frequent reactions of women to harassment are usually focused internally. The victim denies, minimises and pretends nothing serious has happened; she bears up and stands firm, trying to ignore the harassment; she tries to distance herself from the situation psychologically; she blames herself for the behaviour of the abuser. Of the responses focused externally, the most frequent consist of avoiding situations where she runs the risk of being harassed and trying to keep on friendly terms with the abuser. According to various studies, workers who are victims of harassment and take action against it, such as turning to a superior, do not exceed 5%–10% (Fitzgerald, 1993; Thomas and Kitzinger, 1997).

However, we should bear in mind that power relationships are real, they do not exist only in people's heads: when women do not stay in their place, they are often punished. When harassed workers react, about two thirds suffer retaliation: promotion denied, transfer and dismissal. Of those who take their case to court, more than half lose it. Many leave work through fear, anger or frustration (Fitzgerald et al, 1995). Christine Delphy (Delphy and Leonard, 1984, p 121) recalls that 'it is precisely the real power of the oppressor ... which makes him unattackable, or at least not attackable without enormous risks'. Denying violence, the obstinate insistence on defining objectively offensive and aggressive behaviour as 'jokes', is perhaps less paradoxical and more rational than it may seem at first sight.

Denying oppression and violence suffered is behaviour that is typical of victims and people who are dominated, and not limited to women. In a study of a group of 'difficult' boys, about a third recounted a story that did not correspond to what was in their file at the time of the interview (Delle Femine et al, 1990). In the majority of cases the discrepancies consisted of omissions of violence suffered in the family or in reformulations of it in terms of disciplinary measures, for example. Even in this case, the mechanisms for denying made reference to elements of an individual and social type. The boys used the strategy of 'interpretative control', through which, if it is not possible to control reality, an attempt is made at least to control its meaning. They tried to forget the violence in order to protect the image of the abusive parent and the illusion of being loved. For their self-esteem it was also necessary to maintain a virile, macho front, which is incompatible with recognising the violence and suffering endured. The evidence of adults, men and women, who have been abused since childhood by their father, is often touching: we witness the desperate attempt to make sense of what has happened in order to allow the figure of the abusive parent to be reconstructed as positive, at least in certain aspects: rare good times are made the most of, the violence is partly justified ('it was the alcohol', 'it was to teach me a lesson', 'it was good in the end'). There is the need to be reconciled with the torturer, even though he has not recognised the harm he has done and has not asked for forgiveness.[44]

Many homosexual boys also deny the violence suffered. Sometimes a deep and tragic masochism emerges from the evidence of those who have become prostitutes, for example when they maintain that they experienced pleasure when they were subject to group rape (Jeffreys, 1990). In this case there is also a web of factors of a social and individual nature. On the one hand, denying or even laying claim to the humiliation and violence suffered may be necessary in order not to give way and to protect self-esteem and sense of self. On the other hand, in gay culture there is traditionally no space to name abuses of power and the violence and suffering this involves (Trexler, 1995). It is only recently, thanks to the women's movement and its capacity to break through the secrecy surrounding incest and rape, that boys and men may also talk about sexual violence suffered. For Jeffreys (1990, p 205), 'masochism could emerge from the necessity of gay men to reconcile themselves to their oppression, a survival ethic, and from a pulverised sense of self, resulting from growing up gay in a homophobic society'.

Still, the question of whether denying abuse suffered represents an advantage for the victims on an individual and psychological level remains controversial. Some experimental studies show that denying strategies tend to have a negative effect on mental health, a tendency also confirmed by work on the consequences of violence and its moderating factors.[45] One study shows that suffering rape is associated with negative psychological consequences – whether or not the victim labels the experience as 'rape' (Schwartz, 1997). According to another study, among women who had been objectively abused during childhood, those who recognised that they had been abused were more subjectively depressed. It has to be said that this group had suffered more serious abuse (Carlin et al, 1994).

In short, denying violence seems to show few or contradictory advantages in terms of alleviating suffering on an individual level. On a social level, attempts to deal with the situation psychologically in order to make it more bearable inevitably end up instead obscuring the reality of domination and making change more difficult.

At this time there is a bitter debate in progress on the concept of the 'victim', a concept that now seems to annoy many people. On the one hand, the supporters of the 'counterattack', including writers such as Camille Paglia and Katie Roiphe in the US and philosophers such as Elisabeth Badinter in France, attack what they define as 'victimist feminism', which encourages taking pleasure in the role of victim, and accuses women of shouting 'rape' in order not to assume responsibility for unsatisfactory sexual encounters, or inappropriately calling abuse or violence what are only normal everyday interactions between men and women (Faludi, 1991; Thomas and Kitzinger, 1997). I wish to emphasise that all the proof discussed in this book leads in the opposite direction to these accusations. On the other hand, even many feminists seem uncomfortable with the term victim with its indication of passive suffering and in fact have replaced it with that of survivor, which takes better account of the activity, resistance and courage of those who have suffered violence. It is a discussion that leaves me perplexed: if you are subject to an objectively superior power, in fact, you may continue to suffer violence, even if you resist in all ways. This is what the stories of girls who have been victims of incest show, for example (Russell, 1997, 1999). What is more, the cognitive strategies of denying violence put into operation by the victims, which are analysed in this section, suggest that active behaviour may be used for denying and therefore maintaining the status quo. In fact, the incessant intellectual work of the victims, their waste of emotional and cognitive energy do not serve automatically to free them from violence.

### Silence by women about male violence

> Not knowing has a function for both the dominating and the dominated, which is to maintain the order of things.... It is precisely among the oppressed that denial of oppression is strongest. (Mathieu, 1991, pp 10, 218)

Women may also be responsible for abuse and violence. Although the myth of the 'battered husband' is confirmed as a myth, in fact (Kurz, 1997), there is violence in a considerable percentage of lesbian couples (Renzetti, 1997). Mothers may abuse children with moral and physical abuse; as far as sexual abuse against children is concerned, a minority is committed by women (see the subsection 'Violence against children' in Chapter One on p 15). These statements do not detract in any way from the fact that violence against women and children is mostly the work of men. Given the frequency of the various forms of violence, no woman is safe from it; each one has also been witness to abuse and violence against other women: relatives, friends, colleagues, pupils, patients. And yet, in spite of this shared experience, there is no unanimity among women on the meaning of this experience or solidarity on the subject, indeed, there are many who deny male violence emphatically, stubbornly, sometimes almost blindly. The teachers who do not see the suffering of boys and girls or refuse to report it are women above all, just as the social workers and psychologists who, faced with an abusive father and a protective mother, even an imperfect one, believe the first and are on his side, are women above all. Some of the police officers, lawyers and magistrates who approve these decisions are women.

I often find myself speaking about violence to an audience of health and social workers, men and women. Rarely do the men attack me; if they take part, they usually do so cautiously. On many of these occasions

I am attacked, often viscerally, by some women instead: 'it's not true that women are discriminated against and that we all suffer major or minor abuse', 'I've never had any problems', 'I'm not like them, they were looking for it, they wanted it and provoked it', 'I'd leave at once, I wouldn't stay for a minute, I'd fight, I'd refuse', 'it's not true that violence against children is male above all ... and what about the mothers then? The incestuous mothers, the violent mothers, the mothers who commit sexual abuse?'; 'it's not right to set men and women against each other, we need solidarity, we're on the same side, it's society that's violent, not men'. There has also been no occasion where I have not spoken about the project of this book without somebody – a woman, since I have spoken about it mostly to women – saying one of two typical phrases or both of them: 'And men, poor things, they suffer violence, too!', or: 'And women, they can be violent (or wicked) as well, in fact they're even more violent (or wicked)!'.

According to Nicole-Claude Mathieu (1991), oppressive relationships lead to an anaesthesia of the conscience that is inherent in the actual, material and intellectual limitations imposed on the oppressed; indeed, the greatest violence consists of limiting the possibility of portraying oppression in its entirety from personal experience. To confirm this analysis, in fact, extensive psychosocial literature shows that women and children considerably underestimate the discrimination to which they are subject (Foster and Dion, 2003). Steve Biko maintained that the most powerful weapon in the hands of the oppressor was the minds of the oppressed.[46]

Recognising discrimination and violence requires emotional reaction and concrete action. Still 'no-one grows angry with a person on whom there is no prospect of taking vengeance and we feel comparatively little anger or none at all with those who are much our superiors in power'. So said Aristotle, quoted by Susan Brison (1998, p 20), a philosopher who, after suffering dreadful rape, asked herself why she could not feel hate or anger towards the man who had made mincemeat of her. Her theory is that the terror the man continued to inspire in her, even months afterwards, in spite of the fact he was in prison, was such as to preclude her having an appropriate reaction. Her analysis is valuable for understanding another paradoxical phenomenon, that is the fact that girls who are victims of paternal rape often feel more resentment towards their mother than their father. In fact, the mother has not only disappointed expectations of protection, but often is not strong enough or cruel enough to strike real fear, a fear that the father, who is more powerful and able to enforce his will, often continues to inspire (Romito et al, 2001). On the other hand, some mothers, who through fear or dependence on the man are incapable of attributing responsibility for the incest clearly to him, accuse the children of being seductresses; maternal anger is thus directed towards the daughter and not the partner. It is well to remember that alienating mothers from daughters, separating them and dividing them, represents one aspect making up the strategy of incestuous fathers (Herman, 1981; Hooper, 1992; Candib, 1999). As Ann Oakley (2002, p 75) recalls, in a patriarchal society maternity is a 'colonised territory': in this context women may become the worst enemies of other women.

It may be objected that not all women who are victims or witnesses of male violence feel terror towards the abusers. Many seem rather immersed in that anaesthesia of the conscience Mathieu talks about; others prefer simply to be on the side of the strongest; others still want to keep the coherence of a life spent in the emotional and material service of men at all costs.

What do women get in exchange for this loyalty, this silence? At best the crumbs of power, received more as a favour from those dominating them than as rights they have earned. Crumbs they are so afraid of losing that they prefer to deny the evidence and practice that lack of knowledge of themselves and the world that allows the dominating and the dominated to keep the order of things intact. The silence of many women about male violence, a silence that becomes complicity with the torturers, in fact, is tragic. Still, we are wrong if we consider it behaviour typical of women, when instead it is behaviour typical of the dominated. Denied and dominated for a good part of history, even though not without resistance, acts of courage and periods of respite, it is not surprising that many women deny the violence of the oppressors. It is therefore unjust, even though it is easy, to ask why they do not join forces with other victims, just as it is unjust, even though it is easy, to be horrified at the inability of some mothers to protect their children from paternal sexual abuse, when the health and social services or the police or the legal system do not wish to do so.

What is surprising instead is that, in spite of everything, so many women, even though not the majority, throughout the world have been able to analyse subordination, oppose it and construct solidarity, resistance, political action and utopia. On the scientific and political level a burning question is understanding how this could happen, through what social and individual routes, and above all what to do so as not to turn back.

## Notes

[1] Ranke-Heinemann, 1988; Virgilio, 1997; Boneschi, 1998; Kirkwood and Cecil, 2001.

[2] See Bellamy, 2000; Awwad, 2001; Sev'er and Yurdakul, 2001; Amnesty International, 2004.

[3] Baker et al, 1999; Shalhoub-Kevorkian, 1999, 1999b; Awwad, 2001; Seager, 2003.

[4] Ernè, C. (1999), 'Shock sentence for killer of ex-fiancée', *Il Piccolo*, 16 June.

[5] Wilstein, S. (2002), 'O.J.'s history conveniently overlooked by admirers', *Hamilton Spectator*, Ontario, 31 December.

[6] Van Derbeken, J. (2003), 'Slain boy's mom had sought help', *San Francisco Chronicle*, 1 July.

[7] There is a lot of research on this subject. See Smart and Sevenhuijsen, 1989; Eriksson and Hester, 2001; Graycar and Morgan, 2002; Rhoades, 2002; Radford and Hester, 2006.

[8] Smart and Sevenhuijsen, 1989; Rhode, 1997; Dufresne, 1998.

[9] Corneau belongs to an, alas, age-old tradition of philosophers, thinkers and writers, for whom women have no capacity for abstraction and are incapable of objectivity. See Le Doeuff (1998).

[10] For example, I have heard the idea repeated in legal circles that a boy growing up with his mother alone runs the risk of becoming gay. Some judges, those who grant violent fathers the right to visit, must think it is better to run the risk of being killed than becoming gay (of course it is absolutely untrue that growing up without a father increases the likelihood of being gay). For examples in Finland, see Keskinen, 2005.

[11] See research by Boyd, 1989; Brophy, 1989; Graycar, 1989; Moloney, 2001; Graycar and Morgan, 2002.

[12] Saposnek, 1998; Mahoney, 1991; Williams et al, 2001; Rhoades, 2002.

[13] Hoigrad and Finstad, 1992; Monzini, 2002; Nixon et al, 2002; and from Italian daily newspapers on the 5th and 12th of August 1998.

[14] See research by Morgan, 1984, 1992; Sturdevant and Stoltzfus, 1992; Enloe, 1993; Jeffreys, 1997; Monzini, 2002.

[15] See accounts by Nordstrom, 1998; Grandits et al, 1999; Hughes et al, 1999; Amnesty International, 2004.

[16] It is pointed out that traditionally the Catholic Church has shared this image of male desire or 'concupiscence', which is understood as an instinct that is difficult to control, and has proposed marriage as a remedy or lesser evil (Ranke-Heinemann, 1988). According to this logic, marriage and prostitution are neighbours as both meet the need to contain the sexual needs of men.

[17] See the work of Mary Jane Sherfey (in Morgan, 1970), for example.

[18] 'John' is the perjorative term English-speaking prostitutes use to denote their clients.

[19] Sexology arose in this context, taking the sex of prostitution as a model and in fact suggesting to women techniques typical of prostitution to satisfy their partners (Szasz, 1980; Jeffreys, 1997).

[20] This is the *Manual of psychiatry* by F. Gilberti and R. Rossi, published in 1996 (IVth edition) by an influential publishing house, Piccin in Padua.

[21] This version probably draws inspiration from Ovid (*Metamorfosis* I, vv. 452-567), in whose poetic description the aspect of violence ends up by fading into the background.

[22] 'Le plaisir absolu', Interview by C. Rihoit with F. Dolto, *Marie Claire*, April 1984, p 101. In the same interview Dolto maintains that African women who have their clitoris cut out are privileged, because in this way they have direct access to vaginal sexuality without being hampered by the clitoris, which is considered as a vestige of infantile sexuality in the Freudian model.

[23] In France an analysis of court documents relating to the years between 1870 and 1939 supplies numerous details about the victims and perpetrators. Youth, poverty, physical weakness and ignorance in sexual matters made children vulnerable, who were often servants or without protection (illegitimate daughters or orphans). The criminals were mostly friends of the family or relatives. In some rare cases they were 'perverts'; most often they admitted that they abused the children because they were in their hands, they found it difficult to convince an adult woman or, in the case of incestuous fathers, they were certain of their right to use their daughters sexually (Sohn, 1992). This description of the types of abuse against children corresponds to what

Linda Gordon (1988) outlines from analysing the cases of the child protection service in Boston from 1880 to 1960 and it is surprisingly similar to what emerges from more recent research on the subject (Fleming et al, 1997).

[24] There are also no references to one of his studies of a case of physical violence and thus the subject of the 'abused child' seems to appear suddenly on the medical and social scene barely a century later in 1962 with the famous article by the paediatrician Kempe and his colleagues (Masson, 1984).

[25] This is a strategy that is still practised. For the US, see Rush (1980) and Armstrong (1993). For Britain, see the autobiographical account of Rachel Pearce interviewed by Catherine Itzin (2000).

[26] Freud admits replacing the father with the uncle as the perpetrator of abuse in a note to the 1924 edition of his *Studies of hysteria* published in 1895 and also in a letter to a colleague (Rush, 1980; Masson, 1984).

[27] For a detailed analysis of the retraction of the theory of hysteria by Freud, see Rush (1980) and Masson (1984). For a more general criticism of the Freudian model, see Timpanaro (1974); O'Connell Davidson and Layder (1994); and Webster (1995). For a feminist criticism, see Millett (1970).

[28] For example, in 1931 he tried to oppose publication of an essay where Sandor Ferenczi, his ex-pupil, maintained the frequency of incest and its devastating consequences. On the death of Ferenczi in 1933 Ernest Jones, pupil and biographer of Freud, obtained consent to destroy the English translation of the essay from Freud himself. An English translation of the work of Ferenczi was published only in 1949 ('Confusions of tongues between adults and the child: the language of tenderness and the language of passion', *International Journal of Psychoanalysis*, 30: 225-30). Another shadow was thrown over the matter by the fact that Jones was repeatedly accused of sexual abuse against his patients and even against children (Masson, 1984).

[29] I will not go into the details of the scientific controversy about the existence of memories that have been recovered or implanted, as there are excellent reviews of the literature on the subject: see Myers, 1994; Pope and Brown, 1996; Déttore and Fuligni, 1999; Malacrea and Lorenzini, 2002; Brewin, 2003. Another element of ambiguity is introduced by the behaviour of the psychologist and researcher Elizabeth Loftus, who is considered as one of the most authoritative experts supporting the theory of false memories. Loftus agreed to

appear as expert for the defence in the case of Furundzija, the first Croatian militiaman tried by the International Court of the Hague for raping a Muslim woman. The decision by Loftus to give evidence on the FMSF is particularly questionable, since the problem of the woman in question was not that she had forgotten the violence, but rather that she could not forget it (Russell, 1999).

[30] In June 2003 the Supreme Court of the US annulled a measure by the State of California, which since 1994 had extended the time limits within which it was possible to report sexual violence and abuse, a measure that took into account the difficulties many victims of child sexual abuse find when reporting it. Dozens of men already convicted, many of whom had confessed, will be freed. There is a debate between those identifying this decision as an expression of the counterattack and those considering it instead proper rethinking of a measure arising in the context of the so-called hysteria of repressed memories (Finz, S., 2003, 'Repressed memory hysteria prompted molestation ruling', *San Francisco Chronicle*, 29 June). Trying someone for events that happened decades previously is problematic. Still, in some circumstances magistrates and legislators have considered that prosecuting these crimes criminally represents a duty towards the victims and is necessary to keeping a sense of social justice, such as in the case of Nazi criminals and Argentine or Chilean generals, for example.

[31] These associations are often close to chauvinist or masculinist groups that have sprung up overnight throughout the industrialised world to defend 'men's rights', who say they have been oppressed and victimised by women, whom some of them compare to Nazis (hence the English term 'nazifeminist') (Faludi, 1991). In Italy we find Uomini3000, Maschiselvatici, Cruelguys.

[32] *New fatherhood: Information and culture bulletin of the Separated Fathers' Association*, 4(11), May 1999. The bulletin has a page of electoral publicity for the candidate of a political party in the European elections, as confirmation of the connections of these groups and their lobbying capacity.

[33] www.gesef.it/documento.htm; http://associazioni.comune.firenze.it/crescereinsieme/articoli/malice.htm

[34] See McMahon and Pence, 1995; Zorza, 1995; Radford et al, 1997; Williams et al, 2001; Harne, 2002; Radford and Hester, 2006.

[35] Foucault, like all postmodernists, also ignores the power relationships between men and women and therefore male violence against women (Brodribb, 1992).

[36] Gesef – Document presented to the City Council of Rome – Table on paedophilia, 25 September 2001, downloaded from www.gesef. it/documento.htm

[37] 'Le plaisir absolu', Interview by C. Rihoit with F. Dolto, *Marie Claire*, April 1984, p 101.

[38] *New fatherhood: Information and culture bulletin of the Separated Fathers' Association*, 1999, 4(11): 1.

[39] For a criticism of the theory of attachment, see Rutter (1995). For a criticism of the theory of bonding, see Sluckin et al (1983).

[40] This quotation, which is taken from an interview with a police officer from the Flying Squad (Bascelli and Romito, 2000), describes the feelings of many violent men and summarises the essence of patriarchy. It is admirable that this young man was capable of such a clear analysis (from which he dissociated himself completely).

[41] Socolovsky, J., *Spain's domestic violence fatalities rising*, in www. womensenews.org

[42] Other forms of pressure used by this association include besieging the homes of judges involved in custody cases. In Australia, on the other hand, there have been numerous terrorist attacks against the staff of family courts in the last 20 years: a judge and an adviser have been killed. A fathers' rights association, the Men Confraternity, has declared that it feels morally close to these attackers (Graycar, 1989).

[43] Still in Britain, in 1997 the government approved two laws that were important for preventing male violence against women and children: the Protection from Harassment Act and the Sex Offenders Act. Still, in both cases the formulation of the law and the media coverage on the subject emphasised the traditional view of the violent man as a pervert, the 'bogeyman', the stranger who attacks you on the street or persecutes you, ignoring or pretending not to know that the real danger for women and children comes from men they know well: husband, fiancé, ex, father, uncle (Kelly and Humphreys, 2000).

[44] See autobiographical accounts by Guénard, 1999, and Starnone, 2000. It seems to me that these efforts to embellish the figure of the abusive parent are made more frequently in relation to fathers than mothers. The examples quoted concern fathers.

[45] See the work of Pennebaker, 1993, and Pennebaker and Keough, 1999, and the reviews of Scott Heller et al, 1999, and Dufour et al, 2000.

[46] Steve Biko, black South African, born in 1946, anti-apartheid activist, killed by the police in 1977.

# Conclusions

> The challenge ... is to recognise that eradication of violence
> against women is complicated, difficult, and entails tackling
> some of the most deeply-entrenched beliefs in human
> society; that it is a long-term project and will need sustained
> allocation of resources over a long period; that it requires
> commitment and dedication to continue when results seem
> elusive and hard to demonstrate; and that we must keep
> faith with those millions of women who are subjected to
> torture of all kinds just because they were born female.
> (Pickup, 2001, p 306)

Some months ago one of my students came to thank me: he had
discovered during my lectures that rape was a cruel act that may leave
the victim devastated. Until that time, like his friends, he had thought
it was nothing serious, only rather ardent sex, in short. What meaning
should we give to this fact? Must we despair that a man, who was 20
years old in 2004, had never heard it said that rape is violence and
violence is devastating, or be happy because, when he was told, he
thought about it, understood and started changing his way of thinking
and it is hoped also his way of behaving?

The dilemma posed by this episode represents the dilemma to be
faced when we try to assess the results of the struggle to prevent
male violence. Initiatives are flourishing throughout the world, run
by women of extraordinary courage, determination and intelligence.
But these groups always run the risk of giving way, because they are
overloaded with requests for help and limited by lack of resources.
Even when their action is successful, it is a question of repairing the
damage from male violence rather than preventing it. Paradoxically,
there may also be a double meaning to the tragedy of the murders of
wives and companions, which in the last few years have been murders of
ex-wives or companions in particular. Women are no longer accepting
being subject to abuse by their partners and are leaving. Because they
have refused to be subject, in some cases the man kills them. More
systematic attempts at assessment may also arrive at uncertain and
contradictory conclusions: it is possible that in some countries and in
some circumstances some forms of violence are decreasing while in
other countries and in other circumstances other forms of violence
are increasing instead.

If we want to be optimistic, and we need to be in order to continue to act, it must be the optimism of reason and not illusion that guides us. Reason tells us that awareness of women's and children's rights is now global and there is no going back from this awareness, which is the heritage of many women and more than a few men. But the road is long, the fatigue is growing and sometimes faith wavers. At these times we must turn and look at the path we have already travelled and be grateful because, as Christa Wolf suggests (1994, p 165), perhaps 'it has been given to us to enjoy the greatest privilege that exists, bringing a tiny strip of the future into the obscure present'.

# Afterword to the English edition

The first version of this book, in Italian, was published in 2005; the second version, in French, in 2006. The book had a positive reception in both countries and I had the pleasure of presenting it and discussing it publicly on many occasions. Since I have continued to take an interest in male violence against women and children in the meantime, as researcher, teacher and activist, I would like to use the occasion of the English edition to add some points for reflection that have arisen during these years.

The first concerns the use of language to talk about this violence, use that seems to be more and more problematic. Although historically it has been of crucial importance 'to give a name to things' – and therefore invent terms such as 'domestic violence', 'femicide' and 'child sexual abuse' – talking about violence today, even among activists, who share many theoretical and political assumptions, has become difficult. Part of the problem is connected with the internationalisation of the debate: some terms that are preferred in some languages, cultures and countries are not accepted elsewhere. Thus, when the English version was being prepared, I discovered that 'incest' is a term it is preferable to avoid in the UK and the concept of 'domestic abuse' may be preferred to 'domestic violence', because the first also includes psychological violence. On the other hand, in France the term 'abuse' is abhorred, because it is considered euphemistic with reference to the stronger term 'violence' and also because, if we take its Latin etymology literally, 'abuse' refers to excessive use in cases where even 'use' is unacceptable. In Mexico and Central America feminists have changed the English term 'femicide', which was originally coined by Jill Radford and Diane Russell (1992), into 'feminicidio' to oppose the discourse of the State, which puts 'homicide' and 'femicide' on an equal footing (Lagarde, 2005).

On the one hand, these differentiations are a positive sign of the liveliness of the debate on violence against women; on the other hand, they appear as an echo of the more general postmodernist fragmentation of the social world and entail the risk of becoming lost in linguistic nuances and no longer finding common language or strategies.

The linguistic question naturally returns to a conceptual question. The debate on the term 'victim' is exemplary in this sense, but also worrying. As Lorraine Radford and Marianne Hester (2006, p 40) rightly recall, 'the language of victimization has become so invested with these cultural images of individual responsibility and blame that it is very difficult to find alternatives'. This reticence may appear in an extreme way. In a recent article published in a feminist journal the author felt obliged to write a note 18 lines long to justify use of the word 'victim' with reference to women killed by their husbands (Morgan, 2006). On the other hand, in many countries anti-feminists of both sexes have attacked so-called 'victimist feminism', accusing feminists of brainwashing many women, convincing them they have suffered violence, where instead it was a matter of conflict on both sides, passionate courtship or simply unsatisfactory sexual relationships (Romito, 2003). Paradoxically, in short, the term 'victim' is refused by many feminists and anti-feminists today, leaving a gap – which is linguistic, but also political – for defining anyone who, through no fault of their own, suffers injury at the hands of someone or following disasters or calamities (which is the meaning of the term 'victim'). We must ask ourselves why we find it acceptable to talk about victims of accidents at work or an earthquake or terrorist attack and instead are filled with embarrassment if we talk about women who are the victims of male violence. The doubt arises that, in spite of ambiguities and limits, the term 'victim' comes closest to giving a clear indication of the power relationships at work – an abuser, who causes injury; a victim who suffers it – and the term is disturbing for this reason. Carine Mardorossian (2002, p 770) reports the fact that 'the meaning of the term victimization itself has simultaneously changed from an external reality imposed on someone to a psychologized inner state that itself triggers crises'. She therefore proposes reclaiming the term 'victim'. But, of course, if language refers us to concepts, language and concepts refer us to power relationships. As Judith Herman (1992) has shown, it is possible to recognise yourself as victim and claim this status only in a political context that supports and sustains you; otherwise, there is the risk of giving way. I would not like the reluctance to talk about 'victims', which even I am experiencing by now, to be another symptom of the continuing social difficulty of facing up to the question of male violence completely and therefore another hiding tactic in the final analysis.

A subject I have not dealt with in the book is the intersection between patriarchy and other forms of oppression, particularly racism. It is a subject that has been around in North American and English society for some time, which attracted attention more recently in France and even more recently in Italy. The concept of 'intersectionality' shows how various forms of oppression – patriarchy and male violence; racism and discrimination; and class structure and poverty – are all fundamental in modelling the experience of black and minority ethnic women who are victims of violence, and must all be taken into account if we wish to meet their needs appropriately (Crenshaw, 1994). To these systems of domination must be added heterosexism and hatred of lesbians (Lorde, 1984, 2005).

These intersections influence the experience of 'racialised' women suffering violence in many ways: they will have to face up to racism as well as sexism from police officers and health workers; they will have more difficulties and will be more alone in seeking help; and they will suffer greater consequences from this search for help; think only of the risk of being deported from the country in the case of immigrant women without a residence permit or whose permit depends on an abusive husband.

Still, this overlap interests us here particularly because it becomes another way of trivialising and hiding male violence, which, when it is committed by men from 'other' cultures, is considered typical and exclusive to that culture, rather than patriarchy. This interpretation 'naturalises' other cultures, which then become something monolithic from which people cannot distance themselves consciously, almost a 'culture-instinct'. Through this mechanism it is then possible to excuse the behaviour of these violent men, trivialising the violence and abandoning the women who are victims of it to their fate. In various Western countries men belonging to minority groups have received very light sentences for crimes committed against women from their group, as such violence is considered 'normal' in that culture. Thus in the UK an Asian man received a very light (non-custodial) sentence for almost beating his wife to death with the justification that he was an 'immigrant' (Patel, 2000). In Canada three Inuit men were sentenced to seven days in prison for having sex with an underage girl, also an Inuit. The decision of the judge, who was white, was based on the fact that according to his information in the Inuit culture girls mature early and start sexual activity earlier than 'whites' (Razack, 1994), incidentally the same justification – dehumanising the victims – as Western males who practise sex tourism in the Southern countries of the world.[1]

These discourses and these racist and misogynist practices allow violence in other cultures, which is then treated as legitimate, to be trivialised, and at the same time allow it to be hidden in Western culture. In France we have witnessed the proliferation of a public discourse in the last few years, in which violence against women is presented as typical and exclusive to Muslim or 'Islamic' culture. One aspect concerns so-called '*viols par tournants*', gang rape, in which sometimes the victim, a young woman or adolescent, is enticed by a man she knows and to whom she may have formed a sentimental attachment. These rapes have been presented by the press and many French intellectuals as typical of the suburbs of large towns and carried out exclusively by young men of African origin or, as they euphemistically say in France, by 'young people [of undefined gender!] born of emigration'.[2] To this must be added the campaign against the use of the Islamic veil in schools – the veil is never considered as an identity choice by girls facing racism in French society but always, necessarily, as proof of Islamic oppression and violence towards women (Delphy, 2006).[3] Today in France it has become acceptable to say and write that violence against women is a problem of other cultures that has nothing to do with Western culture or white, Western males, a discourse also held recently in Italian newspapers, when in the summer of 2006 there were some rapes committed by immigrant men from Africa or Eastern European countries. The philosopher Elizabeth Badinter, who has also railed against 'victimist feminism' on several occasions, declared that:

> It would not be reasonable to put violence against women in democratic countries and violence in non-democratic, patriarchal States on the same footing. In these last, violence against women is based on philosophical, traditional and religious principles that have nothing to do with ours.... Violence against women in our society instead is absolutely against our principles ... reveals above all a pathology ... that requires medical treatment.[4]

And in the US Leti Volpp (2000) described the different legal and medical treatment of phenomena such as forced marriages or girls marrying adult men according to whether those involved were 'white Americans' or belonged to other cultures.

It is ironic that in this context Islam as a religion is indicated as the origin of violence against women, forgetting the active role of the Christian and particularly the Catholic religion in this violence: from the torture and extermination of thousands of women considered witches during the Holy Inquisition to the epidemic of sexual violence against children committed by priests in Catholic institutions more recently, violence that was sanctioned and hidden by the highest religious authorities,[5] including the New Catechism edited by Cardinal Ratzinger a few months before he became Pope of the Catholic Church, in which adultery, masturbation and rape are put on the same footing as sins against chastity with a chilling confusion between free and conscious sexual and sentimental choices and sexual violence.[6]

Thus, according to the effective expression of Christine Delphy, racism makes a platform for anti-feminist theory, according to which patriarchy has now been overcome and has disappeared. To take up the tools for analysis developed in this book again, racism in this particular formulation perhaps is taking the shape of a new strategy for hiding male violence, involving many of the tactics already analysed: naturalising, dehumanising, psychologising and removing responsibility from the abusers and, of course, separating. It is obvious that taking racism into account is a necessary condition for continuing the fight to prevent male violence against women and children.

## Notes

[1] In Italy in March 2007, nine years after promulgation of the law on sex tourism, there was the first conviction of a man for sexual violence against children committed abroad (*La Repubblica*, 8 March 2007).

[2] The sociologist Laurent Mucchielli (2005) dismantles mystification by the media and shows how gang rape is common even in other contexts and in other historical periods. Unfortunately, even Mucchielli cannot face up to the evidence of male violence. In the concluding section of his book, as a measure to prevent this type of rape, he suggests improving the social and economic conditions of young men of African origin and living conditions in the suburbs in general, without touching on the question of sexism and patriarchal violence in the slightest.

[3] A law has prohibited the display of any obvious religious sign and therefore the veil at school in France since March 2004.

[4] Badinter, E. (2005) 'The truth about marital violence', *l'Express*, 20 June, quoted by Delphy, 2006, p 77.

[5] A letter (*De delictis gravioribus*) written in 2001 by the then Cardinal J.Ratzinger, prefect of the Congregation for the Doctrine of the Faith, became known recently, which obliges priests to maintain 'Pontifical secrecy' strictly regarding all crimes of sexual violence committed by priests against children, subject to the severest sanctions, including excommunication (*La Repubblica*, 11 April 2007). In short, a priest reporting another priest responsible for sexual abuse against children to the social services or the magistrature, as required to do ethically, out of concern for the victims and by Italian law, if the priest in question also holds public office, would incur serious sanctions, including excommunication.

[6] It seems to be a fixed idea in the Catholic hierarchy. Angelo Bagnasco, chair of the Italian Episcopal Conference, declared that recognising the civil rights of heterosexual or homosexual unmarried couples

would also open the way to incest and paedophilia (*La Repubblica*, 31 March 2007).

# Information boxes

## Box 1: 'New fatherhood' movements in the US

Here we give a brief summary (dealt with by Williams et al, 2001) of the recent history of 'new fatherhood' movements in the US, which is useful for providing a context for similar movements that have sprung up in other countries. While these movements grew out of the activities of separated fathers in the 1970s, a milestone came in 1994, the year when Vice President Al Gore maintained in a public speech that the social crisis in the country was caused by estrangement between fathers and children, a consequence of children born outside marriage and of divorce. The fact that 90% of children remain with the mother after divorce and many lose contact with the father became even more visible and problematic. In 1995 President Clinton asked all government agencies to review their programme so as to strengthen the role of the father in families. Three main movements developed during these years:

**Father Involvement Program**: the objective of this programme is to 'bring fathers back home' so that they can provide for the family financially. The existence of domestic violence is recognised, but attributed to the men's feeling of powerlessness (due to unemployment, poverty and so on).

**Responsible Fatherhood Groups**: the objective of these groups is to make men more responsible as husbands and fathers. These groups consider the absence of the biological father to be a disaster and encourage traditional marriage. When they admit the existence of domestic violence, they attribute it to society and the loss of traditional values, as well as immutable male biological characteristics. Since male aggressiveness is inborn, the presence of women and children is essential to absorb it and soften it. They actively promote the practice of family mediation in divorces as a tool to maintaining family ties. Many groups form part of Responsible Fatherhood Groups, all of them conservative: the Institute for American Values, the National Fatherhood Initiative and the National Congress for Fathers and Families. This last promoted a measure to oblige unmarried mothers to name the father of the child; otherwise they are deprived of state financial support. This proposal goes hand in hand with a law in Florida in 2001, according to which unmarried women who decided to have their child adopted could be forced to publish their sexual history in the local newspaper in order to inform the biological father of the existence of a child. The law was repealed in 2003 and replaced with a 'softer' measure: men who thought they had made a woman pregnant were encouraged to register in a confidential file so they could be contacted if a child presumed to be theirs was put up for adoption (Dahlburg, 2003).

**Fathers' Rights Groups**: these have existed since 1960 and bring together middle-class divorced fathers in particular. The leaders are often well-known lawyers. They deny the existence of domestic violence and maintain that the majority of reports of incest against fathers are invented or suggested by hostile and vindictive mothers. They consider themselves victims.

## Box 2: Violence by the partner after separation and visits to the children – Italy

Piera, Lea and Nora are three women who are separated from violent men who do not accept separation and continue to attack them, threaten them and persecute them in every way. The women are not opposed to contact between father and children, but ask for a system of visits to be organised that protects the children and themselves and takes some practical requirements into account (working hours, the routines of small children and so on). Instead, social services support requests by the fathers for greater access to the children in ways that are more convenient for them. For example, the social worker is putting pressure on Piera to leave the shelter where she has taken refuge (her husband refused to leave their joint home, which is owned by Piera) and rent a bungalow on a campsite at her expense, so that the father can visit their little girl more easily. In another case the father's visiting times do not take into account the working hours of the mother, who must take a taxi (at her expense) to hand over the child in time; if she arrives late, the father calls the police. When these women resisted the father's requests, the conflict increased to such an extent that the court asked for a psychological report on the parents. Analysis of the documents shows that male violence is left out and denied; the behaviour of the women thus becomes unreasonable and incomprehensible, a sign of personal limitations and difficulties. With reference to Lea who is opposed to joint custody (not very practical with a two-year-old boy), although recognising that she is an excellent mother, the psychologist wrote: 'The lady showed a certain hostility towards the husband that prevents her from exercising a proper and generous role as mother'. For these reasons it was the father who was given custody. Some months later the father returned the child to the mother; the court then gave custody to her. Lea, who earns a living from temporary work, had to pay a huge sum for the psychologist's report. The case of Nora is also significant: when she leaves her ex-cohabitee, he threatens to kill her, to kill himself and to kill the child, he starts persecuting her and her family (chasing them by car, ramming them deliberately on the motorway, insulting them, attacking them) and continues doing this so that he soon collects some convictions as well as many reports. The child witnesses all this violence. Supported by the Separated Fathers' Movement, the man gets social services to increase his visiting time. In the psychologist's reports the only reference to the violence committed by this man is as follows: Nora has 'a persecutory type experience such as to distort the image of her tireless "suitor" to the point of being terrorised by him'. With objective references to abuse and threats removed, the reasonable fear of Nora becomes paranoia and a man already convicted several times for violence becomes an innocent, even though tireless, suitor (Romito, 1999b).

## Box 3: Paternal sexual abuse after separation or divorce – the US

The jurists Joan Pennington and Laurie Woods (1990) describe many cases of this type that have occurred in the US. In the case of A.H. the paediatrician discovers that the child shows signs of suspected sexual violence; a specialist intervenes, who concludes at the end of the diagnosis that the child has been sodomised by her father. The father has a history of paedophilia, but the judge gives him the right to visit without supervision, in spite of this information. The mother refuses to hand over the little girl to her father and hides her with friends to protect her. Not obeying the court is a crime: the mother is arrested and will be released only a month later, when the FBI finds the little girl again. The judge decides to give custody to the father. The mother must follow psychological treatment and may see the child for a few hours a week under the supervision of a person chosen and paid by the father.

In another case, in spite of the child repeatedly mentioning paternal sexual abuse, the judge guaranteed the father the right to visit without supervision. The mother hid the child to protect him and was imprisoned for almost a year, until the little boy was found by the FBI and put in the care of a foster family.

In yet another case, although the medical evidence and declarations by the child agreed on sexual abuse by the father, the man was acquitted. In the reasonable fear that he would be given custody of the child, the mother hid with her, but was caught nine months later. While waiting for a decision by the judge, the child was accommodated in various foster families; the mother could see her for only a few hours a week. In 1990 the judge finally decided to give the father custody of the child.

In the case of Chrissy F. the child had said repeatedly that her father 'touched her'; there was objective gynaecological proof on the matter. Still, the judge did not allow the mother to supply this proof of abuse suffered by the child in the trial because, he said, 'she was a liar'. The mother ran away with the child under a false name. When she became seriously ill, she did not go into hospital, because she was afraid of being discovered. She died because of lack of care and the father was given custody of the child.

## Box 4: Violence against women prostitutes

In the study by Silbert and Pines (1993) in a town in the US, 78% of the women interviewed had suffered sexual violence from clients, 16.6 episodes per woman on average; 41% had suffered other violence, such as sexual relations imposed by police officers or physical abuse, 2.6 times on average; 65% had been beaten by clients, 4.3 times on average. More recently in France in the six months prior to the study 41% of the prostitutes interviewed – women, transvestites and homosexuals – had been seriously attacked; the abusers were clients, pimps/lovers, groups of passers-by, police officers or other prostitutes (Mathieu, 2002). Considering only violence by clients, in England 50% of prostitutes working on the street and 26% of those working at home suffered serious sexual or physical violence in the previous six months. During their working life (four years on average) 81% of the former and 48% of the latter suffered violence (Church et al, 2001). According to a study carried out in London, the probability of a prostitute dying – particularly as a result of violence or Aids – is 12 times greater than that of women of the same age who are not prostitutes (Ward et al, 1999).

## Box 5 : Some information to refute the theories of the unreliable, lying child and false reports

To recall some information, in Western countries 20-30% of children and adolescents have suffered sexual abuse; the victims of abuse by a man in the family circle vary from 5 to 12% (Finkelhor et al, 1990; Russell, 1999; Vogeltanz et al, 1999). A reasonable estimate of the risk of child sexual abuse makes it about 33% for girls and between 3 and 13% for boys (Bolen et al, 2000). Children who are victims of sexual abuse often do not talk about it through fear or shame. In the US in a sample of adult women who had suffered serious sexual violence in childhood, 25% had never revealed it to anyone: the smaller the child at the time of the abuse, the more frequent the episodes and the closer the relationship with the abuser, the less likely she was to talk about it (Smith et al, 2000). In Geneva 36% of girls and 11% of boys interviewed had suffered abuse, which involved physical contact in the majority of cases; more than a third of females and almost two thirds of males had not revealed it to anyone. Of those who had talked about it, adolescents had confided particularly in friends and parents, but often only on condition that these people keep it secret. Less than 5% of the victims had confided in a health worker and even more rarely teachers and police officer (Halpérin et al, 1996). It is estimated that not more than 2% of sexual abuse against children committed by men in the family and about 6% of that carried out by men outside the family is reported to the services (Koss, 1992, 1993).

According to various research, so-called false reports make up between 2 and 8% of the total, but this percentage often also includes situations where abuse is likely but difficult to prove, because the child is too small and unable to explain, for example.

In an Italian study involving 15 centres specialising in the field of abuse, out of 1,111 children monitored for suspected abuse, cases of 'false positives' amounted to 7.6%: half consisted of cases that could not be validated and the other half consisted of 'incorrect suspicions' (Malacrea and Lorenzini, 2002). Malacrea and Lorenzini (2002) discuss the large amount of scientific work on the subject of the memory, suggestibility and reliability of children, concluding that the risk of a 'false negative' is much greater than that of a 'false positive', that is, it is much more likely that the abused child will not talk about it or, if they say something, will end up retracting; this also happens when the abuse is proven because the abuser has confessed, the child has suffered ano-genital trauma or has contracted a sexually transmitted disease, for example. In short, the problem of sexual abuse against children is not that it is exaggerated but that it is underestimated; the abusers, rather than being victims of a witch-hunt, almost always remain in the background and go unpunished.

## Box 6: Paternal sexual abuse after separation or divorce – France

Here we report some cases dealt with by research by the Collectif Féministe Contre le Viol (1999). When his parents separate, X reveals to the teacher of the nursery that he has suffered repeated anal rape. The teacher informs social services and the juvenile police (*Brigade des Mineurs*) of the fact. The child also talks about this violence to a psychiatrist, who reports the fact to the Public Prosecutor's Office and the Children's Judge: no investigation is carried out and no protective measure is put into operation. The child is questioned by the juvenile police only when the mother makes a report: he then recalls the abuse suffered in front of the police officers. But the report is filed, without the mother even being informed of it. The mother makes another report, the child's psychiatrist makes another report and the mother brings a civil action, but the father is not even summoned by the examining magistrate. This time the report ends without giving rise to proceedings. In the meantime civil procedure runs its course: the judge in charge of family matters asks for a psychological report, in which it is recommended that the child sees his father, but in the presence of a third party. The judge decides instead that the child will see his father without supervision at alternate weekends and for half the school holidays. The child refuses, the workers at the medico-psychological centre monitoring him report to the judge that the little boy says he 'wants to kill himself, jump out of the window, get away from his father by killing himself'; still, this attestation goes unheeded. The mother refuses to hand over the child to his father, who reports her: she will be given a suspended sentence of four months in prison, released on bail for 18 months and fined 20,000 francs (case No. 4).

In another case Olivier, who is three years old, returns from a visit to his father very upset and says repeatedly that 'daddy put his willy [penis] in my bottom'. Olivier's story is so complex it is impossible to summarise it briefly, we therefore report only some elements of it. From 1996 to 1999 (date the report was drawn up) the child is more and more disturbed and suffering; he shows highly sexualised behaviour (practises repeated anal masturbation, mimics anal rape on another child); desperately refuses to see his father; presents numerous psychophysical symptoms and also shows positive in the blood test for a sexually transmitted disease. In spite of reports by the mother and at least nine reports from six professionals and various institutions, the criminal enquiry is carried out in a completely unsatisfactory way. The father continues to be given custody of the child for long periods, from which he returns disturbed, recounting sexual abuse by his father and a friend of his. The mother is given a suspended sentence of six months in prison for refusing to hand over the child to his father. In 1998 the judge gives custody of Olivier to the father with the justification that the mother is not giving the child 'a positive image of the father'. A psychoanalyst, an expert for the father in the civil proceedings, presents the following diagnosis of the woman, without ever having seen her: 'hysterical neurosis, which means putting the father and the man in a position of weakness, to maintain her own self with imaginary powerlessness and using her son as an object of her unconsciously incestuous desire [it is therefore the mother who is incestuous!]. In this situation, if the law does not accept the father as its symbolic representative, Olivier may have only this fate: homosexual or delinquent or retarded' (p 9). In 1999, in spite of him showing his desperation and his wish to live with his mother, Olivier was put in a home; however, he must spend one month a year on holiday with his father.

# References

Abel, G., Becker, J., Cunningham-Rathner, J., Mittelman, M. and Rouleau, J. (1988), 'Multiple paraphilic diagnosis among sex offenders', *Bulletin of the American Academy of Psychiatry and the Law*, 16(2): 153-68.

Acker, J., Barry, K. and Esseveld, J. (1983), 'Objectivity and truth: problems in doing feminist research', *Women's Studies International Forum*, 6(4): 423-35.

Adamo, P. (2004), *Il porno di massa*, Cortina, Milan.

Afkhami, M. (1984), 'Iran: a failure in the past: the "prerevolutionary" women's movement', in Morgan, R. (ed), *Sisterhood is global*, Anchor Press, New York, pp 330-37.

Alemany, C. (2000), 'Violences', in Hirata, H., Labories, F., Le Doaré, H. and Senotier, D. (eds), *Dictionnaire critique du féminisme*, Presses Universitaires de France, Paris, pp 245-50.

Améry J. (1996), *At the mind's limits: Contemplations by a survivor on Auschwitz and its realities*, trad. it. di E. Ganni, *Un intellettuale ad Auschwitz*, Bollati Boringhieri, Turin.

Amnesty International (2004), *It's in our hands: Stop violence against women*, (www.amnesty.org).

Anderson, K. (2002), 'Perpetrator or victim? Relationships between intimate partner violence and well-being', *Journal of Marriage and Family*, 64(4): 851-63.

Arata, C. (1999), 'Coping with rape: the role of prior sexual abuse and attributions of blame', *Journal of Interpersonal Violence*, 14(1): 62-78.

Armstrong, L. (1978), *Kiss daddy goodnight*, Hawthorn, New York.

Armstrong, L. (1993), *And they call it help: The psychiatric policing of America's children*, Addison-Wesley, London and New York.

Armstrong, L. (1996), *Rocking the cradle of sexual politics: What happened when women said incest*, Addison-Wesley, London and New York.

Armstrong, L. (2000), 'What happened when women said incest', in Itzin, C. (ed), *Home truths about child sexual abuse*, Routledge, London, pp 27-48.

Ashford, L. and Clifton, D. (2005), *Women of our world*, Population Reference Bureau, (www.prb.org).

Awwad, A. (2001), 'Gossip scandal, shame and honor killing: a case for social constructionism and hegemonic discourse', *Social Thought and Research*, 24(1-2): 40-52.

Babu, A., Biletta, I., Bonnoure-Aufiere, P., David-Jougneau, M., Ditchev, S., Girot, A. and Mariller, N. (1997), *Médiation familiale, regards croisés et perspectives*, Ed. Erès, Ramonville.

Bacon, H. and Richardson, S. (2000), 'Child sexual abuse and the continuum of victim disclosure', in Itzin, C. (ed), *Home truths about child sexual abuse*, Routledge, London, pp 235-76.

Baker, N., Gregware, P. and Cassidy, M. (1999), 'Family killing fields: honor rationales in the murder of women', *Violence Against Women*, 5(2): 164-84.

Baldwin, M. (1992), 'Split at the root: prostitution and feminist discourses of law reform', *Yale Journal of Law and Feminism*, 5(1): 47-120.

Bandura, A. (1999), 'Moral disengagement and the perpetration of inhumanities', *Personality and Social Psychology Review*, 3(3): 193-209.

Bandura, A., Underwood, B. and Fromson, M.E. (1975), 'Disinhibition of aggression through diffusion of responsibility and dehumanization of victims', *Journal of Research in Personality*, 9(4): 253-69.

Barbagli, M. and Colombo, A. (1996), 'La criminalità in Emilia-Romagna: un profilo statistico', in *Quaderni di Città Sicura, 5: La sicurezza in Emilia Romagna*, II(5): 21-56.

Barbagli, M. and Saraceno, C. (1998), *Separarsi in Italia*, Il Mulino, Bologna.

Barrett, M. (1992), 'Words and things: materialism and method in contemporary feminist analysis', in Barrett, M. and Phillips, A. (eds), *Destabilizing theory: Contemporary feminist debates*, Polity, Oxford, pp 201-19.

Bartky, S.L. (1990), *Femininity and domination: Studies in the phenomenology of oppression*, Routledge, New York.

Bascelli, E. and Romito, P. (2000), 'L'intervento della polizia nei casi di maltrattmento domestico', in Romito, P. (ed), *Violenze alle donne e risposte delle istituzioni: Prospettive internazionali*, Angeli, Milan, pp 169-79.

Beck, C. and Sales, B. (2001), *Family mediation: Facts, myths, and future prospects*, American Psychological Association, Washington.

Beckett, K. (1996), 'Culture and the politics of signification: the case of child sexual abuse', *Social problems*, 43(1): 57-76.

Bellamy, C. (2000), 'Unicef executive director targets violence against women', www.unicef.org/newsline/00pr17.htm

Belsky, J. (1993), 'Etiology of child maltreatment: a developmental-ecological analysis', *Psychological Bulletin*, 114(3): 413-34.

Berry, J. (1992), *Lead us not into temptation: Catholic priests and the sexual abuse of children*, Doubleday, New York.

Bianchi, B. (2001a), *La follia e la fuga: Nevrosi di guerra, diserzione e disobbedienza nell'esercito iteliano, 1915-1918*, Bulzoni, Rome.

Bianchi, B. (2001b), 'Deportazione e memoria femminile: la guerra in Sud Africa (1899-1902)', *Rassegna Italiana di Sociologia*, 42(3): 423-39.

Biggerman, M. (1993), 'State v. Shane: confessions of infidelity as a reasonable provocation for voluntary manslaughter', *Ohio Northern University Law Review*, 19: 977-86.

Biletta, I. and Mariller, N. (1997), 'Médiation familiale et droits des femmes: réflexion institutionnelle', in Babu, A., Biletta, I., Bonnoure-Aufiere, P., David-Jougneau, M., Ditchev, S., Girot, A. and Mariller, N. (eds), *Médiation familiale: Regards croisés et perspectives*, Ed. Erès, Ramonville, pp 213-46.

Bingham, C. and Gansler, L. (2002), *Class action*, Anchor Books, New York.

Blaffer Hrdy, S. (1999), *The woman that never evolved*, Harvard University Press, Cambridge.

Bograd, M. (1984), 'Family systems approaches to wife battering: a feminist critique', *American Journal of Orthopsychiatry*, 54(4): 558-68.

Bolen, R., Russell, D. and Scannapieco, M. (2000), 'Child sexual abuse prevalence: a review and re-analysis of relevant studies', in Itzin C. (ed), *Home truths about child sexual abuse*, Routledge, London, pp 169-96.

Boneschi, M. (1998), *Santa pazienza: La storia delle donne italiane dal dopoguerra a oggi*, Mondadori, Milan.

Boserup, E. (1970), *Women's role in economic development*, St. Martin's Press, New York.

Bouchard, P. (2002), 'Faire réussir les garçons ou en finir avec le féminisme? La montée d'une idéologie conservatrice', (www.sisyphe. org/article.php36id_article=329).

Bourdieu, P., Chamboredon, J.C. and Passeron, J.C. (1968), *Le métier de sociologue*, Mouton, Paris.

Boyd, S. (1989), 'From gender specificity to gender neutrality? Ideologies in Canadian child custody law', in Smart, C. and Sevenhuijsen, S. (eds), *Child custody and the politics of gender*, Routledge, London, pp 126-57.

Boyd, S. (2002), *Child custody law and women's work*, Oxford University Press, Oxford.

Brady, S., Briton, J. and Grover, S. (2001), *The sterilisation of girls and young women: Issues and progress*, available at: www.humanrights.gov. au//disability_rights/sterilisation/index.html

Breines, W. and Gordon, L. (1983), 'The new scholarship on family violence', *Signs: Journal of Women in Culture and Society*, 8(3): 490-531.

Brewin, C. (2003), *Posttraumatic stress disorder*, Yale University Press, New Haven, CT.

Brison, S. (1998), 'Surviving sexual violence: a philosophical perspective', in French, S., Teays, W. and Purdy, L. (eds), *Violence against women: Philosophical perspectives*, Cornell University Press, Ithaca, NY, pp 11-26.

Brodribb, S. (1992), *Nothing mat(t)ers: A feminist critique of postmodernism*, Spinifex Press, Melbourne.

Brophy, J. (1989), 'Custody law, child care and inequality in Britain', in Smart, C. and Sevenhuijsen, S. (eds), *Child custody and the politics of gender*, Routledge, London, pp 217-42.

Brown, J., Cohen, P., Johnson, J. and Salzigi, S. (1998), 'A longitudinal analysis of risk-factors for child maltreatment: findings of a 17-year prospective study of officially recorded and self-reported child abuse and neglect', *Child Abuse & Neglect*, 22(11): 1065-78.

Brown Travis, C. (ed) (2003), *Evolution, gender, and rape*, MIT Press, Cambridge, MA.

Brownmiller, S. (1975), *Against our will: Men, women and rape*, Simon & Schuster, New York.

Bruckner, M. (2001), 'Reflections on the reproduction and transformation of gender differences among women: the shelter movement in Germany', *Violence Against Women*, 7(7): 760-78.

Bulman, R. and Wortman, C. (1977), 'Attributions of blame and coping in the "real world": severe accident victims react to their lot', *Journal of Personality & Social Psychology*, 35(5): 351-63.

Cairns, K. (1997), '"Femininity" and women's silence in response to sexual harassment and coercion', in Thomas, A. and Kitzinger, C. (eds), *Sexual harassment: Contemporary feminist perspectives*, Open University Press, Philadelphia, PA, pp 91-112.

Campbell, B. (1988), *Unofficial secrets*, Virago Press, London.

Campbell, J. (1992), ' "If I can't have you, no one can": power and control in homicide of female partners', in Radford, J. and Russell, D. (eds), *Femicide: The politics of woman killing*, Twayne, New York, pp 99-113.

Campbell, J. and Soeken, K. (1999), 'Forced sex and intimate partner violence: effects on women's risk and women's health', *Violence Against Women*, 5(9): 1017-35.

Campbell, J.C., Webster, D., Koziol-McLain, J. et al (2003), 'Risk factors for femicide in abusive relationships: results from a multisite case control study', *American Journal of Public Health*, 93(7): 1089-97.

Candib, L. (1999), 'Incest and other harm to daughters across cultures: maternal complicity and patriarchal power', *Women's Studies International Forum*, 22(2): 185-201.

Caplan, P. (1985), *The myth of women's masochism*, Signet Book, New York.

Caplan, P. (1998), 'Mother-blaming', in Ladd-Taylor, M. and Umansky, L. (eds), *'Bad' mothers: The politics of blame in twentieth-century America*, New York University Press, New York, pp 127-44.

Carlin, A., Kemper, K., Ward, N., Sowell, H., Gustafson, B. and Stevens, N. (1994), 'The effect of differences in objective and subjective definitions of childhood physical abuse on estimates of its incidence and relationship to psychopathology', *Child Abuse & Neglect*, 18(5): 393-9.

Carroll, M. (1989), 'The erotics of absolutism: Rubens and the mystification of sexual violence', *Representations*, 25(1): 3-30.

CFCV (Collectif Féministe Contre le Viol) (1999), *Agressions sexuelles incestueuses dans un contexte de separation des parents: déni de justice?*, CFCV, Paris.

Chesler, P., Rothblum, E. and Cole, E. (1995), *Feminist foremothers: Women's studies, psychology and mental health*, Harrington Park Press, New York.

Church, S., Henderson, M., Barnard, M. and Hart, G. (2001), 'Violence by clients towards female prostitutes in different work settings: questionnaire survey', *British Medical Journal*, 322(7285): 524-5.

Clément, M.-E., Bouchard, C., Jetté, M. and Laferrière, S. (2000), *La violence familiale dans la vie des enfants du Québec, 1999*, Institut de la statistique du Québec, Santé Québec, Montréal.

Cline, S. and Spender, D. (1988), *Reflecting men at twice their natural size*, Fontana, Glasgow.

Conley, F. (1998), *Walking out on the boys*, Farrar, Straus & Giroux, New York.

Conte, J., Wolf, S. and Smith, T. (1989), 'What sexual offenders tell us about prevention strategies', *Child Abuse & Neglect*, 13: 293-301.

Corneau, G. (1998) *Père manquant, fils manqué*, Ed. de l'Homme, Montreal.

Cortina, L., Swann, S., Fitzgerald, L. and Waldo, C. (1998), 'Sexual harassment and assault: chilling the climate for women in academia', *Psychology of Women Quarterly*, 22(3): 419-41.

Covre, P. (1999), 'Comitato diritti civili delle prostitute', in Fiorensoli, M.P. (ed), *Donne, ch'avete intelletto d'amore*, Conference reprints (Modena, 7 November 1998), pp 47-53.

Coyne, J. (2003), 'Of vice and men: a case study in evolutionary psychology', in Brown Travis, C. (ed), *Evolution, gender, and rape*, MIT Press, Cambridge, MA, pp 171-90.

Creazzo, G. (2000), 'I luoghi dell'accoglienza: un punto di vista privilegiato sul fenomeno della violenza', in Romito, P. (ed), *Violenze alle donne and risposte delle istituzioni: Prospettive internazionali*, Angeli, Milan, pp 65-82.

Creazzo, G. (2003), *Mi prendo e mi porto via: Le donne che hanno chiesto aiuto ai centri antiviolenza in Emilia-Romagna*, Angeli, Milan.

Crenshaw Williams, K. (1994), 'Mapping the margins: intersectionality, identity politics, and violence against women of color', in Fineman Albertson, M. and Mykitiuk, R. (eds), *The public nature of private violence*, Routledge, New York, pp 93-118.

Cresson, G. (2000), 'Mediazione familiare e violenza domestica', in Romito, P. (ed), *Violenze alle donne and risposte delle istituzioni: Prospettive internazionali*, Angeli, Milan, pp 123-36.

Crisma, M., Bascelli, E., Paci, D. and Romito, P. (2004), 'Adolescents who experienced sexual abuse: fears, needs and impediments to disclosure', *Child Abuse & Neglect*, 28(10): 1035-48.

Cutrufelli, M.R. (1996), *Il denaro in corpo*, Tropea, Milan.

Dahlburg, J.-T. (2003), 'Sex-history law repealed in Florida', *San Francisco Chronicle*, 31 May.

Daly, M. (1978), *Gyn/ecology: The methaethics of radical feminism*, Beacon Press, Boston, MA.

Dankwort, J. and Rausch, R. (2000), 'Men at work to end wife abuse in Quebec', *Violence Against Women*, 6(9): 936-59.

de Beauvoir, S. (1984), 'France: feminism alive, well and in constant danger', in Morgan, R. (ed), *Sisterhood is global*, Anchor Press, New York, pp 2229-35.

de Beauvoir, S. (1999) *Il secondo sesso*, Il Saggiatore, Milan.

de Young, M. (1988), 'The indignant page: techniques of neutralization in the publications of pedophile organizations', *Child Abuse & Neglect*, 12: 583-91.

Deblinger, E., Lippmann, J., Stauffer, L. and Finkel, M. (1994), 'Personal versus professional responses to child sexual abuse allegations', *Child Abuse & Neglect*, 18(8): 679-82.

DeFronzo, J. and Prochnow, J. (2004), 'Violent cultural factors and serial homicide by males' *Psychological Reports*, 94: 104-8.

Delaney, C. (1998), *Abraham on trial*, Princeton University Press, Princeton, NJ.

Dell, P. (1989), 'Violence and the systemic view: the problem of power', *Family Process*, 28(1): 1-14.

Delle Femine, D., Yeager, C. and Otnow Lewis, D. (1990), 'Child abuse: adolescent records vs adult recall', *Child Abuse & Neglect*, 14: 227-31.

Delphy, C. (1991), 'Penser le genre: quel problème?', in Hurtig, M.C., Kail, M. and Rouch, H. (eds), *Sexe et genre: De la hiérarchie entre les sexes*, Editions du CNRSS, Paris, pp 89-101.

Delphy, C. (1998), *L'ennemi principal*, Syllepse, Paris.

Delphy, C. (2000), 'Patriarcat (théories du)', in Hirata, H., Labories, F., Le Doaré, H. and Senotier, D. (eds), *Dictionnaire critique du féminisme*, Presses Universitaires de France, Paris, pp 141-6.

Delphy, C. (2002), 'Violence économique et violence masculine', *Nouvelles Questions Féministes*, 21(2): 4-7.

Delphy, C. (2006), 'Antisexisme ou anti racisme? Un faux dilemma', *Nouvelle Questions Féministes*, 25(1): 59-83.

Delphy, C. and Leonard, D. (1984), *Close to home: A materialistic analysis of women's oppression*, Hutchinson, London.

Déttore, D. (2001), *Psicologia e psicopatologia del comportamento sessuale*, McGraw-Hill, Milan.

Déttore, D. (2002), 'La prevenzione dell'abuso sessuale sui minori', in Fuligni, C. and Romito, P. (eds), *Il counselling in adolescenza*, McGraw-Hill, Milan, pp 181-200.

Déttore, D. and Fuligni, C. (1999), *L'abuso sessuale sui minori: Valutazione e terapia delle vittime e dei responsabili*, McGraw-Hill, Milan.

Deutsch, H. (1945), *The psychology of women: A psychoanalytic interpretation. 1: Girlhood*, Grune & Stratton, New York.

Dobash, R. and Emerson Dobash, R. (1992), *Women, violence & social change*, Routledge, London.

Dobash, R., Emerson Dobash, R., Cavendish, K. and Lewis, R. (1996), 'Re-education programmes for violent men: an evaluation', *Research Finding*, no 46, Research and Statistics Directorate, Home Office, Croydon.

Doise, W., Deschamps, J.C. and Mugny, G. (1991), *Psychologie sociale expérimentale*, Colin, Paris.

Dolgopal, U. (1995), 'Women's voices, women's pain', *Human Rights Quarterly*, 17(1): 127-54.

Ducret, V. (1993), *Harcelement sexuel*, Bureau de l'Egalité des Droits Entre Homme et Femme, Geneva.

Dufour, M., Nadeau, L. and Bertrand, M. (2000), 'Les facteurs de résilience chez les victimes d'abus sexuel: état de la question', *Child Abuse & Neglect*, 24(6): 781-97.

Dufresne, M. (1998), 'Masculinisme et criminalité sexiste', *Nouvelles Questions Féministes*, 19(2,3,4) and *Recherches Féministes*, 11(2): 125-37.

Dufresne, M. (2002), 'Face aux conjoints agresseurs: la danse avec l'ours', Interview with Quebec psychologist Rudolf Rausch by Martin Dufresne, *Nouvelles Quéstions Féministes*, 21(3): 28-46.

Dufresne, M. and Palma, H. (2002), 'Autorité parentale conjointe: le retour de la loi du père', *Nouvelles Questions Féministes*, 21(2): 31-54.

Dworkin, A. and MacKinnon, C. (1988), *Pornography and civil rights: A new day for women's equality*, Organizing Against Pornography, Minneapolis, MN.

Edleson, J. (1999), 'The overlap between child maltreatment and woman battering', *Violence Against Women*, 5(2): 134-54.

Ehrenreich, B. and English, D. (1979), *For her own good: 150 years of the experts' advice to women*, Pluto Press, London.

Eldridge, H. (2000), 'Patterns of sex offending and strategies for effective assessment and intervention', in Itzin, C. (ed), *Home truths about child sexual abuse*, Routledge, London, pp 313-34.

Enloe, C. (1993), *Sexual politics at the end of the Cold War: The morning after*, University of California Press, Berkeley, CA.

Erdenet, G. (1992), 'RU486, le chiffre de la Bête: le mouvement contre le droit des femmes à l'avortement en France', *Nouvelles Questions Féministes*, 13(3): 29-43.

Eriksson, M. (1997), *Relazione sulla necessità di organizzare una campagna a livello dell'Unione Europea per la totale intransigenza nei confronti della violenza contro le donne*, Commissione per i Diritti Della Donna, European Parliament, Strasburg.

Eriksson, M. and Hester, M. (2001), 'Violent men as good-enough fathers?', *Violence Against Women*, 7(7): 779-98.

Eriksson, M., Hester, M., Keskinen, S., Pringles, K. (eds) (2005), *Tackling men's violence in families: Nordic issues and dilemmas*, The Policy Press, Bristol.

Faller Coulborn, K., Corwin, D. and Olafson, E. (1997), 'Research on false allegations of sexual abuse in divorce', in Myers, J. (ed), *A mother's nightmare-incest: A practical legal guide for parents and professionals*, Sage, Thousand Oaks, CA, pp 199-210.

Faludi, S. (1991), *Backlash: The undeclared war against American women*, Crown, New York.

Farley, M. (eds) (2003), *Prostitution, trafficking and traumatic stress*, Haworth Press, New York.

Fausto-Sterling, A. (1992), *Myths of gender*, Basic Books, New York.

Fausto-Sterling, A. (2000), *Sexing the body*, Basic Books, New York.

Feinauer, L. and Stuart, D. (1996), 'Blame and resilience in women sexually abused as children', *American Journal of Family Therapy*, 24(1): 31-40.

Fergusson, D., Horwood, J. and Lynskey, M. (1997), 'Childhood sexual abuse, adolescent sexual behaviors and sexual revictimization', *Child Abuse & Neglect*, 21(8): 789-803.

Ferraro, K. (2003), 'The words change, but the melody lingers', *Violence Against Women*, 9(1): 110-29.

Fetherston, A. (1995), 'UN peacekeepers and cultures of violence', *Cultural Survival Quarterly*, 19(1): 19-23.

Finkelhor, D. (2003), 'The legacy of the clergy abuse scandal', *Child Abuse & Neglect*, 27(11): 1225-9.

Finkelhor, D. and Dziuba-Leatherman, J. (1995), 'Victimization prevention programs: a national survey of children's exposure and reactions', *Child Abuse & Neglect*, 19(2): 129-39.

Finkelhor, D., Hotaling, G., Lewis, I. and Smith, C. (1990), 'Sexual abuse in a national survey of adult men and women: prevalence, characteristics, and risk factors', *Child Abuse & Neglect*, 14(1): 19-28.

Fitzgerald, L. (1993), 'Sexual harassment: violence against women in the workplace', *American Psychologist*, 48(10): 1070-6.

Fitzgerald, L., Swan, S. and Fisher, K. (1995), 'Why didn't she just report him? The psychological and legal implications of women's responses to sexual harassment', *Journal of Social Issues*, 51(1): 117-38.

Fleming, J., Mullen, P. and Bammer, G. (1997), 'A study of potential risk factors for sexual abuse in childhood', *Child Abuse & Neglect*, 21(1): 49-58.

Fleming, J., Mullen, P., Sibthorpe, B. and Bammer, G. (1999), 'The long-term impact of childhood sexual abuse in Australian women', *Child Abuse & Neglect*, 23(2): 145-59.

Foster, M. and Dion, K. (2003), 'Dispositional hardiness and women's well-being relating to gender discrimination: the role of minimization', *Psychology of Women Quarterly*, 27(3): 197-208.

French, M. (1992), *The war against women*, Simon & Schuster, New York.

French, S., Teays, W. and Purdy, L. (1998), *Violences against women: Philosophical perspectives*, Cornell University Press, Ithaca, NY.

Frenken, J. and Van Stolk, B. (1990), 'Incest victims: inadequate help by professionals', *Child Abuse & Neglect*, 14: 253-63.

Furnham, A. (2003), 'Belief in a just world: research progress over the past decade', *Personality and Individual Differences*, 34(5): 795-817.

Gardner, R. (1987), *The parental alienation syndrome and the differentiation between fabricated and genuine child sexual abuse*, Creative Therapeutics, Cresskill.

Gardner, R.A. (1991), *Sex abuse hysteria: Salem witch trials revisited*, Creative Therapeutics, Cresskill.

Gardner, R.A. (1992), *True and false accusations of child sex abuse*, Creative Therapeutics, Cresskill.

Gardner, R. (1993), 'A theory about the variety of human sexual behavior', *Issues in Child Abuse Accusation*, 5(2): 115.

Garrity, R. (2003), 'Movement activism versus professionalism: domestic violence offender programs as tools of oppression: how cooptation works to silence truth and excuse men's violence against women', *The Voice: Newsletter of the National Coalition Against Domestic Violence*, 10(2): 18-25.

Gianini Belotti, E. (1983), *Non di sola madre*, Rizzoli, Milan.

Gibbons, J. (1996), 'Services for adults who have experienced child sexual assault: improving agency response', *Social Science & Medicine*, 43(12): 1755-63.

Gillioz, L., DePuy, J. and Ducret, V. (2000), 'La violenza domestica in Svizzera: nuovi dati su un fenomeno antico', in Romito, P. (ed), *Violenze alle donne and risposte delle istituzioni: Prospettive internazionali*, Angeli, Milan, pp 83-94.

Giobbe, E. (1990), 'Confronting the liberal lies about prostitution', in Leidholdt, D. and Raymond, J. (eds), *The sexual liberals and the attack on feminism*, Pergamon Press, New York, pp 67-81.

Glover, J. (2001), *Humanity: A moral history of the twentieth century*, Random House, London.

Gonzo, L. (2000), 'I servizi sociosanitari a Bologna: dai risultati di una ricerca a un progetto di formazione', in Romito, P. (ed), *Violenze alle donne e risposte delle istituzioni: Prospettive internazionali*, Angeli, Milan, pp 153-65.

Gordon, L. (1988), *Heroes of their own lives: The politics and history of family violence*, Penguin Books, New York.

Gordon, M. and Riger, S. (1989), *The female fear: The social cost of rape*, University of Illinois Press, Chicago, IL.

Gould, S. (1998), *The mismeasure of man,* trad. it. di A. Zani, Il Saggiatore, *Intelligenza and pregiudizio*, Milan.

Gowaty, P.A. (2003), 'Sexual natures: how feminism changed evolutionary biology', *Signs: Journal of Women in Culture and Society*, 28(3): 901-21.

Graham-Bermann, S. and Edleson, J. (eds) (2001), *Domestic violence in the lives of children*, American Psychological Association, Washington, DC.

Grandits, M., Wipler, E., Baker, K. and Kokar, E. (eds) (1999), *Rape is a war crime*, Proceedings of a conference, International Centre for Migration Policy Development, Vienna, 18-20 June.

Graycar, R. (1989), 'Equal rights versus fathers' rights: the child custody debate in Australia', in Smart, C. and Sevenhuijsen, S. (eds), *Child custody and the politics of gender*, Routledge, London, pp 158-89.

Graycar, R. and Morgan, J. (2002), *The hidden gender of law*, The Federation Press, Sydney.

Guénard, T. (1999), *Plus fort que la haine*, Flammarion, Paris.

Guillaumin, C. (1992), *Sexe, race et pratique du pouvoir*, Coté-femmes, Paris.

Gulotta, G. (1997), 'Le fonti di errore nelle valutazioni di abuso sessuale', in de Cataldo Neoburger, L. (ed), *Abuso sessuale di minore e processo penale: Ruoli e responsabilità*, CEDAM, Padova, pp 151-86.

Hagemann-White, C. (2001), 'European research on the prevalence of violence against women', *Violence Against Women*, 7(7): 732-59.

Halpérin, D., Bouvier, P., Jaffé, P., Monoud, R.-L., Pawlak, C., Laederach, J., Rey Wicky, F. and Astié, F. (1996), 'Prevalence of child sexual abuse among adolescents in Geneva: results of a cross sectional survey', *British Medical Journal*, 312: 1326-9.

Hanmer, J. (1990), 'Men, power and the exploitation of women', *Women's Studies International Forum*, 13(5): 443-56.

Harne, L. (2002), 'Nouveaux pères, violence et garde des enfants', *Nouvelles Questions Féministes*, 21(2): 8-30.

Hart, T., Bogner, J., Whyte, J. and Polansky, M. (2003), 'Attribution to blame in accident and violence related traumatic brain injury', *Rehabilitation Psychology*, 48(2): 86-92.

Haskett, M., Marziano, B. and Dover, E. (1996), 'Absence of males in maltreatment research: a survey of recent literature', *Child Abuse & Neglect*, 20(12): 1175-82.

Hawking, S. (1993), *Black holes and baby universes and other essays*, Bentam, New York.

Heilbrun, C. (1997), 'The end of a long marriage', in Oakley, A. and Mitchell, J. (eds), *Who's afraid of feminism? Seeing through the backlash*, Hamish Hamilton, London, pp 111-29.

Herman, J. (1981), *Father-daughter incest*, Harvard University Press, Cambridge, MA.

Herman, J. (1992), *Trauma and recovery*, Basic Books, New York.

Hester, M. and Radford, L. (1996), *Domestic violence and child contact arrangements in England and Denmark*, The Policy Press, Bristol.

Hirata, H., Labories, F., Le Doaré, H. and Senotier, D. (eds) (2000), *Dictionnaire critique du féminisme*, Presses Universitaires de France, Paris.

Hirigoyen, M.-F. (2005), *Femmes sous emprise: Les ressorts de la violence dans le couple*, Editions Robert Laffont, Paris.

Hoigrad, C. and Finstad, L. (1992), *Backstreets: Prostitution, money and love*, Polity Press, Cambridge.

hooks, b. (1994), *Teaching to transgress: Education as the practice for freedom*, Routledge, New York.

hooks, b. (1997), 'Violence in intimate relationships: a feminist perspective', in O'Toole, L. and Schiffman, J. (eds), *Gender violence: Interdisciplinary perspectives*, New York University Press, New York, pp 279-84.

Hooper, C.A. (1992), *Mothers surviving child sexual abuse*, Routledge, London.

Hughes, D. (2000), 'The "Natasha" trade: the transnational shadow market of trafficking in women', *Journal of International Affairs*, 53(2): 625-51.

Hughes, D., Sporcic, L.J., Mendelsohn, N.Z. and Chirgwin, V. (1999), *Factbook on global sexual exploitation*, Coalition Against Trafficking in Women, Kingston, www.uri.edu/artsci/wms/hughes/factbook. htm

Human Rights Watch (ed) (2001), *Scared at school: Sexual violence against girls in South African schools*, Human Rights Watch, New York, (www. hrw.org/reports/2001/safrica/).

Humphreys, C. (1997), 'Child sexual abuse allegations in the context of divorce: issues for mothers', *British Journal of Social Work*, 27(4): 529-44.

Humphreys, C. (1999), 'Avoidance and confrontation: social work practice in relation to domestic violence and child abuse', *Child and Family Social Work*, 4(1): 77-87.

Humphreys, C. and Thiara, R. (2003), 'Mental health and domestic violence: "I call it symptoms of abuse"', *British Journal of Social Work*, 33: 209-26.

Ingrao, C. and Scoppa, C. (eds) (2001), *Donne 2000: A cinque anni dalla conferenza mondiale di Pechino: Le cose fatte, gli ostacoli incontrati, le cose da fare*, Cabinet of the Prime Minister, Equal Opportunities Department, Rome.

Itzin, C. (2000a),'Child sexual abuse and the radical feminist endeavour: an overview', in Itzin, C. (ed), *Home truths about child sexual abuse*, Routledge, London, pp 1-24.

Itzin, C. (2000b), 'Incest,"paedophilia", pornography and prostitution: conceptualizing the connections', in Itzin, C. (ed), *Home truths about child sexual abuse*, Routledge, London, pp 87-99.

Jackson, S. (1996), *Christine Delphy*, Sage Publications, London.

Jackson, S. (2001), 'Why a materialist feminism is (still) possible and necessary', *Women's Studies International Forum*, 24(3/4): 283-93.

Jaffee, S., Moffitt, T., Caspi, A. and Taylor, A. (2003), 'Life with (or without) father: the benefits of living with two biological parents depend on the father's antisocial behavior', *Child Development*, 74(1): 109-26.

Janoff-Bulman, R. and Frieze, I. (1983), 'A theoretical perspective for understanding reactions to victimization', *Journal of Social Issues*, 39(1): 1-17.

Jaspard, M., Brown, E., Condon, S., Fougeyrollas-Schwebel, D., Houel, A., Lhomond, B., Maillochon, F., Saurel-Cubizolles, M.J. and Schiltz, M.A. (2003), *Les violences envers les femmes en France*, La Documentation Française, Paris.

Jeffreys, S. (1990), *Anticlimax: A feminist perspective on sexual revolution*, New York University Press, New York.

Jeffreys, S. (1997), *The idea of prostitution*, Spinifex Press, Melbourne.

Johnson, C. (2000), *Gli ultimi giorni dell'impero americano*, Garzanti, Milan.

Jones, A. (2000), *Next time, she'll be dead*, Beacon Press, Boston, MA.

Jones, L. and Finkelhor, D. (2003), 'Putting together evidence on declining trends in sexual abuse: a complex puzzle', *Child Abuse & Neglect*, 27: 133-5.

Juergensmeyer, M. (2000), *Terror in the mind of God: The global rise of religious violence*, University of California Press, Berkeley, CA.

Juristat (1994), 'Résultats d'une enquête nationale sur l'aggression contre la conjointe', ed K. Rodgers, *Statistique Canada*, no 85, 14(9): 1-22.

Kahn, A., Jackson, J., Kully, C., Badger, K. and Halvorsen, J. (2003), 'Calling it rape: differences in experiences of women who do or do not label their sexual assault as rape', *Psychology of Women Quarterly*, 27(3): 233-42.

Kaufman Kantor, G. and Little, L. (2003), 'Defining the boundaries of child neglect: when does domestic violence equate with parental failure to protect?', *Journal of Interpersonal Violence*, 18(4): 338-55.

Kelley, S. (1990), 'Responsibilities and management strategies in CSA', *Child Welfare*, 69(1): 43-51.

Kelly, L. (1988), *Surviving sexual violence*, Polity Press, Cambridge.

Kelly, L. and Humphreys, C. (2000), 'Stalking and paedophilia: ironies and contradictions in the politics of naming and legal reform', in Radford, J., Friedberg, M. and Harne, M. (eds), *Women, violence and strategies for action*, Open University Press, Philadelphia, PA, pp 10-23.

Kelly, L., Lovett, J. and Regan, L. (2005), *A gap or a chasm? Attrition in reported rape cases*, Home Office, London.

Kelly, L., Regan, L. and Burton, S. (2000), 'Sexual exploitation: a new discovery or one part of the continuum of sexual abuse in childhood?', in Itzin, C. (ed), *Home truths about sexual abuse*, Routledge, London, pp 70-86.

Kerény, K. (1994), *Gods of the Greeks*, rad. it. di V. Tedeschi, *Gli dei della Grecia*, Il Saggiatore Economici, Milan.

Keskinen, S. (2005), 'Commitments and contradictions: linking violence, parenthood and professionalism', in Eriksson, M., Hester, M., Keskinen, S. and Pringles, K. (eds), *Tackling men's violence in families: Nordic issues and dilemmas*, The Policy Press, Bristol, pp 31-48.

Kirkwood, M. and Cecil, D. (2001), 'Marital rape', *Violence Against Women*, 7(11): 1234-53.

Kitzinger, J. (1998), 'The gender politics of news production: silenced voices and false memories', in Carter, C. (ed) *News, Gender and Power*, Routledge, New York, pp 186-203.

Kitzmann, K., Gaylord, N., Holt, A. and Kenny, E. (2003), 'Child witnesses to domestic violence: a meta-analytic review', *Journal of Consulting and Clinical Psychology*, 71(2): 339-52.

Kolodny, A. (1996), 'Paying the price of antifeminist intellectual harassment', in Clark, V., Nelson-Garner, S., Higonnet, M. and Katak, K. (eds), *Anti feminism in academy*, Routledge, New York, pp 3-33.

Koss, M. (1985), 'The hidden rape victim: personality, attitudinal and situational characteristics', *Psychology of Women Quarterly*, 9(3): 193-212.

Koss, M. (1992), 'The underdetection of rape: methodological choices influence incidence estimates', *Journal of Social Issues*, 48(1): 61-76.

Koss, M. (1993), 'Rape: scope, impact, interventions and public policy responses', *American Psychologist*, 48(10): 1062-9.

Koss, M. (2000), 'Shame, blame and community: justice responses to violence against women', *American Psychologist*, 55(11): 1332-43.

Koss, M. (2003), 'Evolutionary models of why men rape: acknowledging the complexities', in Brown Travis, C. (ed), *Evolution, gender, and rape*, MIT Press, Cambridge, MA, pp 191-205.

Koss, M. and Oros, C. (1982), 'Sexual experiences survey: a research instrument investigating sexual aggression and victimization', *Journal of Consulting and Clinical Psychology*, 50(4): 455-7.

Koss, M., Bailey, J., Yuan, N., Herrera, V. and Lichter, E. (2003), 'Depression and PTSD in survivors of male violence: research and training initiatives to facilitate recovery', *Psychology Of Women Quarterly*, 27(2): 130-42.

Koss, M., Goodman, L., Browne, A., Fitzgerald, L., Keita, P.G. and Russo, N.F. (1994), *Male violence against women at home, at work, and in the community*, American Psychological Association, Washington, DC.

Kotch, J., Browne, D., Dufort, V., Winsor, J. and Catellier, D. (1999), 'Predicting child maltreatment in the first 4 years of life from characteristics assessed in the neonatal period', *Child Abuse & Neglect*, 23(4): 305-19.

Krug, E., Dahlberg, L., Mercy, J., Zwi, A. and Lozano, R. (eds) (2002), *World report on violence and health*, World Health Organization, Geneva.

Kurki-Suonio, K. (2000), 'Joint custody as an interpretation of the best interests of the child in critical and comparative perspective', *International Journal of Law, Policy and the Family*, 14(3): 183-205.

Kurz, D. (1997), 'Violence against women or family violence? Current debates and future directions', in O'Toole, L. and Schiffman, J. (eds), *Gender violence: Interdisciplinary perspectives*, New York University Press, New York, pp 443-53.

La Mendola, S. (1995), *Con gli occhi di Caronte*, Cluep, Bologna.

Ladd-Taylor, M. and Umansky, L. (eds) (1998), *'Bad' mothers: The politics of blame in twentieth-century America*, New York University Press, New York.

Lagarde, M. (2005), 'Por la vida y la libertad de las mujeres, fin al feminicidio', in *Resistencia y alternativa de las mujeres frente al modelo globalizado*, Red Nacional Género y Economia, Mexico DF, pp 114-26.

Lagostena Bassi, T. (1991), *L'avvocato delle donne: Dodici storie di ordinaria violenza*, Mondadori, Milan.

Lamb, S. (1996), *The trouble with blame: Victims, perpetrators and responsibility*, Harvard University Press, Cambridge, MA.

Lamb, S. and Keon, S. (1995), 'Blaming the perpetrator: language that distorts reality in newspaper articles on men battering women', *Psychology of Women Quarterly*, 19(3): 209-20.

Laplante-Edward, S. (1996), 'December 6, 1989: putting a face on the victims', in proceedings of the international conference 'Violence, abuse and women's citizenship', Brighton, 10-15 November, p 105.

Lasch, C. (1982), *Haven in a heartless world*, Basic Books, New York.

Le Carré, J. (2001), *The constant gardener*, trad. it. di A. Biavasco and V. Guani, *Il giardiniere tenace*, Mondadori, Milan.

Le Doeuff, M. (1998), *Le sexe du savoir*, Aubier, Paris.

Lees, S. (1997), *Carnal knowledge: Rape on trial*, Penguin, Harmondsworth.

Leidholdt, D. and Raymond, J. (eds) (1990), *The sexual liberals and the attack on feminism*, Pergamon Press, New York.

Leigh Butler, M. (2001), 'Making waves', *Women's Studies International Forum*, 24 (3/4): 387-99.

Lerner, G. (1986), *The creation of patriarchy*, Oxford University Press, Oxford.

Lerner, M.J. and Miller, D.T. (1978), 'Just world research and the attribution process: looking back and ahead', *Psychological Bulletin*, 85(6): 1030-51.

Levi, P. (1958), *Se questo è un uomo*, Einaudi, Turin.

Lezin Jones, R. and Kaufman, L. (2003), 'Mental wards at New Jersey hospitals are made to double as foster homes', *The New York Times*, 30 June.

Limber, S. (1995), 'Ethical and legal issues in case of child sexual abuse in the United States', in Ney, T. (ed), *True and false allegations of child sexual abuse*, Brunner-Mazel, New York.

Locke, D. (2000), 'Family homicide', in Pottie Bunge, V. and Locke, D. (eds), *Family violence in Canada: a statistical profile 2000*, Canadian Centre for Justice Statistics, Ottawa, pp 39-44.

Lorde, A. (2005), 'Age, race, class and sex', in Baca Zin, M., Hondagneu-Sotelo, P. and Messner, M. (eds), *Gender through the prism of difference*, Oxford, Oxford University Press, pp 245-50.

Lovett, B. (1995), 'Child sexual abuse: the female victim's relationship with her nonoffending mother', *Child Abuse & Neglect*, 19(6): 951-64.

Luo, T.-Y. (2000), '"Marrying my rapist?!" The cultural trauma among Chinese rape survivors', *Gender & Society*, 14(4): 581-97.

MacDonald, B. (2003), 'The politics of aging', in Morgan, R. (eds), *Sisterhood is forever: The women's anthology for a new millennium*, Washington Square Press, New York, pp 152-61.

McLeer, S. and Anwar, R. (1989), 'A study of battered women presenting in an emergency department', *American Journal of Public Health*, 79(1): 65-6.

McMahon, M. and Pence, E. (1995), 'Doing more harm than good? Some cautions on visitation centers', in Peled, E., Jaffe, P. and Edleson, J. (eds), *Ending the cycle of violence: Community responses to children of battered women*, Sage Publications, Thousand Oaks, CA, pp 186-206.

MacMillan, H., Fleming, J., Trocmé, N., Boyle, M., Wong, M., Racine, Y., Beardslee, W. and Offord, D. (1997), 'Prevalence of child physical and sexual abuse in the community', *Journal of American Medical Association*, 278(2): 131-5.

Maeterlinck, M. ([1901]1968) *La vie des abeilles*, Plon, Paris.

Mahoney, M. (1991), 'Legal images of battered women: redefining the issue of separation', *Michigan Law Review*, 90(1): 1-94.

Malacrea, M. and Lorenzini, S. (2002), *Bambini abusati*, Cortina, Milan.

Malamuth, N., Addison, T. and Koss, M. (2000), 'Pornography and sexual aggression: are there reliable effects and can we understand them?', *Annual Review of Sex Research*, 11(1): 26-91.

Malinosky-Rummell, R. and Hansen, D. (1993), 'Long-term consequences of childhood physical abuse', *Psychological Bulletin*, 114(1): 68-79.

Mardorossian, C. (2002), 'Toward a new feminist theory of rape', *Signs: Journal of Women in Culture and Society*, 27(3): 743-5.

Masson, J. (1984), *The assault on truth*, Farrar, Straus & Giroux, New York.

Mathieu, L. (2002), 'La prostitution, zone de vulnerabilité sociale', *Nouvelles Questions Féministes*, 21(2): 55-75.

Mathieu, N.C. (1991), *L'anatomie politique: Catégorisations et idéologies du sexe*, Coté Femmes, Paris.

Mathieu, N.C. (2000), 'Sexe et genre: différenciation biologique, différenciation sociale', in Hirata, H., Labories, F., Le Doaré, H. and Senotier, D. (eds), *Dictionnaire critique du féminisme*, Presses Universitaires de France, Paris, pp 191-200.

Maxfield, M. and Widom, S.C. (1996), 'The cycle of violence: revisited 6 years later', *Archives of Pediatrics and Adolescent Medicine*, 150(4): 390-5.

May-Chahal, C. and Cawson, P. (2005), 'Measuring child maltreatment in the United Kingdom: a study of the prevalence of child abuse and neglect', *Child Abuse & Neglect*, 29: 969-84.

Merrill, L., Thomsen, C., Gold, S. and Milner, J. (2001), 'Childhood abuse and premilitary sexual assault in male navy recruits', *Journal of Consulting and Clinical Psychology*, 69(2): 252-61.

Meyer Williams, L. (1994), 'Recall of childhood trauma: a prospective study of women's memories of child sexual abuse', *Journal of Consulting and Clinical Psychology*, 62(6): 1167-76.

Miccio, K. (1995), 'In the name of mothers and children: deconstructing the myth of the passive battered mother and the "protected child" in child neglect proceedings', *Albany Law Review*, 58(4): 1087-107.

Miller, J. (2002), 'Violence and coercion in Sri Lanka's commercial sex industry', *Violence Against Women*, 8(9): 1044-73.

Millett, K. (1970), *Sexual politics*, Doubleday, New York.

Moloney, L. (2001), 'Do fathers "win" or do mothers "lose"? A preliminary analysis of closely contested parenting judgments in the Family Court of Australia', *International Journal of Law, Policy and the Family*, 15(3): 363-96.

Montecchi, F. (1994), *Gli abusi all'infanzia: Dalla ricerca all'intervento clinico*, Carocci, Rome.

Monzini, P. (2002), *Il mercato delle donne: Prostituzione, tratta e sfruttamento*, Donzelli, Rome.

Morbois, C., Vayssade, M.-C. and Villerbu, L. (1994), *Rapport de la commission 'Violences à l'encontre des femmes'*, (unpublished), Regional Committee on Women's Rights, Paris.

Morgan, K. (2006), 'Cheating wives and vice girls: the construction of a culture of resignation', *Women's Studies International Forum*, 29: 489-98.

Morgan, R. (ed) (1970), *Sisterhood is powerful*, Vintage Books, New York.

Morgan, R. (ed) (1984), *Sisterhood is global*, Anchor Press, New York.

Morgan, R. (1992), *The word of a woman: Feminist dispatches 1968-1992*, Norton & Company, New York.

Morgan, R. (ed) (2003), *Sisterhood is forever: The women's anthology for a new millennium*, Washington Square Press, New York.

Morley, R. (2000), 'Domestic violence and housing', in Itzin, C. (ed), *Home truths about child sexual abuse*, Routledge, London, pp 228-45.

Moro, L. (2003), *L'abuso sessuale sul minore: Un'analisi dei fascicoli giudiziari del tribunale ordinario e del tribunale per i minorenni*, Tesi di laurea in psicologia sociale, (unpublished) Facoltà di Psicologia, Università degli Studi di Trieste.

Morris, A. (1997), *Women's safety survey 1996*, Victimisation Survey Committee, Wellington.

Mott, H. and Condor, S. (1997), 'Sexual harassment and the working lives of secretaries', in Thomas, A. and Kitzinger, C. (eds), *Sexual harassment: Contemporary feminist perspectives*, Open University Press, Philadelphia, PA, pp 49-90.

Mucchielli, L. (2005), *Le scandale des 'tournants': Dérives médiatiques, contre-enquete sociologique*, La Découverte, Paris.

Mullen, P., Martin, J., Anderson, J., Romans, S. and Herbison, G. (1996), 'The long-term impact of the physical, emotional and sexual abuse of children: a community study', *Child Abuse & Neglect*, 20(1): 7-21.

Mullender, A. (1996), *Rethinking domestic violence: The social work and probation response*, Routledge, London.

Murray, C. and Herrnstein, R. (1994), *The Bell curve: Intelligence and class structure in American life*, Free Press, New York.

Myer, M. (1985), 'A new look at mothers of incest victims', *Journal of Social Work and Human Sexuality*, 3(1): 47-58.

Myers, J. (1994), *The backlash: Child protection under fire*, Sage Publications, Thousand Oaks, CA.

Myers, J. (1997), *A mother's nightmare-incest: A practical legal guide for parents and professionals*, Sage Publications, Thousand Oaks, CA.

Nelson, S. (2000), 'Confronting sexual abuse: challenging for the future', in Itzin, C. (ed), *Home truths about child sexual abuse*, Routledge, London, pp 387-402.

Nixon, K., Tutty, L., Downe, P., Gorkoff, K. and Ursel, J. (2002), 'The everyday occurrence: violence in the lives of girls exploited through prostitution', *Violence Against Women*, 8(9): 1016-43.

Nordborg, G. (2005), 'Children's peace? The possibility of protecting children by means of criminal law and family law', in Eriksson, M., Hester, M., Keskinen, S. and Pringles, K. (eds), *Tackling men's violence in families: Nordic issues and dilemmas*, The Policy Press, Bristol, pp 101-18.

Nordstrom, C. (1998), 'Girls behind the (front) lines', in Lorentzen, L. and Turpin, J. (eds), *The women and war reader*, New York University Press, New York.

Novick, P. (2001), *The Holocaust and collective memory*, Bloomsbury, London.

O'Connell Davidson, J. and Layder, D. (1994), *Methods, sex and madness*, Routledge, London.

O'Connell Davidson, J. and Sanchez Taylor, J. (1996a), 'Child prostitution and sex tourism: Goa', www.ecpat.net/eng/Ecpat_inter/IRC/ePublicTitle.asp

O'Connell Davidson, J. and Sanchez Taylor, J. (1996b), 'Child prostitution and sex tourism: Costa Rica', www.ecpat.net/eng/Ecpat_inter/IRC/ePublicTitle.asp

Oakley, A. (2002), *Gender on planet earth*, The New Press, New York.

Olafson, E., Corwin, D. and Summit, R. (1993), 'Modern history of child sexual abuse awareness: cycle of discovery and suppression', *Child Abuse & Neglect*, 17(1): 7–24.

Osborn, M. (1998), 'Facts and figures still show little room at the top for women in science in most EU countries', in Colosimo, A. and Dewandre, N. (eds), *Women and science*, Proceedings of the conference Women and Science, European Commission, Brussels, pp 83–108.

Paci, D. and Romito, P. (2000), 'Trattamenti o mal-trattamenti? Gli operatori sociosanitari di fronte alle donne che hanno subito violenza', in Romito, P. (ed), *Violenze alle donne e risposte delle istituzioni: Prospettive internazionali*, Angeli, Milan, pp 137–52.

Patel, P. (2000) 'Southall Black Sisters: domestic violence campaigns and alliances across the division of race, gender and class', in Hanmer, J. and Itzin, C. (eds) *Home truths about domestic violence*, Routledge, London, pp 167–84.

Pateman, C. (1988), *The sexual contract*, Polity Press, Cambridge.

Peled, E. (1997), 'The battered women's movement response to children of battered women', *Violence Against Women*, 3(4): 424–46.

Peled, E. (2000), 'Parenting by men who abuse women: issues and dilemmas', *The British Journal of Social Work*, 30(1): 25–36.

Pellai, A. (2004), *Un'ombra sul cuore*, Angeli, Milan.

Pennebaker, J. (1993), 'Putting stress into words: health, linguistic and therapeutic implications', *Behavior Research and Therapy*, 31(5): 539–48.

Pennebaker, J. and Keough, K. (1999), 'Revealing, organizing, and reorganizing the self in response to stress and emotion', in Contrada, R. and Ashmore, R. (eds), *Self, social identity, and physical health: Interdisciplinary explorations*, Oxford University Press, Oxford and New York, pp 101–21.

Pennington, J. and Woods, L. (1990), *Legal issues and legal options in civil child sexual abuse cases: Representing the protective parent*, National Center on Women and Family Law, New York.

Petit, J.M. (2004), *Rights of the child (Addendum: Mission to France, 25–29/11/2002)*, http://ap.ohchr.org/documents/dpage_e.aspx?m=102 (scaricato da Internet il 29/12/2004)

Phillips, L. (2000), *Flirting with danger: Young women's reflections on sexuality and domination*, New York University Press, New York.

Phillips, L. and Henderson, M. (1999), 'Patient was hit in the face by a fist: a discourse analysis of male violence against women', *American Journal of Orthopsychiatry*, 69(1): 116–21.

Pickup, F. (2001), *Ending violence against women: A challenge for development and humanitarian work*, Oxfam Publishing, Oxford.

Pisanty, V. (1998), *L'irritante questione delle camere a gas*, Bompiani, Milan.

Pope, K. and Brown, L. (1996), *I ricordi delle antiche violenze: Come riemergono, come si interpretano, come si superano*, McGraw-Hill, Milan.

Pearce, R. (2000), 'Paternal incest: an autobiographical account', Rachel Pearce interviewed by Catherine Itzin in Itzin, C. (ed), *Home truths about child sexual abuse*, Routledge, London, pp 103-22.

Radford, J. and Russell, D. (1992), *Femicide: The politics of woman killing*, Twayne, New York.

Radford, L. and Hester, M. (2006), *Mothering through domestic violence*, Kingsley, London.

Radford, L., Hester, M., Humphries, J. and Woodfield, K. (1997), 'For the sake of the children: the law, domestic violence and child contact in England', *Women's Studies International Forum*, 20(4): 471-82.

Ramazanoglu, C. (1989), *Feminism and the contradiction of oppression*, Routledge, London.

Ranke-Heinemann, U. (1988), *Eunuchs for the Kingdom of Heaven: Women, sexuality and the Catholic Church*, Doubleday, New York.

Raymond, J. (2002), 'The new UN trafficking protocol', *Women's Studies International Forum*, 25(5): 491-502.

Razack, S. (1994), 'What is to be gained by looking white people in the eye? Culture, race and gender in cases of sexual violence', *Signs*, 19(4): 894-923.

Rennison, C.M. and Welchans, S. (2000), *Intimate partner violence (Special report, NCJ 178247)*, Department of Justice, Washington, DC.

Renzetti, C. (1997), 'Violence in lesbian and gay relationships', in O'Toole, L. and Schiffman, J. (eds), *Gender violence: Interdisciplinary perspectives*, New York University Press, New York, pp 285-93.

Resnick, H., Acierno, R. and Kilpatrick, D. (1997), 'Health impact of interpersonal violence 2: medical and mental health outcome', *Behavioral Medicine*, 23: 65-78.

Rhoades, H. (2002), 'The "no contact mother": reconstructions of motherhood in the era of the "new father"', *International Journal of Law, Policy and the Family*, 16(1): 71-94.

Rhode, D. (1997), *Speaking of sex: The denial of gender inequality*, Harvard University Press, Cambridge, MA.

Robinson, L. (1997), 'Touring Thailand's sex industry', in Hennessy, R. and Inghraham, C. (eds), *Materialist feminisms*, Routledge, London, pp 253-8.

Roccia, C. and Foti, C. (1994), *L'abuso sessuale sui minori, educazione sessuale, prevenzione, trattamento*, Unicopli, Milan.

Rochefort, C. (1988), *La porte du fond*, Grasset, Paris.

Romito, P. (1990), *La naissance du premier enfant*, Delachuax et Niestlé, Lausanne.

Romito, P. (1999a), *The response of health and social institutions to the problem of violence against women*, The Women's Association 'La Settima Onda', Trieste, the European Daphne Initiative, unpublished report.

Romito, P. (1999b), 'Dalla padella alla brace: donne maltrattate, violenza privata and complicità pubbliche', *Polis*, 13(2): 235-54.

Romito, P. (2000), 'Private violence, public complicity: the response of health and social services to battered women', in Sherr, L. and St Lawrence, J. (eds), *Women, health and the mind*, Wiley & Sons, New York, pp 59-74.

Romito, P. (2003), 'Les attaques contre les enquêtes sur les violences envers les femmes ou qui a peur des chiffres sur les violences commises par les hommes', *Nouvelles Questions Féministes*, 22(3): 82-7.

Romito, P. and Cresson, G. (1994), '"Non ho fatto niente": come le madri parlano di quello che fanno: vita di relazione, svalorizzazione di sé e sofferenza mentale', in Leonardi, P. (ed), *Curare nella differenza*, Angeli, Milan, pp 226-45.

Romito, P. and Gerin, D. (2002), 'Asking patients about violence: a survey of 510 women attending social and health services in Trieste, Italy', *Social Science & Medicine*, 54(12): 1813-24.

Romito, P. and Volpato, C. (2005), 'Women inside and outside academia: a struggle to access knowledge, legitimacy and influence', *Social Science Information*, 44(1): 41-63.

Romito, P., Molzan Turan, J. and De Marchi, M. (2005), 'The impact of current and past interpersonal violence on women's mental health', *Social Science & Medicine*, 60: 1717-27.

Romito, P., Saurel-Cubizolles, M.J. and Crisma, M. (2001), 'The relationship between parents' violence against daughters and violence by other perpetrators: an Italian study', *Violence Against Women*, 7(12): 1429-63.

Romito, P., De Marchi, M., Molzan Turan, J., Ciociano Bottaretto, R. and Tavi, M. (2004), 'Identifying violence among women patients attending family practices: the role of research in community change', *Journal of Community and Applied Social Psychology*, 14(1): 1-16.

Rose, H. and Rose, S. (eds) (2000), *Alas, poor Darwin*, Harmony Books, New York.

Rose, S., Lewontin, R. and Kamin, E. (1983), *Il gene e la sua mente: Biologia, ideologia and natura umana*, Mondadori, Milan.

Rothman, B.K. (2005), *Weaving a family: Untangling race and adoption.* Beacon Press, Boston, MA.

Roy, A. (2001), *The god of small things*, trad. it. di C. Gabutti, *Il dio delle piccole cose*, Guanda, Parma.

Ruggiero, K., McLeer, S. and Dixon, F. (2000), 'Sexual abuse characteristics associated with survivors' psychopathology', *Child Abuse & Neglect*, 24(7): 951-64.

Rush, F. (1980), *The best kept secret: Sexual abuse of children*, McGraw-Hill, New York.

Russ, J. (1983), *How to suppress women's writing*, University of Texas Press, Austin, TX.

Russell, D. (1984), *Sexual exploitation: Rape, child sexual abuse and sexual harassment*, Sage Publications, Thousand Oaks, CA.

Russell, D. (1990), *Rape in marriage*, Indiana University Press, Bloomington, IN.

Russell, D. (1993), *Making violence sexy: Feminist views on pornography*, Columbia University Press, New York.

Russell, D. (1997), *Behind closed doors in white South Africa: Incest survivors tell their stories*, St. Martin Press, New York.

Russell, D. (1999), *The secret trauma: Incest in the lives of girls and women*, Basic Books, New York (1st edition, 1986).

Russell, D. and Bolen, R. (2000), *The epidemic of rape and child sexual abuse in the United States*, Sage Publications, Thousand Oaks, CA.

Rutter, M. (1995), 'Clinical implications of attachment concepts: retrospect and prospect', *Journal of Child Psychology and Psychiatry*, 36(4): 549-71.

Ryan, W. (1976), *Blaming the victim*, Vintage Books, New York.

Sabbadini, L. (1998), *La sicurezza dei cittadini*, (unpublished report), Istat, Rome.

Saposnek, D. (1998), *Mediating child custody disputes: A strategic approach*, Jossey-Bass Publishers, San Francisco, CA.

Saraceno, C. (2004), 'Lavoro, famiglia e tempo per sé: intervista a Luisa Stanzani', *Alla Pari. Periodico del Servizio per le politiche delle pari opportunità della Regione Emilia Romagna*, pp 11-12, www.regione.emilia-romagna.it/allapari

Sariola, H. and Uutela, A. (1992), 'The prevalence and context of family violence against children in Finland', *Child Abuse & Neglect*, 16: 823-32.

Saunders, H. (2004), *Twenty-nine child homicides: Lessons still to be learnt on domestic violence and child protection*, Women's Aid, Bristol, www.womensaid.org.uk

Schechter, S. (1982), *Women and male violence: The visions and the struggles of the battered women's movement*, South End Press, Boston, MA.

Schinaia, C. (2001), *Pedofilia pedofilie: La psicoanalisi e il mondo del pedofilo*, Bollati Boringhieri, Turin.

Schneider, E. (2000), *Battered women & feminist lawmaking*, Yale University Press, New Haven, CT.

Scholder, A. (1993), *Critical condition: Women on the edge of violence*, City Lights Books, San Francisco, CA.

Schopler, E. (1985), 'Parents of psychotic children as scapegoats', in Donnellan, A. (ed), *Classic readings in autism*, Teacher's College Press, New York, pp 236-41.

Schwartz, M. (ed) (1997), *Researching sexual violence against women*, Sage Publications, Thousand Oaks, CA.

Scott Heller, S., Larrieu, J., D'Imperio, R. and Boris, N. (1999), 'Research on resilience to child maltreatment: empirical considerations', *Child Abuse & Neglect*, 23(4): 321-38.

Scully, D. and Marolla, J. (1984), 'Convicted rapists' vocabulary of motive: excuses and justifications', *Social problems*, 31(5): 530-44.

Scully, D. and Marolla, J. (1985), '"Riding the bull at Gilley's": convicted rapists describe the rewards of rape', *Social Problems*, 32(3): 251-63.

Scutt, J. (1988), 'The privatization of justice: power differentials, inequality, and the palliative of counselling and mediation', *Women's Studies International Forum*, 11(5): 503-20.

Seager, J. (2003), *The Penguin atlas of women in the world*, Penguin, Harmondsworth.

Seligman, M. (1975), *Helplessness: On depression, development and death*, Freeman & Co, San Francisco, CA.

Sen, A. (1990), 'More than 100 million women are missing', *New York Review of Books*, 20 November.

Sev'er, A. and Yurdakul, G. (2001), 'Cultur of honor, culture of change', *Violence Against Women*, 7(9): 964-98.

Shalhoub-Kevorkian, N. (1999a), 'The politics of disclosing female sexual abuse: a case study of Palestinian society', *Child Abuse & Neglect*, 23(12): 1275-93.

Shalhoub-Kevorkian, N. (1999b), 'Towards a cultural definition of rape: dilemmas in dealing with rape victims in Palestinian society', *Women's Studies International Forum*, 22(2):157-73.

Sherman, R. (1993), 'Gardner's law', *The National Law Journal*, August, 16: 45-6.

Showalter, E. (1985), *The female malady*, Penguin Books, New York.

Sideris, T. (2003), 'War, gender and culture: Mozambican women refugees', *Social Science & Medicine*, 56(4): 713-24.

Silbert, M. and Pines, A. (1993), 'Pornography and sexual abuse of women', in Russell, D. (eds), *Making violence sexy: Feminist views on pornography*, Columbia University Press, New York, pp 113-19.

Silverman, A., Reinherz, H. and Giaconia, R. (1996), 'The long-term sequelae of child and adolescent abuse: a longitudinal community study', *Child Abuse & Neglect*, 20(8): 709-23.

Sirles, E. and Franke, P. (1989), 'Factors influencing mothers' reactions to intrafamily sexual abuse', *Child Abuse & Neglect*, 13: 131-9.

Sluckin, W., Herbert, M. and Sluckin, A. (1983), *Maternal bonding*, Blackwell, Oxford.

Smart, C. (1989), 'Power and the politics of child custody', in Smart, C. and Sevenhuijsen, S. (eds), *Child custody and the politics of gender*, Routledge, London, pp 1-26.

Smart, C. and Sevenhuijsen, S. (eds) (1989), *Child custody and the politics of gender*, Routledge, London.

Smith, D., Letourneau, E., Saunders, B.E., Kilpatrick, D.G., Resnick, H.S. and Best, C.L. (2000), 'Delay in disclosure of childhood rape: results from a national survey', *Child Abuse & Neglect*, 24(2): 273-87.

Smyth, A. (2002), 'Résistance féministe à la violence masculine: quelles perspectives?', *Nouvelles Questions Féministes*, 21(2): 4-7.

Sohn, A.-M. (1992), 'L'oltraggio al pudore sulla persona delle bambine e la sessualità nella vita quotidiana (Francia, 1870-1939)', in Corbin, A. (ed), *La violenza sessuale nella storia*, Laterza, Bari, pp 63-104.

So-Kum Tang, C., Wong, D. and Mui-Ching Cheung, F. (2002), 'Social construction of women as legitimate victims of violence in Chinese societies', *Violence Against Women*, 8(8): 968-96.

Soothill, K., Francis, B., Ackerley, E. and Collett, S. (1999), *Homicide in Britain*, Scottish Executive Central Research Unit, Edinburgh.

Sorenson, S., Stein, J., Siegel, J., Golding, J. and Burnam, A. (1987), 'The prevalence of adult sexual assault', *American Journal of Epidemiology*, 126(6): 1154-64.

Spatz, M. (1991), 'A "lesser" crime: a comparative study of legal defense for men who kill their wives', *Columbia Journal of Law and Social Problems*, 24(4): 597-638.

Spender, D. (1980), *Man made language*, Routledge & Kegan Paul, London.

Stark, E. and Flitcraft, A. (1996), *Women at risk: Domestic violence and women's health*, Sage Publications, London.

Starnone, D. (2000), *Via Gemito*, Feltrinelli, Milan.

Staub, E. (1999), 'The roots of evil: social conditions, culture, personality and basic human needs', *Personality and Social Psychology Review*, 3(3): 179-92.

Stefanizzi, S. and Terragni, L. (1993), 'La violenza nel matrimonio a Milano', *Sociologia del Diritto*, 3(1): 45-67.

Stern, A.E. (1995), 'Behavior and family functioning in sexually abused children', *Journal of Child Psychology and Psychiatry*, 36(6): 1077-89.

Stoltenberg, J. (1993), 'Male sexuality: why ownership is sexy', *Michigan Journal of Gender & Law*, 1(1): 59-64.

*Stop Trafficking* (2002), Proceedings of an international conference, Bologna, 23-24 May.

Sturdevant, S. and Stoltzfus, B. (1992), *Let the good times roll: The sale of women's sexual labor around U.S. military bases in the Philippines, Okinawa, and the Southern part of Korea*, New Press, New York.

Swann, S. (2000), 'Helping girls involved in "prostitution": A Barnardos experiment', in Itzin, C. (ed), *Home truths about child sexual abuse*, Routledge, London, pp 277-89.

Swanson, J. (2002), 'Acid attacks: Bangladesh's efforts to stop the violence', *International Health. Harvard Health Policy Review*, 3(1): 1-3.

Sykes, G. and Matza, D. (1957), 'Techniques of neutralization: a theory of delinquency', *American Sociological Review*, 22(6): 663-70.

Szasz, T. (1980), *Sex: Facts, frauds and follies*, Blackwell, Oxford.

Talbot, M. (1988), *Language and gender*, Polity Press, Cambridge.

Tavris, C. (1992), *The mis-measure of women*, Simon & Schuster, New York.

Taylor McDonnell, J. (1998), 'On being the "bad" mother of an autistic child', in Ladd-Taylor, M. and Umansky, L. (eds), *'Bad' mothers: The politics of blame in twentieth-century America*, New York University Press, New York, pp 220-9.

Temkin, J. (1997), 'Plus ça change', *British Journal of Criminology*, 37(4): 507-27.

The Boston Women's Health Book Collective (1971), *Our bodies, ourselves*, Simon & Schuster, New York.

Thibault, M.C., Laperrière, E., Chatigny, C. and Messing, K. (2003), *Des intervenantes à tout faire: Analyse du travail en maison d'hébergement: Rapport de recherche*, Université du Québec à Montréal et Cinbiose, Montréal.

Thoennes, N. and Tjaden, P. (1990), 'The extent, nature and validity of sexual abuse allegations in custody/visitations disputes', *Child Abuse & Neglect*, 14: 151-63.

Thomas, A. and Kitzinger, C. (1997), *Sexual harassment: Contemporary feminist perspectives*, Open University Press, Philadelphia, PA.

Thornhill, R. and Palmer, C. (2000a), 'Why men rape', *The Sciences*, Jan-Feb: 30-6.

Thornhill, R. and Palmer, C. (2000b), *A natural history of rape: Biologial bases of sexual coercion*, MIT Press, Cambridge, MA.

Timpanaro, S. (1974), *Il lapsus freudiano*, La Nuova Italia, Florence.

Todorov, T. (2000), *Memoire du mal: Tentation du bien*, Laffont, Paris.

Tortolani, D. (1998), 'Il rilevamento e la diagnosi in ambito ospedaliero delle famiglie abusanti', 'L'intervento familiare: nodi problematici', in Montecchi, F. (ed), *I maltrattamenti e gli abusi sui bambini*, Angeli, Milane, pp 229-42 and pp 271-97.

Toubia, N. (1994), 'Female circumcision as a public health issue', *The New England Journal of Medicine*, 331(11): 712-16.

Trexler, R. (1995), *Sex and conquest: Gendered violence, political order, and the European conquest of the Americas*, Cornell University Press, Ithaca, NY.

Trocmé, N. and Bala, N. (2005), 'False allegations of abuse and neglect when parents separate', *Child Abuse & Neglect*, 29, 1333-45.

Ullman, S. (1996), 'Social relations, coping strategies, and self-blame attributions in adjustment to sexual assault', *Psychology of Women Quarterly*, 20(4): 505-26.

Unesco (1986), *Final report: International meeting of experts on the social and cultural causes of prostitution and strategies for the struggle against procuring and the sexual exploitation of women (SHS-85/Conf. 608/14, 7)*, Unesco, Division of Human Rights and Peace, Paris.

Unicef (2003), *A league table of child maltreatment deaths in rich nations (V Report Card)*, Unicef Innocenti Research Centre, Florence, www. unicef-icdc.org

US Conference of Catholic Bishops (2004), '4450 priests accused of sex abuse', http://edition.cnn.com/2004/US/02/16/church.abuse/

Virgilio, M. (1997), *Violenza sessuale and norma: Legislazioni penali a confronto*, Casa Editrice Nuove Ricerche, Ancona.

Vogeltanz, N., Wilsnack, S., Harris, R., Wilsnack, R., Wonderlich, S. and Kristjanson, A. (1999), 'Prevalence and risk factors for childhood sexual abuse in women: national survey findings', *Child Abuse & Neglect*, 23(6): 579-92.

Volpp, L. (2000), 'Blaming culture for bad behavior', *Yale Journal of Law and the Humanities,* 12(89): 89-116.

Wadman, M.C. and Muelleman, R.L. (1999), 'Domestic violence homicides: ED use before victimization', *American Journal of Emergency Medicine*, 17(7): 689-91.

Walby, S. and Allen, J. (2004), *Domestic violence, sexual assault and stalking: Findings from the British Crime Survey*, Home Office Research, Development and Statistics Directorate, London.

Walker, L. (2000), *The battered woman syndrome*, Springer, New York.

Walker, R., Logan, T.K., Jordan, C. and Campbell, J. (2004), 'An integrative review of separation in the context of victimization', *Trauma, Violence & Abuse*, 5(2): 143-93.

Ward, H., Day, S. and Weber, J. (1999), 'Risky business: health and safety in the sex industry over a 9 year period', *Sexually Transmitted Infections*, 75(5): 340-43.

Warin, C. (2005), 'Pérou: stérilisées malgré elles', *L'Express*, 7 February: 74-5.

Warshaw, C. (1993), 'Limitations of the medical model in the care of battered women', in Bart, P. and Geil Moran, E. (eds), *Violence against women*, Sage Publications, London, pp 134-46.

Watkins, B. and Bentovim, A. (1992), 'The sexual abuse of male children and adolescents: a review of current research', *Journal of Child Psychology and Psychiatry*, 33(1): 197-248.

Wattleton, F. (2003), 'Unfinished agenda: reproductive rights', in Morgan, R. (ed), *Sisterhood is forever: The women's anthology for a new millennium*, Washington Square Press, New York, pp 17-27.

Webster, R. (1995), *Why Freud was wrong: Sin, science and psychoanalysis*, Harper & Collins, London.

Wenneras, C. and Wold, A. (1997), 'Nepotism and sexism in peer-review', *Nature*, 387: 341-43.

WHO (World Health Organization) (1997), *Violence against women. Women's health and development programme*, WHO, Geneva.

Whyte, J., Hall Smyth, P., Koss, M. and Figueredo, A. (2000) 'Intimate partner aggression: what have we learned? Comment on Archer (2000)', *Psychological Bulletin*, 126(5): 690-6.

Wigmore, J. (1961), *Wigmore on evidence* (3rd edition), Little Brown, Boston, MA.

Williams, O., Boggess, J. and Carter, J. (2001), 'Fatherhood and domestic violence: exploring the role of men who batter in the lives of their children', in Graham-Bermann, S. and Edleson, J. (eds), *Domestic violence in the lives of children*, American Psychological Association, Washington, pp 157-87.

Williamson, C. and Cluse-Tolar, T. (2002), 'Pimp-controlled prostitution', *Violence Against Women*, 8(9): 1074-92.

Wolf, C. (1993), *Introduction to Cassandra*, Trad. it. di A. Raja, *Premesse a Cassandra*, Edizioni E/O, Rome.

Wolf, C. (1994), *Cassandra*, Trad. it di A. Raja, *Cassandra*, Edizioni E/O, Rome.

Wolfe, D.A., Jaffe, P., Jetté, J. and Poisson, S. (2003), 'The impact of child abuse in community institutions and organizations: advancing professional and scientific understanding', *Clinical Psychology: Science and Practice*, 10(2): 179-91.

Yoshihama, M. (2002), 'Policies and services addressing domestic violence in Japan: from non-interference to incremental changes', *Women's Studies International Forum*, 25(5): 541-53.

Yunus, M. (1997), *Il banchiere dei poveri*, Feltrinelli, Milan.

Zingarelli (2004) *Vocabolario della lingua italiana* (*Dictionary of the Italian language*), Zanichelli, Bologna.

Zorza, J. (1995), 'How abused women can use the law to protect their children', in Peled, E., Jaffe, P. and Edleson, J. (eds), *Ending the cycle of violence: Community responses to children of battered women*, Sage, Thousands Oaks, CA, pp 147-69.

# Index

NOTE: Page numbers followed by *n* refer to information in a note; page numbers followed by *App* refer to information in the Appendix.